Shadows of the Soul

This volume brings together fourteen highly accessible chapters on negative emotions, written by established experts in the philosophy of emotions for a non-specialized audience. Topics covered range from general questions, such as the nature of valence and the role of negative emotions in fiction, to the study of specific emotions, such as disgust, grief, anxiety, shame, contempt, hatred and jealousy.

Christine Tappolet is Full Professor at the Département de philosophie at the Université de Montréal. Her research interests lie mainly in ethics, moral psychology, and emotion theory. She has edited a number of volumes, including, with Sarah Stroud, *Weakness of Will and Practical Rationality* (2003), and is the author of two books, *Émotions et valeurs* (2000) and *Emotions, Values, and Agency* (2016).

Fabrice Teroni is Associate Professor at the Philosophy Departments at the Universities of Geneva and of Fribourg. He has published several articles and monographs on the general theory of emotions (*The Emotions: A Philosophical Introduction*, 2012), on the nature of shame (*In Defense of Shame: The Faces of an Emotion*, 2011) and on memory. He has recently edited, with Hichem Naar, *The Ontology of Emotions* (2017).

Anita Konzelmann Ziv was Senior Research and Teaching Assistant at the Philosophy Department at the University of Geneva. Her research focuses on shared and moral emotions. She co-edited *Self-Evaluation—Affective and Social Grounds of Intentionality* (2011) and *Institutions, Emotions, and Group Agents: Contributions to Social Ontology* (2013).

Shadows of the Soul

Philosophical Perspectives on
Negative Emotions

Edited by Christine Tappolet,
Fabrice Teroni and Anita
Konzelmann Ziv

Routledge
Taylor & Francis Group

NEW YORK AND LONDON

Published 2018
by Routledge
711 Third Avenue, New York, NY 10017

and by Routledge
2 Park Square, Milton Park, Abingdon, Oxon, OX14 4RN

Routledge is an imprint of the Taylor & Francis Group, an informa business

Library of Congress Cataloging-in-Publication Data
A catalog record for this book has been requested

ISBN: 978-1-138-68969-5 (hbk)
ISBN: 978-1-315-53746-7 (ebk)

Typeset in Goudy
by Apex CoVantage, LLC

This volume is published in honor of Professor Kevin Mulligan and commemorates his dedication to his students during his time at the University of Geneva. The choice of topic mirrors both Kevin's interest in emotions and his ability to open up new lines of research. We hope that exploring the shadows of the soul will make for an enjoyable, or at least interestingly mixed, experience.

Contents

Notes on Contributors   ix

Introduction   1
CHRISTINE TAPPOLET, FABRICE TERONI AND ANITA
KONZELMANN ZIV

1 **Emotionally Charged—The Puzzle of Affective
   Valence**   10
   FABRICE TERONI

2 **Nasty Emotions and the Perception of Values**   20
   CHRISTINE TAPPOLET

3 **Imaginative Resistance: Negative Emotions,
   Values and Fiction**   30
   ANNE REBOUL

4 **Who is Afraid of Contrary Emotions?**   39
   CLOTILDE CALABI AND MARCO SANTAMBROGIO

5 **Bitter Joys and Sweet Sorrows**   50
   OLIVIER MASSIN

6 **The Emotion of Being Moved**   60
   JULIEN A. DEONNA

7 **The Uncanny and Other Negative Existential
   Feelings**   69
   JÉRÔME DOKIC

 8 Disgustingly Handsome: Nausea in the Face of
    Physical Beauty   77
    ANITA KONZELMANN ZIV

 9 Stench and Olfactory Disgust   86
    VIVIAN MIZRAHI

10 Anxiety: A Case Study on the Value of Negative
    Emotion   95
    CHARLIE KURTH

11 Grief   105
    CAROLYN PRICE

12 The Moral Shadows of Shame and Contempt   113
    RAFFAELE RODOGNO

13 Negative Emotions and Racism   122
    LUC FAUCHER

14 How to Think Yourself Out of Jealousy   132
    RONALD DE SOUSA

    Index   143

Contributors

Clotilde Calabi is Associate Professor of Philosophy of Mind and Language at the University of Milano. She has written extensively on philosophy of perception, on attention and joint attention and on emotions. Among her publications are an introduction to *The Philosophy of Perception* (*Filosofia della Percezione*, Laterza, 2009) and a book on intentionality co-authored with A. Voltolini (*I Problemi dell'intenzionalità*, Torino, 2009). She is the editor of a collection of essays on perceptual illusions (*Perceptual Illusions: Philosophical and Psychological Essays*, 2012).

Julien A. Deonna is Associate Professor in Philosophy at the University of Geneva and Project Leader at CISA, the Centre Interfacultaire en Sciences Affectives. He works in philosophy of mind, in particular the philosophy of emotions, on moral emotions and moral psychology. In addition to many articles in the area, he is the coauthor of *In Defense of Shame* (2011) and *The Emotions: A Philosophical Introduction* (2012).

Ronald de Sousa is Professor Emeritus of Philosophy at the University of Toronto. His current research bears on emotions, sex and love, and the bearing of the dual mental processing hypothesis on emotional rationality. His books include *The Rationality of Emotion* (1987), *Why Think? Evolution and the Rational Mind* (2007), *Emotional Truth* (2011) and *Love, a Very Short Introduction* (2015).

Jérôme Dokic is Professor of Cognitive Philosophy at the École des Hautes Études en Sciences Sociales and a member of Institut Jean-Nicod in Paris. His research interests are perception, memory, imagination and more recently epistemic feelings and metacognition. He has published many essays on these topics, including the books *La philosophie du son* with Roberto Casati (1994), *L'esprit en mouvement. Essai sur la dynamique cognitive* (2001), *Qu'est-ce que la perception?* (2nd ed., 2009) and *Ramsey: Truth and Success* with Pascal Engel (2002).

Luc Faucher is Professor of Philosophy at the Université du Québec à Montréal. His research interests cover philosophy of cognitive sciences, philosophy of race, philosophy of emotions and philosophy of psychiatry. He is the co-editor (with Christine Tappolet) of *The Modularity of Emotions* (2008) and the editor of *Philosophie et psychopathologie* (2006). His journal articles have appeared in *Philosophy of Science*, *Philosophy of Social Sciences*, *Emotion Review*, *Journal of Social Philosophy*, *Synthese* and *The Monist*.

Anita Konzelmann Ziv was a Senior Research and Teaching Assistant at the Philosophy Department, University of Geneva. Her research interests focus on shared and moral emotions, in particular indignation. She co-edited the volumes *Self-Evaluation—Affective and Social Grounds of Intentionality* (2011) and *Institutions, Emotions, and Group Agents: Contributions to Social Ontology* (2013).

Charlie Kurth is Assistant Professor of Philosophy at Washington University in St. Louis. His book, *The Anxious Mind: An Investigation into the Varieties and Virtues of Anxiety* (2018), develops an extended philosophical defense of what anxiety is and why it matters for moral and social life. The book is part of a larger set of published papers and ongoing projects at the intersection of emotion research, moral psychology and ethical theory.

Olivier Massin is Associate Professor of Philosophy at the University of Zurich and Research Scientist at the CNRS, Institut Jean-Nicod, Paris. He has published several papers in metaphysics, philosophy of mind and philosophy of values and has co-edited the book *Aristote chez les Helvètes* (with Anne Meylan) and is finishing a book entitled *Hedonic Goodness*.

Vivian Mizrahi's research is mostly in the philosophy of mind and the philosophy of perception. She is currently working on the nature of odors, the perception of stuff and the role of perceptual media, but her previous research has mostly focused on the nature of colors. She has written several papers on colors and smells and coedited a *Dialectica* special issue on the nature of colors.

Carolyn Price is Senior Lecturer in Philosophy at the Open University. She works in the philosophy of mind, and has a particular interest in the philosophy of emotion. She has published papers on the nature of emotion and mood, on what emotions and moods tell us about the world, and on the possibility of collective emotion. She has published *Emotion* (2015), a short monograph in which she investigates the current literature on emotion and presents her own account. She is currently exploring some further questions about emotional action and about the relationship between emotion and the self.

Anne Reboul has a Ph.D. in Linguistics and a Ph.D. in Philosophy and is Senior Researcher at CNRS (National Center for Scientific Research, France), head of the team Pragmatics and Cognition and Vice Director of the Laboratory on Language, Brain and Cognition. She is President of the Language Sciences section at the National Committee for Scientific Research (France). She has published numerous papers in philosophy of language, as well as seven books, and has recently edited the two-volume project *Mind, Values and Metaphysics: Philosophical Papers Dedicated to Kevin Mulligan* (2013, 2014), as well as a special issue of the review *Neuropsychologia*.

Raffaele Rodogno is Associate Professor at the Department of Philosophy and History of Ideas at Aarhus University. His research interests lie mainly at the intersection of ethics, the psychology and the politics of shame, guilt, anger and contempt, and the philosophy and social science of well-being. He has also published in other areas of ethics, namely, euthanasia, cultural and religious conflicts, robot-assisted elderly care, the ethics of algorithmic decisions and environmental ethics. He is the coauthor of *In Defense of Shame* (2011) and the editor of *The Ethics of Social Robotics* (2016).

Marco Santambrogio was one of the founding members of the European Society for Analytic Philosophy and of the Italian Society for Analytic Philosophy. He taught philosophy of language at the Universities of Bologna, Cagliari and Parma and has published extensively on proper names, direct reference and fictional entities.

Christine Tappolet is Professor at the Département de philosophie at the Université de Montréal. Her research interests lie mainly in ethics, moral psychology and emotion theory. She has edited a number of volumes, including, with Sarah Stroud, *Weakness of Will and Practical Rationality* (2003), and is the author of numerous articles and chapters on themes such as values, normativity, weakness of will, procrastination, autonomy and emotions, and of two books, *Émotions et valeurs* (2000) and *Emotions, Values, and Agency* (2016).

Fabrice Teroni is Associate Professor at the Philosophy Departments, Universities of Geneva and Fribourg. He works in the philosophy of mind and epistemology. He has published several articles and monographs on the general theory of emotions (*The Emotions: A Philosophical Introduction*, 2012), on the nature of shame (*In Defense of Shame: The Faces of an Emotion*, 2011) and on memory. He has recently co-edited, with Hichem Naar, *The Ontology of Emotions* (2017).

Introduction

*Christine Tappolet, Fabrice Teroni
and Anita Konzelmann Ziv*

The emotions we feel color many of our thoughts and actions, often in rather dark shades. We have at our disposal a rich lexicon of negative emotions, such as disgust, sadness, fear, shame, guilt, regret, remorse, resentment, despair, indignation, scorn, contempt, jealousy, hatred, anger, etc. In fact, we are more prone to draw fine distinctions among negative emotions than among positive emotions. While it would certainly strain things too far to say with the French philosopher Alain that "we are built such that all our emotions are sorrows" (1934, 12), many of our everyday discussions turn around negative emotions, aiming at a better understanding of their causes and moderation of their sometimes devastating consequences.

This is not to say that we harbor univocal attitudes towards negative emotions; we do not always undergo them reluctantly, for instance. Not only do we think that some situations or objects merit negative emotions, but we also actively pursue them—the aim of many recreational and artistic activities is to elicit fear, and we sometimes enjoy undergoing emotions such as anger and disgust. So, even if we try to get rid of some negative emotions, we certainly do not aim at a purely positive affective life, a life whose interest and coherence can itself be questioned. Indeed, the interest and depth of episodes of satisfaction and joy often appear to be significantly enhanced by the negative emotions to which we are prone. Moreover, is it not difficult, perhaps even incoherent, to attribute the sorts of attachments to values (justice, generosity, friendship), persons and institutions that prove so central in our self-conception to an individual deprived of negative affect? What would remain of a sense of justice in an individual who lacks the disposition to be outraged when confronted with a blatant injustice?

Despite their importance and the complexity of our attitudes towards them, negative emotions have rarely been a topic of study in their own right. Part of the explanation for why is found in the dramatic rehabilitation of emotions that has taken place in the recent philosophical literature. The traditional suspicion with which emotions, positive and negative, were regarded is nicely expressed by Immanuel Kant, according to whom "the principle of apathy—namely, that the wise man must never be in a state of affect . . . is an entirely correct and sublime moral principle of the Stoic school; for affect makes us more or less blind" (2006, 142). Prominent among the traditional charges against the emotions is the idea that they threaten the exercise of our reasoning capacities and foster a variety of vices. Many contributions in this volume contain critical echoes of this traditional outlook. However, this outlook has been progressively replaced by a near-consensus regarding the indispensable roles played by emotions in relation to the ability to make decisions, the gathering of evaluative knowledge and the ability to conduct moral reasoning.[1] For instance, as Ronald de Sousa hypothesized, emotions such as fear or anger are plausibly seen as having the crucial function to focus the agent's attention on what matters. Thus, it would be thanks to our fear that we avoid the sad destiny of the robot that sat on a bomb, spending time considering the effects of its options, including whether the price of tea might increase, instead of simply saving its skin.[2] Given that many negative emotions may seem more difficult to rehabilitate in a similar way, they have been somewhat neglected within this scholarly trend. Many of the contributions to this volume argue that this is a mistake and that negative emotions have the potential to contribute positively to our lives.

More generally, the exploration of negative emotions raises several fundamental issues. Obviously, it presupposes a grasp of the way we distinguish negative and positive emotions. This distinction between negative and positive emotions may well be the central distinction governing our apprehension of the affective domain. Within the contemporary literature, scholars attempt to develop accounts of what they describe as the "valence" or "polarity" of affective states, often emphasizing this central distinction and the various reasons for which we may speak of positive or negative emotions. The papers by Fabrice Teroni and Christine Tappolet, which open this volume, concentrate on these fundamental theoretical issues raised by the very idea of affective valence.

In *Emotionally Charged: The Puzzle of Affective Valence*, Teroni's aim is to understand what it is that makes certain emotions positive and others negative. To that end, he insists that valence is supposed to be a fundamental contrastive property of emotions, which should not be explainable in terms of other properties that they have. Teroni uses this constraint to criticize accounts of valence that appeal to desires—e.g., the idea that negative emotions are those emotions that frustrate the subject's desires—and hedonic states—e.g., the idea that negative emotions are those that contain an irreducible, unpleasant phenomenal quality. According to him, the explanatory power of these accounts is illusory, since the relevant desires need to be explained by hedonic states, and hedonic states are in turn partly composed of emotions. For that reason, trying to explain affective valence by means of desires and hedonic states is to go around in circles. This conclusion leads Teroni to explore an alternative, evaluative explanation of valence and to give some reasons favoring a specific evaluative account that emphasizes the role of emotional attitudes. In this context, he raises doubts regarding the possibility of explaining valence in terms of what the emotions represent, and favors an approach centered around the bodily dimension of emotional experience. Emotions are embodied attitudes, and this is key to understanding their valence, according to Teroni.

Nasty Emotions and the Perception of Values, by Tappolet, starts with the observation that, in some contemporary discussions, the emotions of regret and shame have been rehabilitated alongside emotions like compassion. However, she points out that other negative emotions, such as jealousy, envy or hatred, do not easily lend themselves to similar reappraisals; they appear intrinsically nasty. Tappolet's discussion explores the impact of nasty emotions on one view that she herself favors and that underlies many attempts at rehabilitating the emotions: the view according to which an emotion is a kind of perceptual experience, one which allows us to apprehend the values of things, such as their fearsomeness or admirableness. Tappolet distinguishes several sorts of affective faults of which emotions may be guilty, and explores whether these faults threaten the view that emotions are perception-like experiences. According to her, they do not. As opposed to perceptual experiences, emotions may sometimes be irrational, painful and immoral, but this is to be expected in light of their distinctive characteristics. They are not entirely passive and their concern with values means that they can be intrinsically painful or pleasant as well as morally relevant. The take-home lesson is a sane reminder that the rehabilitation of emotions cannot be wholesale. Emotions are liable to be afflicted by all sorts of faults.

The utter ugliness of some of our emotional reactions raises worries in itself. One can wonder whether we would not be better off without any negative emotions whatsoever. Do negative emotions have a function, however? This is what Anne Reboul discusses in *Imaginative Resistance: Negative Emotions, Values and Fiction*, where she explores the fact that, despite appearances to the contrary, there are limits to what we can imagine. These limits relate to an asymmetry between two kinds of contents, as David Hume emphasized: factual contents and evaluative contents. We can easily imagine factual contents that contradict our beliefs (e.g., suppose that the Earth is flat), but have a much harder time imagining evaluative contents that contradict our convictions (e.g., suppose that killing girls at birth is a good thing). How should we understand this imaginative resistance? What does it reveal about imagination and emotions? These are crucial issues given the widespread and plausible idea that fiction influences our perception of values and our evaluative judgments, for good or for bad. Reboul argues that imaginative resistance does not simply manifest the refusal to imagine; it manifests the inability to imagine evaluative contents that contradict our beliefs, an inability she goes on to explain by the negative emotions that such contents trigger. In imaginative resistance, negative emotions make it impossible to endorse some evaluative thoughts, thereby proving crucial for the delineation of our ethical outlook. In addition, Reboul explains how fiction can refine our emotional sensitivity by making us react differently to subtly different scenarios. The result is a rich picture of the interplay between fiction and emotion, where fiction not only triggers the negative emotions underlying imaginative resistance, but also enriches and extends our emotional repertoire.

As important as the distinction between positive and negative emotions is, the truth is that our emotional lives are sometimes too complex to be categorized univocally in terms of positive or negative affect. Emotional reactions often manifest a kind of ambivalence, as when the objects and situations we confront elicit mixed feelings in us. The very existence of such ambivalence raises interesting issues, which are the topics of the next two chapters.

The exploration of emotional ambivalence provides an insightful and original perspective on the hotly debated issue of the rationality of emotions. Ambivalence is a striking feature of our emotional lives, and understanding the distinctive nature of emotional rationality requires a proper account of ambivalence. *Who is Afraid of Contrary Emotions*, by Clotilde Calabi and Marco Santambrogio, aims at examining emotional rationality and comparing it to the rationality of belief. The authors observe that we do not take ambivalent emotions to be irrational—they seem like a normal and inescapable aspect of our affective lives, as when one is simultaneously pleased and displeased that a team won a game. This differs strikingly from parallel cases involving beliefs: contrary beliefs seem like abnormal aspects of our cognitive lives that we should try to get rid of. It is irrational to simultaneously believe and disbelieve that a team won a game. According to many philosophers, this demonstrates that ambivalent emotions are not genuinely contrary, otherwise they would constitute an irrational pair. Calabi and Santambrogio explain how this observation leads to the claim that ambivalent emotions have different objects. For instance, one is pleased with some aspect of the team's winning the game (e.g., it's one's hometown team) and displeased with another aspect of this event (e.g., they played too defensively). If so, emotions differ from belief and disbelief insofar as their propositional objects are more complex than it may initially seem. In contrast, Calabi and Santambrogio maintain that some opposite emotions directed at the very same object are genuinely contrary. They believe, however, that this does not make them irrational, since, as they argue, emotions and belief obey distinct logics.

In *Bitter Joys and Sweet Sorrows*, Olivier Massin emphasizes that mixed feelings raise two additional issues. The first regards their very existence: at first sight, emotional ambivalence appears incompatible with the contrariety of pleasure and displeasure. How could these seemingly paradoxical fusions of negative and positive affect exist? The second issue concerns a consequence of these fusions: when we experience mixed feelings, does the excess of pleasure or displeasure that we feel itself constitute a new feeling? Massin argues for a conciliatory solution to the first issue. According to him, mixed feelings are possible and do not threaten the relation of contrariety between pleasure and displeasure. As regards the second issue, Massin privileges ontological parsimony and maintains that the resultant feelings do not exist: having a lot of pleasure and a little displeasure does not result in experiencing a mild pleasure. Claiming that there is an extra amount of pleasure or displeasure is to mistake a mathematical fiction for a psychologically real phenomenon. On this basis, Massin argues that skepticism about mixed feelings and belief in the existence of resultant feelings, although mistaken, originate in the correct idea that pleasures and displeasures do fuse in some cases. He further suggests that pleasures and displeasures that have no objects tend to fuse, resulting in pure pleasure or pure displeasure.

Beyond these broad theoretical issues, the study of any negative emotion raises a variety of more specific but no less important questions. The remainder of the contributions to the volume will allow the reader to explore a fair share of them. We begin with two chapters regarding emotions that have an existential significance for us.

The first discusses an ambiguous and undertheorized emotion. *The Emotion of Being Moved*, by Julien Deonna, starts by observing that we often use the expression "being moved" to refer to a specific affective phenomenon, which deserves a place in the taxonomy of emotions alongside more readily recognized emotions. Deonna introduces five criteria to determine whether an affective phenomenon qualifies as an emotion, criteria which concern intentionality, a distinctive evaluative profile, phenomenology, function and action tendency. Deonna argues that being moved meets these criteria. He emphasizes that this emotion can be elicited in different types of conditions: when positive values are made salient (e.g., when kindness or fraternity emerges despite difficult circumstances); when positive values are showcased in ceremonies and celebrations; and when the presence of these values is in itself so extraordinary that it is sufficient to move us. In light of its concern with positive values, Deonna suggests that being moved serves the function of reminding the subject of the values she holds dear, making salient some of the most fundamental aspects of our engagement with the world. According to the resulting picture, this emotion lies on the border between positive and negative emotions. It is an unsettling yet soothing form of pleasureless contentment, occasioned by the contemplation of a positive value making a stand. As such, being moved relates to gratitude, and it is likely to lead to a variety of actions. Deonna concludes that the study of being moved raises intriguing questions regarding its links to other emotions, such as joy, awe and elevation, to aesthetic experience, to sentimentality and to happiness.

The next emotion tackled in the volume is an intriguing negative existential feeling, the feeling of uncanniness that aroused the interest of Sigmund Freud, among others. The aim of Jérôme Dokic's *The Uncanny and Other Negative Existential Feelings* is to explore its nature. Dokic starts by emphasizing that the feeling of uncanniness involves more than a failure of familiarity; it targets something that, although it should be familiar to us, strikes us as being somehow strange. A representative example is the feeling elicited by realistic puppets or wax figures, which answer only some of our expectations regarding the behavior of sentient beings—it is arguably for this reason that they make numerous appearances in horror fiction. Dokic explores the nature of the experienced strangeness involved in this feeling and argues that it constitutes a distinctive experience that cannot be understood as the mere absence of a feeling of familiarity. According to the account he favors, the feeling of uncanniness is a meta-feeling, which is elicited by the cognitive dissonance between the familiarity one expects and the strangeness of what one actually confronts. Dokic helps himself to this role of cognitive dissonance to emphasize the crucial roles played by existential feelings in general, and the feeling of uncanniness in particular, in our cognitive life and behavior.

The remainder of the chapters discuss a number of negative emotions, most of which are all too familiar.

"Disgustingly Handsome"—Nausea in the Face of Physical Beauty, by Anita Konzelmann Ziv, examines the phenomenon of negative emotional responses felt towards positive values. In particular, she asks how it could be that a beautiful person feels disgust at her own beauty. This question is raised by the experience of Solal, the hero of the novel *Belle du Seigneur*, who is described as assessing himself as "disgustingly handsome". Aiming to identify Solal's peculiar feeling, the chapter shows that some approaches can be dismissed altogether. Thus, Solal's disgust is obviously not a perception-based response to potentially harmful substances, nor is it an instance of moral disgust. Moreover, it would be hard to explain it in terms of "disgust of satiation". On the positive side, Konzelmann Ziv argues for two theses. Solal's disgust (i) signals an offense to his personal set of values, and (ii) is a mediated feeling invoking a complex cognitive basis. Within the context of the novel, three interlocking key themes shape this basis: narcissism, *vanitas* and the exploration of love. While the first two themes provide basic conditions for disgust towards the beautiful, the third shows the ultimate value under attack: Solal's ideal of love is in tension with the role played by physical beauty in romantic relationships. Such a strong negative reaction may incite the subject to reflect on the rightness of the values that she holds. In Solal's case, it arguably leads him to a more balanced view of human love.

More often than we would like, we are disgusted by what we smell. What is the nature of this seemingly simple reaction? How does the answer to that question bear on the nature of stench? In *Stench and Olfactory Disgust*, Vivian Mizrahi argues in favor of the idea that stench has to be understood in emotional rather than in strictly perceptual terms. Mizrahi's strategy consists in showing that stench is the object of olfactory disgust. This puts her in a position to maintain that no smell is intrinsically unpleasant—there are, according to her, only smells that are associated with unpleasant emotions. The defense of these claims leads Mizrahi to lay out a view of olfactory disgust and to explain the nature of the relation between smell and stench. In the process, she examines the notion of hedonic value for smells, and offers a non-polar opposition view of olfactory pleasantness. According to this view, olfactory disgust does not have an opposite emotion. A smell can be pleasant for a variety of reasons: it may whet our appetite or evoke various positive associations. Hence no positive olfactory emotion is strictly the opposite of olfactory disgust.

The next contribution moves us from disgust to the apprehension of risk. In *Anxiety: A Case Study on the Value of Negative Emotion*, Charlie Kurth rejects the idea that we should do our best to avoid negative emotions. According to him, negative emotions matter. They matter not only instrumentally, in helping us to manage risks, dangers and threats, but they also matter in themselves *aretically* (from *arete*, virtue in Greek), insofar as they are constitutive of a good or virtuous character. To support this conclusion in the case of anxiety (but his discussion also touches on anger and fear), Kurth argues that much folk and philosophical wisdom is wrong-headed. Anxiety is in fact valuable for our ability to navigate successfully the complexities of social life, and is a central dimension of virtuous agency. In so arguing, Kurth takes issue with a picture fostered by Kant, according to which virtue is purely a matter of self-control and strength in the fulfillment of one's duty—and which thus takes virtue to be incompatible with negative emotions. Kurth argues that this is simply to miss the fundamental role played by negative emotions in general, and anxiety in particular, in self-control. We should not be led astray by the existence of extreme or clinical forms of anxiety, since anxiety sometimes counts as a basic manifestation of self-control. A surgeon feeling anxious before a complex operation is not failing to exercise self-control: it is precisely because she feels this unpleasant emotion that she can summon the focus and caution needed for the operation to succeed. Here lies the instrumental and *aretic* value of anxiety.

Carolyn Price's *Grief* provides the opportunity to pursue these lines of thought in relation to our complex responses to irreversible loss, as well as to our attitudes towards these responses. If given the opportunity, should we dispense with grief? Price's starting point is to present the charges that have been laid against grief—it is painful, disruptive, futile, irrational and it reveals a kind of weakness. She next examines a possible response to these charges. Psychological states, she points out, may be painful and disruptive without being disorders. For a psychological state to be a disorder, it should additionally result from dysfunctions, which is not obviously true of grief. As to the irrationality charge, Price examines the common response that grief is meaningful: it is the recognition of lost value. According to Price, this response does not go far enough. It leaves the possibility open that grief contains irrational or harmful elements besides the appropriate recognition of loss. Moreover, emphasizing the role of grief in value recognition is likely to backfire as there may be less distressing, preferable ways of recognizing loss. This motivates Price to offer an alternative view, which centers on the fact that grief involves different types of sorrow. The griever should recover as quickly as possible from searching grief, in which feelings do not catch up with the situation. This does not apply to despairing grief, however, where the emotions may be in tune with reality.

In *The Moral Shadows of Shame and Contempt*, Raffaele Rodogno takes up the relation of emotions to the moral domain by focusing on shame and contempt, two emotions whose moral standing has been regularly questioned. He starts by examining which considerations determine their moral standing. Are these considerations substantive in that they involve specific views about what is good? Or are they structural considerations regarding the role of specific emotions within morality? With this basis to hand, Rodogno distinguishes two ways emotions relate to the moral domain. First, one may determine the moral standing of an emotion by the moral or immoral nature of the evaluations and action tendencies it involves. This can only be done against the backdrop of a substantive moral view. Second, one may demarcate emotions that belong to the moral domain from emotions that lie outside it—e.g., on the grounds of their diverging relation to moral concepts, to autonomy, or to our moral practices. This requires no reference to substantive moral views. How do shame and contempt relate to these issues? Rodogno raises worries regarding the methodology behind the empirical data used to support the conclusion that shame is immoral. Moreover, according to him, we should not conclude that shame is outside of the moral domain because it need not engage the subject's responsibility. Another worry concerns the globalist nature of shame and contempt, namely that these emotions may deny their target all moral worth and thereby the possibility of improving. Rodogno highlights how complex the issue is: one may reject the claim that shame and contempt are global, or insist that they can be virtuous in their globalist guise.

The volume then turns to hatred and other reactions involved in racism. In *Negative Emotions in Racism*, Luc Faucher starts by airing his misgivings about monistic theories, according to which all forms of racism are reducible to one element, such as disregard, disrespect or hatred. This leads him to develop a pluralistic theory that distinguishes different forms of racism based on the emotions they involve. Faucher takes inspiration from both philosophy and psychology. He relies on the philosopher Bennett Helm's approach, according to which respect is constituted by a rational pattern of emotions (desires, judgments and actions) directed towards a person. Seen through this lens, racism should be explained by the patterns characteristic of hate and contempt. He then puts this idea into dialogue with three theories in psychology. First, the duplex theory, on which hate has potentially three components: negation of intimacy, negative passion and diminution of commitment. According to this approach, different kinds of hate result from combining these components, which are sensitive to the way the hated group is perceived. Second, the Stereotype Content Model, which similarly emphasizes that different types of discrimination result from different conceptions of the out-groups. In this model, social perception revolves around warmth and competence, and different combinations of warmth and competence produce different types of discrimination mediated by different emotions. Third, the threat-management approach to prejudice, which relies on the idea that each type of emotion is a response to a specific problem. These theories contribute to building Faucher's case for pluralism, as they all postulate that the emotions we experience towards members of out-groups are partially determined by the ways we conceptualize these out-groups, thereby fostering a nuanced picture of racism.

Our last negative emotion, jealousy, has arguably devastating effects that do not pale in comparison to those of racism. Ronald de Sousa's *How to Think Yourself out of Jealousy* tries to remedy the situation by explaining how we can avoid this particularly nasty emotion. De Sousa starts by reminding the reader of the trend whose aim is to rehabilitate the emotions, a trend he has contributed to shaping. Insofar as this rehabilitation is supported by considerations regarding the adaptive role of emotions, he observes that emotions that were once adaptive may prove detrimental in our actual environment, such as the emotions that underlie racism, road rage, xenophobia, disgust at gender identities, envy and jealousy. According to de Sousa, jealousy is indeed a paradigm negative emotion: it is painful, potentially harmful for those it targets and motivates mostly counterproductive actions. He takes exception to recent attempts at rehabilitating jealously, and argues that certain forms of jealousy should simply be eradicated. As a consequence, the bulk of his discussion explores how this could be done. De Sousa's key idea here is that we may convert jealousy into a positive mirror image of itself. The resulting emotion, *compersion*, applies to situations that give rise to paradigmatic forms of jealousy, but differs from it in being positively valenced. Compersion consists in being pleased by the pleasure the beloved takes with another, and it expresses the lover's care for the beloved's autonomy and her potential for pleasure. What is striking here is the idea that the valence of a response can be reversed without modifying its content. De Sousa observes that facts do not by themselves determine the attitudes we take to them. Even if valence reversion is not always easy to achieve, a rich literature full of concrete advice about how best to cultivate desirable alternative attitudes can prove handy.

We hope that this overview of the issues raised by the exploration of negative emotions in this volume showcases its intrinsic interest as well as its potential impact on theorizing about the emotions, which must give due attention to the richness and complexity of our affective lives.

Notes

1. See de Sousa (1987) and Damasio (1994). Karen Jones speaks of a new "pro-emotion consensus" (Jones 2006).
2. See de Sousa (1987, 195).

References

Alain. 1934. *Propos de littérature*. Paris: Hartmann.
Damasio, Antonio. 1994. *Descartes' Error*. New York: Putnam.
de Sousa, Ronald. 1987. *The Rationality of Emotion*. Cambridge, MA: MIT Press.
Jones, Karen. 2006. "Metaethics and Emotions Research: A Response to Prinz." *Philosophical Explorations* 9, no. 1: 45–53.
Kant, Immanuel. 2006. *Anthropology from a Pragmatic Point of View*. Translated by Robert B. Louden. Cambridge: Cambridge University Press.

1 Emotionally Charged—The Puzzle of Affective Valence[1]

Fabrice Teroni

We intuitively distinguish between positive emotions (pride, joy, admiration) and negative emotions (shame, sadness, fear). It is true that we also speak of positive or negative perceptual experiences and memories, but these properties accrue to these states only because of the emotions that we feel when we perceive or remember. This suggests that the positivity or negativity of emotions has priority over that of other mental states. Contemporary researchers interested in this feature of emotions speak in terms of "polarity" or "valence". Elucidating these notions, and understanding what it is that makes emotions positive or negative, is a major theoretical task in the field.

As a point of departure, and along with contemporary accounts of valence, I will presuppose that the kind of features we are trying to get at when talking about the valence of an emotion is distinct from moral or prudential evaluations concerning the emotion. So, we are concerned with the sense in which we all classify shame as a negative emotion, quite independently of any argument about its moral or prudential value. Although it is difficult to be informative at this stage of our discussion, we may say that this presupposition is justified because the sorts of positive things that may be said about shame (viz. that it manifests a virtue in specific circumstances or that it motivates self-reform) are actually explained by its negative valence. Reacting with shame to a wrong one has done can manifest one's decency because shame is a negative emotional reaction to this wrong, and the fact that shame may motivate one to avoid committing such wrongs in the future is also rooted in its negative valence. To put it differently, positive or negative valence is supposed to be a feature intrinsic to types of emotions, and so it is independent of the specific objects that elicit emotions or the potential effects emotions may have. Pride has positive valence despite the fact that it sometimes manifests the vice of pridefulness and the fact that it may lead to vile courses of action.

On the basis of this assumption, my aim is to understand what makes certain emotions positive and others negative. I will focus on the following explanatory constraint: *an account of valence must appeal to a fundamental contrastive property of emotions that does not itself in turn require explanation by another of their properties.* It is fair to say that most participants in contemporary debates would accept this constraint, since valence is supposed to be a basic aspect of emotions. In what follows, I will use this constraint to criticize representative accounts of valence that appeal to desires and hedonic states. I will argue that their explanatory power is largely illusory because the relevant desires need to be explained by hedonic states, and hedonic states are themselves in part composed of emotions. On this basis, I will explore an alternative explanation of valence by means of evaluation and give some reasons to favor one specific evaluative account.

Desire-based Accounts

The first account seeks to explain valence in terms of desire representation. It amounts to claiming that an emotion is positive insofar as it represents a desire as potentially or actually satisfied and negative insofar as it represents the desire as potentially or actually frustrated (Lazarus 1991). Fear is negative because it represents, say, the desire to preserve one's physical integrity as potentially frustrated, whereas joy felt following a victory is positive because it represents the desire to succeed as satisfied. What makes emotions positive or negative is this layer of representations concerning desire. Now, it is certainly plausible to say that positive emotions are those that signal that one "gets what one wants", while negative emotions are those that signal that one does not.

This first account turns out not to be convincing, however. Even if we were to admit that all emotions represent a desire as frustrated or satisfied, itself a dubious claim, we would still be forced to concede that it is not possible to use that representation to analyze valence. This is because the account relies on an ambiguity in the meaning of "frustrated" and "satisfied". Suppose that, while lying on a beach, you come to represent the situation as frustrating your desire to go to a meeting. Claiming that you represent this desire as frustrated can simply amount to attributing to you a representation of this desire as something that cannot be fulfilled—the desire is to go to a meeting, and you appreciate that your lying on the beach means that you will not go. Within the project of explaining valence, an appeal to this kind of representation is legitimate because it does not itself presuppose that the subject has any negative emotion. This is the case since, while lying on the beach, your realization that your desire to go to the meeting cannot be satisfied may leave you unmoved, or even amuse you. Yet, such a representation cannot for the same reason account for negative valence. The theory creates the illusion of an explanation because we also use the notion of being "frustrated" (or "satisfied") to refer to a common affective reaction, one that occurs when we notice irreconcilable differences between the world as it is and how we would like it to be. Realizing that your desire to preserve your physical integrity is likely to be frustrated will typically elicit fear, and realizing that your desire for success has been satisfied will typically elicit pride. However, since we are seeking to understand what makes emotions positive or negative, we cannot allow ourselves to appeal to emotions in the analysis. We must conclude that the first account is either unsatisfying or circular.

This problem may nonetheless not be fatal to all accounts that appeal to desires. Indeed, the second account to which we shall now turn our attention claims that emotional valence results from the presence of particular desires about the emotions (Prinz 2010). Some emotions are positive because we want them to persist (pride, admiration), and others are negative because we want them to cease (fear, shame). The crucial difference between the first and second accounts is that the relevant desires in the second account are not directed at the object of the emotions (the lion of which you are afraid or the victory of which you are proud), but rather at these emotions themselves. For that reason, valence is not claimed to consist in the representation of a desire as satisfied or as frustrated—it rather consists in the content of the desire, which is that the emotion either persists or ceases. There is again something attractive in this appeal to desires about the emotions. After all, states of affairs are often assessed positively because we want them to persist, negatively because we want them to cease. Yet, there are reasons to doubt that explaining valence in terms of these emotion-directed desires pitches the explanation at a satisfactory level.

Suppose that I ask you why you want your shame to cease or your joy to persist. We have two options here. We could first consider the presence of these desires as a primitive fact from the first-person point of view. This is tantamount to conceiving of these desires as urges, that is to say, as desires for which we have no reasons. This answer is unconvincing: desires to see shame dissipate or joy persist are desires for which we have reasons. And, if such desires are intrinsically tied to different types of emotions, these reasons must be found among other aspects of these emotions that can explain their presence (Mulligan 2010). What are these reasons for which we intrinsically desire certain emotions and are intrinsically averse to others? They must have to do with a contrastive property of the emotions that gives us a deeper and more complete explanation of their valence. Thus, this desire-based account stops halfway; it is not fully explanatory of valence. It does not meet the constraint by which we have agreed to abide.

From Hedonic States to Values

In order to reach the required level of explanation, why not try to account for valence by means of hedonic states (Goldstein 2002)? Our desires for some emotions and aversion to others can then easily be explained: fear and shame are unpleasant, which is why we want them to cease, whereas admiration and pride are pleasant, which is why we desire that they persist. In short, emotions are positive or negative in virtue of exemplifying positive or negative hedonic properties. This theory posits that the explanation stops here; because these hedonic properties are fundamental psychological properties, there is no further account of them. At best, we may say that positive and negative emotions have one of two phenomenal "glows" in common (Duncker 1941).

As I hope to make clear, the explanatory force of this third account is largely illusory. To do so, I will present two observations that are central to recent research concerning bodily pain, suggesting that they apply *mutatis mutandis* to other kinds of pain. These observations concern respectively the unity of the category of pain and the theoretical consequences of certain cases of dissociation.

The first observation highlights the rich variety of bodily pains, such as the different types of migraines and joint pain, stomach aches, pain associated with cuts or pain resulting from other modifications of skin tissue. We have at our disposal a broad vocabulary to describe these pains: there are shooting, throbbing, stabbing, darting pains, and so on (Clark 2005). The question then arises, why are we tempted to consider these disparate phenomena as pains? Is it, as the third account of valence claims, because they all exemplify the same unanalyzable hedonic property? One initial reaction to the variety of bodily pains is to grant that they do not have one specific "glow" in common, but to insist that each of them has one phenomenal property that belongs to a kind of properties united by a common experiential core (Crisp 2006). In light of the variety of these phenomena, this claim is far from evident: what exactly does it mean to say that pains have different "glows" that share an experiential core? Is this a genuine alternative to the idea that negative valence is an unanalyzable property? In any case, a momentous tradition, starting with Plato[2] and quite dominant in recent research, tends to draw a deeper lesson from the variety of pains: pains do not even share an experiential core (Labukt 2012). If so, we should find an alternative explanation as to why we consider all of them to be pains.

This explanation is motivated by a second observation prompted by certain cases of dissociation revealed by clinical studies of pain (Grahek 2007). The patients with the dissociative condition in these studies have the capacity to refer to and to recognize their bodily pains, but the latter curiously do not move them at all. When an experimenter pierces their skin with a needle, they tend to smile and say something along the lines of "it is painful, but I don't care". These cases of dissociation suggest that we need to make a distinction. Pain is not a single phenomenon, but is comprised of two distinct aspects. First, it involves a sensory aspect that we can regard as a form of proprioception, whose content can vary considerably. This sensory aspect, however, does not explain what makes a pain negative. To explain that, and in light of the dissociation cases, we must introduce a second feature of pain that we can regard as the subject's reaction to what he discriminates by proprioception. A bodily pain is then a complex phenomenon consisting in the subject's reaction to a sensory representation of a part of his body.

At this point, we find ourselves facing a problem for the hedonic account of valence. The reactive feature of pain can be understood in two ways. We could first claim that it consists in the fact that the subject desires her current mental state to cease (Sidgwick 1874). However, this is tantamount to reverting to the second account of valence, which we have deemed unsatisfactory for emotions and which is also most assuredly unsatisfactory for pains. Much as in the case of emotions, it seems that we want to avoid pains because of their negative aspect. If so, then this aspect cannot simply consist in the presence of a desire. Second, and more plausibly, we can understand the reactive feature of pain in a different way, in terms of affective states (Tye 2005). Victims of dissociation tend to share two types of deficiency. They lack desires about the pain, but seem also to remain emotionally unmoved by what is happening in the affected parts of their body. They somehow do not appreciate that something is "going wrong" there, which seems to be constitutive of our experience of pain. This suggests that, due to their neurological deficit, the victims of dissociation cannot have a certain kind of evaluative experience.

In light of most contemporary approaches, this constitutes the central and distinctive aspect of emotions: emotions are experiences that relate to values and evaluations. This should not come as a surprise, as this relation is linguistically manifest. We speak, for instance, of such values as the shameful, the disgusting, the admirable, the funny, and so on. Contemporary approaches to the emotions take heed of this relation between emotions and values by conceiving of the emotions as experiences that track values and make them manifest (Deonna and Teroni 2012, Prinz 2004, Tappolet, this volume). Now, the claim that pain involves an emotion that allows us to appreciate that something is going wrong in a bodily part carries with it a clear advantage. It allows us to say that this emotional aspect of pain explains the desires typically linked to it: they are desires motivated by the realization that something is going wrong in one's body.

If hedonic states are partially affective, advocates of the hedonic account of valence cannot simply appeal to these hedonic states to explain valence. On the contrary, they must choose one of the two following options. The first option is to generalize our observations about pains and apply them to emotional valence, where the latter is understood in terms of bodily pains and pleasures. So, a subject undergoing fear would appreciate that something is wrong in the way his bodily condition is altered, while a subject undergoing pride would appreciate that something is right in this. More generally, an emotion would be positive or negative insofar as it contains a bodily pleasure or pain. This option is hardly convincing, as it is difficult to resist the idea that what is pleasant or unpleasant in most emotions is not what is happening in our body, but rather some given external situation. What is unpleasant in fear is above all, say, the encounter with a predator. Further, the idea that all emotions contain the appreciation that something right or wrong is going on in parts of our body is itself implausible.

The second option, in light of these difficulties, is to draw a deeper lesson from the parallels between positive and negative emotions, on the one hand, and bodily pleasures and pains, on the other (Solomon 2001). The starting point here is the observation that we should not make a mistake similar to the one consisting in claiming that all bodily pains have a phenomenal property in common. Repeating this mistake would involve, much like in the first option, considering bodily pains and pleasures as features shared by negative and positive emotions. The lesson that we must draw instead is that "pleasant" and "unpleasant" should rather be understood as determinables, of which the determinates are *evaluative experiences*. What is this supposed to mean? Take the property of being colored. It is often claimed that being colored is a determinable with different determinates in order to underscore two things (Johnson 1921). First, it underscores that an object is always colored in virtue of exemplifying a determinate color, say a certain nuance of scarlet red. Second, it underscores that the determinate property cannot itself be defined in terms of the determinable together with a determinate property: the nuance of scarlet red cannot be defined in terms of the determinable "being colored" together with a determinate property (the only suitable determinate property is the nuance itself, and this does not constitute a definition).[3] I suggest that we apply this distinction to the case at hand. "Pleasant" and "unpleasant" are determinables of the determinate values to which types of emotions relate. The unpleasant nature of fear consists in the fact that the subject experiences a danger; the unpleasant nature of sadness consists in the fact that he experiences a loss; the pleasant nature of pride consists in the fact that he experiences a success; and bodily pains and pleasures relate to hedonic values. The valence of an emotion is ultimately nothing but the polarity of the value of which it is an experience: fear and pride have negative and positive valence because they are, respectively, experiences of danger and of success.[4]

If viable, this account of valence is explanatorily deeper than those discussed in the preceding sections and is thus more convincing. It allows us to understand what is positive or negative about certain representations of satisfied or frustrated desires. It explains why we desire for certain experiences to persist and for others to cease. It also accounts for what unifies pains, pleasures and emotions. This is all fine and well, but the viability of the account requires that we make sense of the idea that emotions are experiences of values. The aim of the last section is to explore two ways of understanding this idea.

Emotions and Values

The first and by far dominant approach in emotion theory consists in appealing to the notion of representation. According to it, emotions are experiences of values in the sense that they represent these values (Prinz 2004; Tappolet 2016, this volume). Representation is a ubiquitous feature of psychological states: a belief may represent the fact that the moon is round, a visual experience may represent colors and shapes in one's immediate environment, and so on. The idea is to add values to this list and in this way to account for the valence of emotions in terms of the specific value represented by a given type of emotions. It is, for instance, because fear represents a negative value—danger—that it has negative valence. Despite its appeal to an undisputed feature of psychological states, this approach raises some worries.

First, the fact that a psychological state represents a value does not endow it with valence. For instance, judging that one is facing a danger is to represent danger, yet the judgment is not negatively valenced in the way fear is.

A natural move at this stage is to maintain that emotions represent values *in a specific format* that is not shared by evaluative judgments. Perhaps emotions do represent values in a cognitively less demanding way than evaluative judgments: the former do not, as opposed to the latter, require that one deploy the concept of the relevant value. This may well be true, but it offers a purely negative—and, hence, unsatisfactory—characterization of emotions as experiences of values. How exactly can we make sense of emotional valence in terms of a non-conceptual format of representation?

Second, and relatedly, one may question the very idea that emotions are evaluative experiences because they represent values. Consider less controversial cases of experiences that represent properties, such as a visual experience representing a shade of red or an auditory experience representing the timbre and pitch of a given sound. In such cases, it is difficult to convey the nature of the relevant experiences except by mentioning what they represent. They are experiences that make the relevant visual and aural properties manifest, and this is how they are revealed to us from the first-person perspective (Harman 1990). For this reason, it is difficult to deny that these experiences owe part of their nature to the properties they represent. It is much less clear that fear, shame and pride are similarly revealed to us as experiences of the relevant values. If I ask you to describe how it is to undergo these emotions, it is much more likely that you will mention the specific way your body feels. This is why it is more tempting in the case of emotional experiences than in the case of perceptual experiences to deny that the experiences are what they are—in particular, positively and negatively valenced experiences—because of what they represent.

The second approach understands the idea that emotions are evaluative experiences not in terms of what they represent, but in terms of the specific psychological attitudes that they feature (Deonna and Teroni 2012, 2015). It is customary to analyze psychological states in terms of what is represented, on the one hand, and a given attitude towards it, on the other. For instance, the fact that the moon is round may be believed, supposed or desired. The approach under discussion holds that emotions are evaluative experiences, and hence have positive or negative valence, because of the attitudes that they feature. It is not because fear and pride represent danger and success that they are negatively and positively valenced, but because they feature distinct attitudes. Intuitively, the idea is quite attractive, as it makes much sense to conceive of fear as a negative attitude towards danger and of pride as a positive attitude towards success. But we will be in a position to capitalize on this only if we can be more informative regarding the relevant attitudes.[5]

One idea worth exploring consists in emphasizing the bodily dimension of emotional experience. We concluded our discussion of the first approach to value representation by saying that emotions are not revealed to us as experiences that make values manifest, but rather as bodily experiences. But how exactly is the body manifest in an emotion? It may be argued that emotional experiences feature specific bodily attitudes. In fear, we feel the way our body is poised to act so as to contribute to the neutralization of what provokes the fear. In anger, we feel the way our body is prepared for active hostility to whatever causes the anger. In admiration, we feel the way our body is prepared to further attend to and explore what we admire. According to the approach under discussion, these positive and negative attitudes are key to understanding emotional valence. This is likely to raise the following worries, however.

First, we are pursuing the idea that the valence of emotions is due to their relation to values. So, why is the specific felt bodily attitude that fear involves calibrated to danger? One may similarly wonder as to what makes belief an attitude calibrated to truth—hardly an easy question to answer! The difficulty is compounded in our case, since the relation between the attitude and the value is supposed to account for emotional valence. It is tempting to say that emotions involve attitudes that are *merited* by the relevant values—fear is a distinctive form of rejecting disvalue that is merited by danger, pride a distinctive form of welcoming value that is merited by success, and so on. Still, can we make sense of this idea of merit? The second worry regards the explanatory credentials of an account of valence in terms of felt bodily attitudes. After all, this account is close to the idea that positive emotions are linked to a behavioral tendency, one that consists in pursuing the object of the emotion, and negative emotions are linked to one consisting in evading the object (MacLean 1993). Now, suppose that I ask you why fear is a negative emotion, and you answer that it is because it is associated with a tendency to avoid its object. This tendency is surely not, from your perspective, a brute fact. Yet, if it is further explainable, isn't it in terms of another, deeper negative aspect of fear? Answering this question positively would mean that we have once more failed to locate valence at the appropriate level. Let me conclude with two possible reactions.

The first, deflationary reaction consists in adopting a resolutely pluralist understanding of valence (Solomon 2001): there is nothing like "the valence" of an emotion, but rather various considerations that bear on it and that are likely to go in different directions. We have been led on a wild goose chase, thinking that the label "valence" denotes a unified phenomenon and that our intuitions can be used to track a deep level of explanation. Intuitions are unfit for this task, since they are nothing more than a motley crew. One may well end up concluding that all the accounts of valence we have reviewed have something to be said in their favor, given that they correspond to some of the reasons why we deem emotions positive or negative.

The alternative reaction is to insist that the attitudinal account under discussion is right in understanding valence in terms of the different attitudes we take towards values, since this is a fundamental contrastive property of the emotions. This is not to say that the occurrence of attitudes of rejecting or welcoming cannot be explained. The suggestion is rather that the explanation is not to be found in a deeper contrastive aspect of the emotions—emotions are just valenced reactions to what we apprehend, and no deeper aspect of them explains why this is the case. Yet, the relevant behavioral tendency will typically not appear to the subject as a brute fact. He will know why it occurs, since the explanation is to be found in what he believes or perceives, i.e., in the reasons why he undergoes the emotion.

Notes

1. I thank Otto Bruun, Mary Carman, Julien Deonna, Richard Dub, Anita Konzelmann Ziv and Christine Tappolet for their valuable remarks on a previous version of this chapter.
2. "Pleasure . . . comes in many different forms that are quite unlike each other" (*Philebus* 12 c).
3. It is for this reason that the relation between a determinable and its determinates is distinct from the relation between a genus and its species, where such a definition is possible (e.g., "Man is a rational animal").
4. Labukt (2012) suggests that positive experiences have no phenomenal property in common, but rather an evaluative one: they are those experiences that are intrinsically good in virtue of how they feel. I do not have the space to discuss this approach here, so let me simply suggest that emotions are intrinsically good or bad because they are evaluative experiences (e.g., it is because fear is an experience of danger that it is intrinsically bad in virtue of how it feels).
5. Feldman's (2004) account in terms of attitudinal pleasures, i.e. states of being pleased by something, qualifies as a variant of the approach under discussion. The main worry raised by this account is that it is couched in terms of propositional attitudes that have no distinctive feel (Labukt 2012). Appealing, as I am about to do, to felt bodily attitudes is a way to alleviate this worry.

References

Clark, Austen. 2005. "Painfulness Is not a Quale." In *Pain: New Essays on Its Nature and the Methodology of Its Study*, edited by Murat Aydede, 177–97. Cambridge, MA: MIT Press.

Crisp, Roger. 2006. *Reasons and the Good*. Oxford: Oxford University Press.

Deonna, Julien A., and Fabrice Teroni. 2012. *The Emotions: A Philosophical Introduction*. New York: Routledge.

Deonna, Julien A., and Fabrice Teroni. 2015. "Emotions as Attitudes." *Dialectica* 69, no. 3: 293–311.

Duncker, Karl. 1941. "On Pleasure, Emotion, and Striving." *Philosophy and Phenomenological Research* 1: 391–430.

Feldman, Fred. 2004. *Pleasure and the Good Life: Concerning the Nature, Varieties and Plausibility of Hedonism*. New York: Oxford University Press.

Goldstein, Irwin S. 2002. "Are Emotions Feelings? A Further Look at Hedonic Theories of Emotions." *Consciousness and Emotion* 3, no. 1: 21–33.

Grahek, Nikola. 2007. *Feeling Pain and Being in Pain*. Cambridge, MA: MIT Press.

Harman, Gilbert. 1990. "The Intrinsic Quality of Experience." *Philosophical Perspectives* 4: 31–52.

Johnson, William. 1921. *Logic (Part 1)*. Cambridge: Cambridge University Press.

Labukt, Ivar R. 2012. "Hedonic Tone and the Heterogeneity of Pleasure." *Utilitas* 24, no. 2: 172–99.

Lazarus, Richard S. 1991. *Emotion and Adaptation*. New York: Oxford University Press.

MacLean, Paul. 1993. "Cerebral Evolution of Emotion." In *Handbook of Emotions*, edited by Michael Lewis and John Haviland, 67–83. New York: The Guilford Press.

Mulligan, Kevin. 2010. "Emotions and Values." In *The Oxford Handbook of Philosophy of Emotion*, edited by Peter Goldie, 475–500. New York: Oxford University Press.

Plato. 1997. *Complete Works*, edited by John Cooper. Indianapolis: Hackett.

Prinz, Jesse J. 2004. *Gut Reactions: A Perceptual Theory of the Emotions*. New York: Oxford University Press.

Prinz, Jesse J. 2010. "For Valence." *Emotion Review* 2, no. 1: 5–13.

Sidgwick, Henry. [1874]1981. *The Methods of Ethics*. New York: Hackett.

Solomon, Robert C. 2001. "Against Valence ('Positive' and 'Negative' Emotions)." In *Not Passion's Slave. Emotions and Choice*, 162–77. New York: Oxford University Press.

Tappolet, Christine. 2016. *Emotions, Value and Agency*. New York: Oxford University Press.

Tye, Michael. 2005. "Another Look at Representationalism about Pain." In *Pain: New Essays on Its Nature and the Methodology of Its Study*, edited by Murat Aydede, 99–120. Cambridge, MA: MIT Press.

2 Nasty Emotions and the Perception of Values

Christine Tappolet

The emotions have long been considered at war with reason. Anger, hatred, jealousy, fear, but also pride and pity, among others, have been accused of disturbing our reasoning, of leading us into error, and above all, of favoring irrational behavior, such as actions manifesting weakness of will. Indeed, the same accusation has been made with respect to morally condemnable behavior—think of the violence incited by hatred or jealousy, for example. Following the work of Ronald de Sousa and Antonio Damasio, a new consensus has become largely established among the community of philosophers and scientists interested in the emotions.[1] These thinkers now for the most part maintain that, far from constituting an obstacle, emotions are at once necessary for the proper functioning of reason and essential to moral action. Emotions, according to them, enable us to act in a manner that is more appropriate, whether from the standpoint of self-interest or ethics. Thus, an emotion like fear is held to enable a rapid response to danger while disgust is taken to have the function of alerting us to toxin risks, each thereby promoting the interests of the person experiencing that kind of emotion. From a moral point of view, many have emphasized the importance of emotions like regret and shame in addition to that of positive emotions like compassion. In short, according to this new consensus, emotions may have some defects, but, overall, they are a boon.

Truth be told, however, a good number of emotions lend themselves poorly to this sort of reappraisal. Jealousy, envy, or hatred, for instance, readily come to mind as examples of emotions that appear to be intrinsically nasty.[2] The general question is, what follows from the existence of such emotions? Does admitting that intrinsically nasty emotions exist cast doubt on the project of reappraising the emotions more generally? Or may we find on the contrary that apparently harmful emotions have hidden virtues?[3]

Rather than taking up this vast question, which would involve an in-depth study of different kinds of emotions, this chapter will focus on the narrower question of determining what the existence of *nasty* emotions (in some sense or other of the term "nasty") implies for a view at the heart of a good number of attempts to reappraise the emotions. The view in question is one according to which an emotion is thought to be a kind of perceptual experience that allows us to apprehend the evaluative properties of things, such as their fear-someness or admirableness.

The plan is as follows. The first section presents, as a dilemma, the difficulty of reconciling the idea that there are nasty emotions with the view according to which emotions are a kind perceptual experience. The second examines the notion of a nasty emotion, or more generally of nasty affects—where the term "affect" designates the larger category comprising both emotions and moods, as well as sentiments—and distinguishes different sorts of affective faults, while the third presents a solution to the initial dilemma.

The Nasty Emotion Dilemma

According to a plausible view, emotions play a crucial role because they allow us to become conscious of the positive and negative values of things.[4] More precisely, on this view, feeling an emotion consists in having a sort of percep-tual experience that allows us to apprehend an object's value. Thus, to be afraid of a wolf, for example, is equivalent to having the perceptual experience of the threatening and fearsome character of the wolf. In the same manner, feel-ing disgust is equivalent to apprehending a thing's disgusting character, while admiration for a person allows us to experience their admirable character.

A first consideration that speaks in favor of this view of emotions, which we can call the *perceptual theory*, is that it possesses the virtue of offering a middle way between two predominant theories of emotions that, though they have some plausibility, are far from problem-free. On the one hand, there is the theory that emotions consist in simple bodily feelings like that of an itch (James 1884), and on the other there is the theory that holds that emotions are kinds of judgments (Solomon 1976; Nussbaum 2001). In short, the first approach does not allow us to account for the fact that emotions are about objects. One is afraid of a wolf, admires a feat, or hopes for good weather, while feelings such as itches are in general thought not to be about anything. Clearly, one is not itchy of or about something or other. The second approach, according to which emotions are judgments, is incompatible with the fact that it is certainly possible to experience an emotion without possessing the concepts that would enable us to make the judgments in question—small chil-dren and cognitively simple animals feel fear, but are not thereby capable of judgments of danger.

None of these problems arises for the perceptual theory. First, in contrast to *feeling theories*, the perceptual theory has no problem with the fact that emo-tions concern objects. This is so because perceptual experiences are obviously about objects. We are apprehending the dangerousness or fearsomeness of the wolf or the admirableness of someone's feat, for instance. Second, in contrast to *judgmental theories*, the perceptual theory holds explicitly that we can apprehend evaluative properties without possessing the corresponding evaluative concepts.

A second consideration that militates in favor of the perceptual theory is that there are a number of important similarities between the emotions and sensory perceptions. First, a sensory experience, like the visual experience of a lemon, and an emotion may both be conscious as well as characterized in general by a rich phenomenology. Additionally, sensory experiences and emotions are in general caused by things in our environment. A third characteristic shared between emotions and perceptual experiences concerns their relation to the will: neither is under its direct control. Even if it is possible to position oneself to see things in a certain way, one can hardly decide not to have the visual experience once one has opened one's eyes. Emotions are not under the direct control of our will in much the same way. We cannot simply decide to feel angry—even though we doubtless have a certain *indirect* control over our emotions, as when we breathe through our nose to stave off a bout of anger.[5]

The perceptual theory of emotions is plausible, but by no means uncontroversial. Indeed, it takes only a little thinking to see that there are also important differences between emotions and sensory perceptions. Thus, paradigmatic perceptual experiences, such as color experiences, depend on sensory organs, something which is clearly not true of emotions. Indeed, emotions often depend on the information gathered by the senses, such as when we experience fear on the basis of having seen an approaching wolf. More generally, emotions depend on cognitive bases, whether these are sensory perceptions, beliefs, memories or indeed mere imaginings. Another point is that emotions seem to admit of reasons, in the sense that one can have reasons to fear something or admire someone, while it seems that one cannot have reasons to have visual experiences. One would not, for example, demand of someone who sees a mature lemon as yellow their reasons for seeing the lemon as yellow. Generally speaking, the question at issue is whether these differences imply that emotions cannot be understood as perceptual experiences. This is a question that depends, in the end, on what perceptions are taken to consist in. Arguably, on a sufficiently liberal conception of perception, which, for instance, does not require inputs from a dedicated sensory organ, nothing forbids us from thinking that emotion is a kind of perceptual experience.[6]

The problem that interests me here concerns a challenging implication of the existence of nasty emotions for the perceptual theory. More specifically, nasty emotions constitute a threat to the perceptual theory to the extent that they highlight a potential asymmetry between emotions and perceptual experiences. Emotions can be evaluated as positive or negative, yet this seems not to be the case for sensory perceptions.

In other words, nasty emotions pose a dilemma. The following two propositions both seem plausible, yet they are difficult to reconcile with each other:

(1) Emotions are perceptual experiences of values, and
(2) In contrast with sensory perceptions, emotions can be nasty.

In a schematic way, this dilemma has three solutions.[7] The first consists in denying (1), which of course amounts to rejecting the perceptual theory. The second is to cast doubt on (2), either by affirming that, like emotions, sensory perceptions can be nasty, or by holding that neither emotions nor sensory perceptions can be nasty. Finally, the third solution looks to show that, contrary to appearances, the two claims do not in reality constitute a dilemma, for they are compatible with each other.

Obviously, to evaluate these solutions it is necessary to clarify the notion of a nasty emotion, and it is to this task that I turn now.

Nasty Affects

As one quickly realizes, the phenomenon of nasty emotions is not as simple as it might have seemed at first sight. To begin with, going by general types of emotions, one can enumerate a variety of emotions likely to be considered problematic: fear, disgust, shame, contempt, jealousy, envy, anger, etc. If one considers moods and sentiments as well, then the list would be even longer. It would include states like depression and anxiety, to name two examples of particularly troublesome moods, as well as hatred, which, like love, is naturally taken to consist in a dispositional state that involves experiencing a number of emotions, something that in turn is generally taken to constitute a sentiment.[8]

Moreover, it must be emphasized that it is open to question whether a particular occurrence of any kind of emotion, mood, or sentiment, is nasty. Thus, even if one admits that as kinds of emotion hope or admiration pose no problem, a particular manifestation of one of these—such as the hope that an adversary suffers a resounding failure, or admiration felt towards the cruelty of a hangman—could be morally questionable.

Next, there is a plurality of faults liable to tarnish the emotions or, more generally, the affects.[9] Thus, affects can be characterized as painful, bothersome, harmful, imprudent, unjustified, unfitting, immoral, repugnant, vile, ugly, shameful, ridiculous, etc. Some of these evaluations depend on the fact that one affect can be about another, as when one is ashamed of being afraid, thus taking the fear to be shameful, or when one is disgusted at one's own shame, thus apprehending the shame as repugnant. Other negative evaluations attribute faults unconnected to affects, as when one says that an emotion is imprudent or unjustified. It must be emphasized that these negative evaluations are not exclusive: one's fear can be at the same time bothersome, imprudent and shameful, for instance. Moreover, negative evaluations can crosscut positive ones: one's pride can be pleasant, but also morally problematic.

It will prove useful to propose a classification of the principal affective faults. Generally speaking, one can distinguish two sorts of defects. On the one hand there are *extrinsic* faults, and on the other *intrinsic* faults. In contrast to the latter, the former have their origin not in the affect itself but in the effects produced by this affect. Extrinsic faults can be of different sorts. Emotions, and more generally affects, can cause faults of a cognitive nature.[10] For example, it's often said that love, which is typically taken to be a sentiment, blinds us. In such a case the affect produces a cognitive bias, since the person loved is seen in a more positive light than is accurate. In the same way, one has a tendency to regard the person one hates in a more negative light than is accurate. Emotions can also have harmful effects on the rationality of our actions. Thus, emotions are often capable of making us act against our better judgment, which is a characteristic feature of weakness of will. For example, one might write an insulting letter out of anger even when perfectly aware that it would have grave consequences for several innocent people and judging that this fact is a decisive reason not to write the letter. Such impulsive motivations can result in acts that we regret, either because they are bad for ourselves and thus imprudent, or worse, because they cause harm to others and are thus morally condemnable. Causing imprudent or immoral actions are two ways in which affects can be extrinsically bad.

One finds the same categories in the domain of intrinsic affective faults. Emotions can be intrinsically faulty from a cognitive point of view. So, an emotion of shame can represent things inaccurately, as when one feels ashamed of something not particularly shameful. It's not difficult to imagine someone who is ashamed to have big ears, even though surely, we'd all agree that this is nothing to be ashamed of. Emotions can also be intrinsically irrational. Thus, fearing a little spider that one judges harmless would be considered irrational. The irrationality of this emotion arises from a conflict between emotion and judgment. Here it must be emphasized that the emotion is considered irrational even if it turns out that, contrary to belief, the spider is an extremely dangerous miniature tarantula. In this case fear is entirely fitting, even if irrational in virtue of its conflict with the person's belief.

We have seen that affects can cause imprudent acts. The intrinsic fault that most closely corresponds to this extrinsic fault is that of being painful. It is generally agreed that most if not all affects have positive and negative hedonic properties.[11] Indeed affects can be quite painful. Think of terror, jealousy, shame, guilt, grief and depression, for instance. In so far as this is an intrinsic feature of an affective state, painfulness can be considered to be an intrinsic affective defect that afflicts emotions and other affective states.

Finally, it also seems that an emotion can be intrinsically immoral, independently of its effects on motivation and action. Consider the case of hatred, one of the most problematic affects from a moral point of view. Hatred can be relatively harmless, as when one hates spinach or zucchini. One can also hate a particular aspect of a thing or person, for example, the green color of spinach or someone's indifference. In general, however, this emotion tends to have an all-encompassing, global character.[12] It consists in a complete and total aversion to someone or something, including to whatever might be good about that person or thing. To hate someone is to perceive his or her entire being as hateful. Often hatred pushes people to the worst—mendacity and murder—but it moreover seems vicious in itself, independently of its destructive effects. It seems there is something fundamentally problematic, from a moral point of view, about considering someone to be entirely hateful and bad.

One might wonder what these intrinsically immoral affects have in common. According to one interesting suggestion, the affects in question manifest the fault of not respecting a principle considered by some to be fundamental, namely that one must love the good and hate the bad.[13] Such a principle comports well with holding that schadenfreude, i.e., delight at others' pain, is morally condemnable. If this principle is to be believed, then it is also morally problematic to be saddened by others' joy. In the same way, in so far as anyone has at least some modicum of positive value, it is morally problematic to apprehend a person as entirely hateful and bad.

Whether this principle is accurate or not, the important point here is that there is a large variety of nasty emotions according to all the ways affects can be intrinsically or extrinsically bad.

The Solution

Now that we have a better understanding of what the idea of a nasty emotion covers, we may return to the dilemma. What we have seen permits us to quickly dismiss the proposed solution according to which neither emotions nor perceptions can be characterized as nasty: that simply isn't true! Whatever the verdict for sensory perceptions, it is clear that emotions are sometimes nasty.

What of the suggestion that sensory perceptions, just like emotions, can be nasty? The answer to that question is less forthcoming. In fact, it depends on the sort of fault at stake. Consider first the case of extrinsic faults. We have seen that the emotions can cause (i) cognitive faults, (ii) irrational actions, (iii) imprudent actions, and (iv) immoral actions. Which of these may be true of sensory perceptions as well?

On a closer look, sensory perceptions do not, in fact, seem to differ from emotions from this point of view. They are liable to cause the same problems as emotions. A sensory perception, like that of an oar submerged in water which seems bent, can surely mislead me. Such a perception can lead me to drop the oar in the water even when I perfectly well know that an optical illusion is causing my perception. This action would be irrational, and if I find myself far from the shore and without any other oar, it would also prove imprudent. If, moreover, there is a child on board with me whom I am trying to bring to land, my action will have bad consequences for others. Perhaps I cannot be accused of a moral wrong since I had no intention of doing harm, but the illusory perception's effect could be characterized as morally regrettable all the same.

So far nothing seems to indicate a difference between emotions and sensory perceptions. However, one might object that an important difference arises from the fact that emotions, but not sensory perceptions, are tightly linked to our motivations. Someone feeling fear, for example, is generally motivated to escape the danger he or she perceives. Yet it seems that sensory perceptions, such as my perception of the yellow lemon, are not as tightly linked to our motivations. Here it is important to notice that we can admit this difference concerning motivation while maintaining the parallel between emotions and sensory perceptions. What matters is that sensory perceptions can figure in causal chains that result in actions. That is perfectly sufficient for us to conclude that sensory perceptions can exhibit an extrinsic fault.

Let us now turn to intrinsic faults. We saw that emotions can be intrinsically faulty in four ways: they can be (i) cognitively faulty, (ii) irrational, (iii) hedonically defective and (iv) immoral. The first category clearly applies to the case of sensory perceptions: if I see the lemon as blue when it is a completely normal yellow lemon in normal lighting, the issue is with my perception. The three other categories, by contrast, do not seem to apply as easily to the case of sensory perceptions. One might say that an illusory perception is irrational, but in general we call such perceptions erroneous without also accusing them of irrationality. Similarly, standard cases of sensory experiences, such as color experiences, do not seem to involve painfulness.[14] The case of the intrinsic moral fault is even clearer. It is hard to see how a sensory perception could of itself be intrinsically immoral. My perception of a yellow lemon as blue can be called all manner of things, but we would hardly call it intrinsically immoral or vicious!

The only option at this stage, therefore, is to turn to the third solution mentioned earlier. What the friend of the perceptual theory must try to show is that with respect to intrinsic moral faults, hedonic defects, and intrinsic irrationality, the asymmetry between emotions and perceptions does not invalidate the perceptual theory.

To evaluate the plausibility of this strategy, let us begin by asking why sensory perceptions cannot be intrinsically irrational or immoral. We can point to two factors. First, sensory perceptions are passive; they are representations induced by the world, entirely independent of our control and based on stable and inflexible dispositions.[15] Second, there is what we can call the "amorality" of sensory perceptions: in contrast to emotions, sensory perceptions do not respond to morally relevant, or more generally normatively relevant, characteristics. The experience of the lemon as yellow is about yellowness whereas that of the oar as bent is about the shape of the oar. These two kinds of properties, colors and shapes, are neither moral nor normative in nature. This seems to be generally true of sensory perceptions. That is why we can say that sensory perceptions are amoral.

The emotions, in contrast, are neither entirely passive nor amoral. Indeed, even if emotions are not under our direct control, we have an indirect control over what we feel, as we have already seen. There are a number of things we can do to influence our emotions, and more generally to modify our emotional dispositions. As I said earlier, simply controlling our respiration may enable us to control a bout of anger, or indeed we can dispel our sadness by listening to music. But we can also start a course of therapy, or adopt a dog to overcome a fear of dogs. Thus, emotions depend on systems that can be characterized as plastic, in the sense that they can be molded over time.

Moreover, emotions are far from being amoral. On the contrary, they are tightly linked to values, and therefore to what is by nature normative. Each type of emotion concerns a specific sort of value: the threatening or the fearsome for fear, the disgusting for disgust, the admirable for admiration, and so on. Indeed, this would be hard to deny, and even those who resist the perceptual theory admit as much.

The question now is whether this double asymmetry threatens the idea that emotion is a kind of perception. Upon reflection, it seems that it does not. First, the fact that emotions concern values is simply something that must be granted. Because values are valenced—they can be positive or negative—it follows that emotions divide into two groups: the positive group that is concerned with positive values, and the negative group that is concerned with negative values.[16] But as such this implies nothing in particular for the perceptual theory. It is entirely possible to allow that positive and negative values, just as colors and shapes, may be objects of perceptual experiences.

The fact that emotions are concerned with positive or negative values allows us to explain a further difference between standard sensory experiences and emotions. According to a plausible hypothesis, the fact that some emotions are intrinsically painful, while color experiences cannot be intrinsically painful, comes from the fact that intrinsically painful emotions, but not standard sensory experiences, are concerned with negative values. Against the view that values may be objects of emotional perceptual experiences, one might hold that values are such queer objects that it is hardly possible to say that a state of any kind could make us conscious of them (Mackie 1977). Discussion on this question would lead us too far away. However, it is worth emphasizing that if we admit the existence of such properties as the fearsome or admirable, nothing obliges us to subscribe to the thesis that these properties are queer and, in some sense, imperceptible objects.

Second, the fact that emotions are not entirely passive but are liable to be indirectly modified also implies nothing particular for the perceptual theory. To see this, it is sufficient to imagine that our visual perceptions depend on plastic systems that evolve with time. Let us imagine, for example that small children see the world in black and white and shift progressively to polychromatic vision. Even if we admitted beyond doubt that their vision was not perfect, we certainly would not want to say that a child does not have a visual perception when she sees the lemon as pale gray!

Conclusion

What to make of these remarks? First of all, sensory perceptions are in reality more similar to emotions than we might have thought. As we have seen, sensory perceptions themselves can have all sorts of faults. Next, if, in contrast to sensory experiences, emotions can be intrinsically irrational and painful as well as immoral, it is because the latter possess distinctive characteristics. Emotions are not entirely passive, and by their link to values they are not amoral. Given that negative emotions are concerned with negative values, it makes sense that in contrast to standard sensory perceptions, emotions can be intrinsically painful. However, we must conclude that these differences with sensory perceptual experiences do not force us to abandon the idea that emotions consist in perceptual experiences that allow us to apprehend values. Put simply: the perceptual theory is not threatened.

What does this imply for the question of the reappraisal of the emotions? Proponents of reappraisal can rejoice that the theory according to which emotions can, when things go well, allow us to grasp the value of things, remains intact. In cases where admiration is fitting, for example, this emotion allows us to apprehend the admirable character of a thing or person. That is an undeniable benefit. But we must nevertheless face the fact that emotions are liable to be afflicted by all sorts of faults of varying degrees of seriousness, from cognitive failures to foul vice, passing through imprudence.

Notes

I had the opportunity to present these ideas at a round table organized at the Congress of the Canadian Philosophical Association in June 2010 as well as to the *Thumos* research group in Geneva. I would like to thank Luc Faucher, David Furrer, Kevin Mulligan, Ronnie de Sousa and especially Fabrice Teroni and Anita Konzelmann Ziv for their helpful comments. Thanks also to Paul Boswell for translating this chapter into English. My work for this chapter was supported by the FQRSC and the SSHRC, which I gratefully acknowledge.

1. See de Sousa (1987); Damasio (1994); and Nussbaum (2001), among others.
2. For a critique of jealousy, see de Sousa, this volume.
3. For such a strategy as applied to anxiety, see Kurth, this volume.
4. See de Sousa (1987); Tappolet (2000 and 2016); Döring (2003); Prinz (2004); Deonna (2006), among others.
5. For more details on these arguments, see Tappolet (2016, Chapter 1).
6. See Deonna and Teroni (2012) and Brady (2013), as well as the discussion in Tappolet (2016).
7. Note that this problem has the same structure as that posed by the existence of irrational emotions; see Tappolet (2012).
8. See Naar (2013).
9. See Kristjánsson (2003) for a classification of different sorts of negative emotions. The classification proposed here is more inclusive.
10. See, for instance, Goldie (2008).
11. See Teroni, this volume.
12. As Rodogno, this volume, emphasizes, shame and contempt appear to have a similar *globalist* nature, in that they involve a nasty evaluation of oneself or of someone else as a whole.
13. See Hurka (2001), who attributes this principle to Aristotle and G. E. Moore.
14. Some consider pain to be a perceptual experience (see Tye 1996, *inter alia*), but even so, everyone would agree that the perception of color or of sound is unlikely to be intrinsically painful.
15. In any case, this is so for sensory perceptions that are not conceptually enriched; see Siegel (2006) for a discussion of how acquired recognitional dispositions modify perceptual content.
16. See Teroni, this volume.

References

Brady, Michael S. 2013. *Emotional Insight*. Oxford: Oxford University Press.

Damasio, Antonio R. 1994. *Descartes' Error: Emotion, Reason and the Human Brain*. New York: Gossett/Putnam.

Deonna, Julien A. 2006. "Emotion, Perception and Perspective." *Dialectica* 60, no. 1: 29–46.

Deonna, Julien A., and F. Teroni. 2012. *The Emotions: A Philosophical Introduction*. New York: Routledge.

de Sousa, Ronald. 1987. *The Rationality of Emotion*. Cambridge, MA: MIT Press.

Döring, Sabine A. 2003. "Explaining Action by Emotion." *The Philosophical Quarterly* 53, no. 211: 214–30.

Goldie, Peter. 2008. "Misleading Emotions." In *Epistemology and Emotions*, edited by Georg Brun, Ulvi Dogluoglu and Dominique Kuenzle, 149–65. Farnham: Ashgate Publishing Company.

Hurka, Thomas. 2001. *Virtue, Vice and Value*. New York: Oxford University Press.

James, William. 1884. "What Is an Emotion?" *Mind* 9: 188–205.

Kristjánsson, Kristján. 2003. "On the Very Idea of 'Negative' Emotions." *Journal for the Theory of Social Behaviour* 33, no. 4: 351–64.

Mackie, John. 1977. *Ethics: Inventing Right and Wrong*. Harmondsworth: Penguin.

Naar, Hichem. 2013. "A Dispositional Theory of Love." *Pacific Philosophical Quarterly* 94, no. 3: 342–57.

Nussbaum, Martha C. 2001. *Upheavals of Thought*. Cambridge: Cambridge University Press.

Prinz, Jesse J. 2004. *Gut Reactions: A Perceptual Theory of Emotion*. New York: Oxford University Press.

Siegel, Susanna. 2006. "Which Properties Are Represented in Perception?" In *Perceptual Experience*, edited by Tamar Szabo Gendler and John Hawthorne, 481–503. New York: Oxford University Press.

Solomon, Robert C. 1976. *The Passions*. Indianapolis, IN: Hackett Publishing Company.

Tappolet, Christine. 2000. *Emotions et valeurs*. Paris: Presses Universitaires de France.

Tappolet, Christine. 2012. "Emotions, Perceptions and Emotional Illusions." In *Perceptual Illusions: Philosophical and Psychological Essays*, edited by Clotilde Calabi, 207–24. Houndsmill: Palgrave Macmillan.

Tappolet, Christine. 2016. *Emotions, Values, and Agency*. Oxford: Oxford University Press.

Tye, Michael. 1996. *Ten Problems of Consciousness: A Representational Theory of the Phenomenal Mind*. Cambridge, MA: MIT Press.

3 Imaginative Resistance

Negative Emotions, Values and Fiction

Anne Reboul

There does not seem to be any limits to what we can imagine, from time travel in H. G. Wells's *Time Machine*, to the magical exploits of the heroes of the Harry Potter saga. What is more, our imagination can take different forms: we can imagine that it is true that Harry Potter is a wizard able, among other things, to speak the language of snakes; we can also mentally visualize the griffins he meets at Hogwarts or hear the sound of the "howler" Mrs. Weasley sends to her son Ron for having borrowed the family's flying car without permission. Thus, our imagination, both as far as the contents imagined (time travel, magic, etc.) and the ways in which we imagine them (visual, auditory, etc.) are concerned, seems not to be constrained in any way other than that we ourselves enforce. In other words, the imagination that we enjoy seems to be entirely under voluntary control.

Yet, at the end of the eighteenth century, the Scottish philosopher David Hume, in an essay devoted to taste in literature (*Of the Standard of Taste*, see Hume 1826), had noted that there is an asymmetry in our faculty of imagination between two sorts of contents, "factual" contents (e.g., "Harry Potter is a wizard") and "evaluative" contents (e.g., "Killing girls at birth is good"). Indeed, while we have no difficulty in imagining a factual content, even when it contradicts our beliefs, we have great difficulties in imagining an evaluative content that contradicts our convictions. Thus, we have no difficulties in imagining that Harry Potter is a wizard, but we find it difficult or impossible to imagine that killing girls at birth is a good deed.

A first thing to note is that the difficulty has nothing to do with imagining that a fictional character could hold moral beliefs contradictory with our own. Rather it has to do with imagining that moral beliefs contradictory with our own could be valid. Thus, we find it easy to imagine that Voldemort, Harry Potter's enemy, believes that killing "muggles" (non-wizards) is a good idea. Yet we find it difficult to think that killing muggles is a good deed. Hume's idea has been discussed in Walton (1994), who has come up with the term *imaginative resistance*, and discussed by Stokes (2006). Here I will stay with Hume's basic notion of an asymmetry between our imagination for factual and evaluative contents.

This asymmetry described by Hume between easy to imagine factual contents and evaluative contents triggering "imaginative resistance" (i.e., which are difficult if not impossible to imagine) seems to go against the imaginative freedom described above. This might be just an appearance, depending on how imaginative resistance is understood: is it a *refusal* to imagine or an *inability* to imagine? If a refusal, then our imaginative freedom remains untouched, because imagination still is under voluntary control. If, on the other hand, it is an inability to imagine, then part of our imagination is not under voluntary control, and our imaginative freedom is not unlimited.

I will defend here the idea that imaginative resistance is the result of an inability to imagine evaluative contents that contradict our beliefs and I will explain that inability by the negative emotions that such contents trigger.

A General Asymmetry

As we have just seen, imaginative resistance is due to an asymmetry between factual and evaluative contents. It is thus an important question whether this asymmetry is specific to fiction. As Kevin Mulligan (1998) has noted, the contrast between factual and evaluative contents is just as striking in ordinary discourse: while we expect evaluative discourses to lead to controversy, we do not expect factual discourse to do so. If I sincerely say "It is raining today", I do not expect contradiction. On the other hand, if I sincerely say "Sexual freedom is a good thing", I do expect contrary opinions to manifest themselves. Thus, it does not seem that the asymmetry between factual and evaluative contents is in any way specific to fiction.

As noted by Mulligan, the two types of content, factual and evaluative, while they both can be evaluated for truth-value, are not open to the same processes of justification. If my interlocutor says "This is not true" in answer to my remark about the weather, I can point out to her the gray sky and the rain to justify the truth of my assertion. This is not the case if my interlocutor contradicts my claim as to the value of sexual freedom. Factual contents outside of fiction are justified directly by their fit with reality, which is not the case for evaluative contents.

This difference in contents is also found in the sentences used to express them. Sentences expressing evaluative contents use evaluative adjectives, such as *good/bad*, *courageous/cowardly*, *beautiful/ugly*, etc. These adjectives correspond to properties (e.g., courage or cowardice) that are not directly perceived in the environment, but which are nonetheless linked to perceivable properties. Mulligan gives the example of Sam who sees a big dog with its hackles up and is afraid. His emotion (fear) is linked to his perception of the dog which justifies his judgment that the dog is dangerous (the evaluative content). Thus, according to Mulligan's paper, emotions are justified by perceptions of natural properties and in turn justify evaluative judgments.

More precisely, Mulligan proposes the four scenarios below:

(1) Perceptual content justifies belief:

- The vision that Sam has of the dog justifies his belief according to which there is a big dog with its hackles up;

(2) Perceptual content justifies emotion:

- The vision that Sam has of the dog justifies his fear;

(3) Belief justifies emotion:

- The fact that Sam believes that there is a big dog with its hackles up justifies his fear;

(4) Emotions justify evaluative judgments:

- Sam's fear justifies his judgment according to which the dog is dangerous.

These four scenarios have to do with the justification of evaluative judgments out of fiction. But what happens in fiction?

Emotions and Imaginative Resistance

It should be noted that, though Hume limited his essay to literary fiction, fiction, which nowadays includes cinema, television, computer games, as well as drama or opera, has different forms, allowing perception, which obviously is not the case for literary fiction.

The spectator of a theatrical, cinematographic, televisual or electronic fiction can, because she has perceptions, follow any of the scenarios described above. On the other hand, the reader of a literary fiction is limited to the last two: belief justifies emotion; emotion justifies evaluative judgment. I will begin by discussing literary fiction even though the explanation of imaginative resistance that I will propose can apply to all forms of fiction.

In literary fictions, the reader's beliefs, though under voluntary control, are dependent for their contents on what the author wrote. Yet, the beliefs induced by the sentences in the novel or by imagination are different from ordinary beliefs in that they don't lead (or don't lead directly) to action. Let us suppose that I believe that a robber is trying to get into my flat (I hear weird noises). I will quite legitimately call the police and ask them to come. Let us suppose on the other hand that I imagine that there is a robber trying to get into my flat. I can imagine calling the police. But if I actually call the police, it seems that I have a major cognitive problem: I do not distinguish between reality (where my belief leads legitimately to action) and fiction or imagination (where it does not). Thus, it seems that there is a difference between beliefs relative to reality and beliefs relative to imaginative contents.

To capture this difference, it has often been said that the second, by contrast with beliefs about reality, are 'quasi-beliefs'. It should be clear that there is a link between the reason for which quasi-belief cannot legitimately lead to action and the fact that quasi-belief about fiction is under voluntary control. Quasi-belief cannot legitimately lead to action because it is not about reality. And it is because it is not about reality that it is under voluntary control. Our ordinary beliefs are not. Being under voluntary control is thus a strong indication to the fact that a mental state of a given kind is a quasi-mental state of that kind. The main question is whether other kinds of mental states, apart from beliefs, can also be quasi- in that sense.

In literary fiction, it is thus quasi-beliefs that justify the reader's emotions, these emotions themselves justifying her evaluative judgments. The central question then is the status both of the emotions triggered by the factual quasi-beliefs of the reader and the status of the evaluative judgments those emotions justify: are they emotions or quasi-emotions and are they evaluative judgments or evaluative quasi-judgments?

It should be remembered that quasi-beliefs, even if induced by what the author says, are under voluntary control. By parity of reasoning, the emotions triggered by the factual quasi-beliefs can only be seen as quasi-emotions if they too are under voluntary control. In the same way, evaluative judgments triggered by a fiction can only be seen as quasi-judgments if they too are under the voluntary control of the reader. And this is where evaluative resistance comes in.

Indeed, imaginative resistance suggests that evaluative judgments are not under voluntary control: we cannot, as we do for a factual content that contradicts our convictions, imagine an evaluative content that contradicts our convictions. In other words, if there are factual quasi-beliefs that are different from factual beliefs because they are both under voluntary control and do not lead to action, there are no evaluative quasi-judgments that are under voluntary control. Thus, while we can imagine, i.e., consider as true in J. K. Rowling's saga, that Harry Potter talks to snakes, we cannot imagine, what is considered as true in the *Odyssey*, that Helen did a good deed when she left her husband and children to follow Paris, leading to the Trojan war, to the destruction of Troy and to numerous deaths on both sides.[1]

Thus, there are no evaluative quasi-judgments, but only evaluative judgments. Given Mulligan's analysis of the justification of evaluative judgments on the basis of the underlying emotions (Sam's fear justifies his judgment that the dog is dangerous), this suggests that there are no quasi-emotions either. In other words, fiction triggers emotions that are strictly identical as far as their nature is concerned to the emotions triggered by the perception of reality and by ordinary beliefs. From that point of view, the evaluative judgments triggered by a fiction are not less justified than are those triggered by reality.

Mulligan notes that his analysis, which sees emotions as justifying evaluative judgments, constitutes a reversal of the commonly postulated order according to which it is an evaluative adjective that is (at least in part) the basis of any emotion (on this debate, see Prinz 2007; Brady 2009, 2013, 2014; Deonna and Teroni 2014; Pelser 2014; Tappolet 2016). Yet, if that reverse order was the case, then, it would be impossible to explain imaginative resistance: nothing would prevent the reader to imagine an evaluative content that contradicts her own convictions. Indeed, given that the reader has no general difficulty in imagining factual contents that contradict what she knows about the world, the same should be true of evaluative contents, if they are dependent on her lexicon or her concepts, rather than on her emotions. Hence, the problem of imaginative resistance, i.e., explaining the asymmetry between imagining factual contents and imagining evaluative content, would gain a new momentum.

Thus, if Mulligan is right in thinking that emotions justify evaluative judgments, given that emotions are not under voluntary control, this suggests the following scenario for imaginative resistance:

(1) The reader builds factual quasi-beliefs on the basis of the descriptive sentences of fiction;
(2) These quasi-beliefs trigger an emotion;
(3) The emotion triggers an evaluative judgment;
(4) This evaluative judgment contradicts another evaluative judgment that is proposed as true by the fiction;
(5) Hence imaginative resistance, i.e., the reader's inability to form an evaluative judgment in agreement with the fiction.

Let us go back to Helen's example:

(1) The reader of the *Iliad* and *Odyssey* forms a number of quasi-beliefs:

- Helen is married to Menelaus, king of Sparta and brother of Agamemnon;
- She goes away with Paris, son of Priam, king of Troy, leaving her husband and children;
- To get her back, the Greeks wage war on Troy;
- Troy is destroyed after numerous and violent fights;

(2) These quasi-beliefs trigger complex emotions: compassion for the dead warriors and for the Trojans' misfortune, anger relative to Helen's acts that have led to this suffering;
(3) These emotions trigger an evaluative judgment:

- Helen has behaved disgracefully and irresponsibly;

(4) This evaluative judgment is in contradiction with that proposed in the fourth canto of the *Odyssey*, where Helen is presented as having behaved in the right way;
(5) Hence imaginative resistance, i.e., the inability of the reader to have a positive judgment of Helen's actions, in agreement with Homer's assessment.

The same type of explanation goes for cinematographic, theatrical, etc., fictions, where it may be the very perception of a situation that triggers directly either a quasi-belief which itself triggers an emotion, or an emotion.

Here, it is interesting to go back to why Homer had such an admiration for the erring Helen, because it highlights the fact that there can be fairly wide cross-cultural variation in imaginative resistance.[2] As Dreyfus and Kelly (2011) point out, Homer's appreciation is based on the appropriateness between Helen's actions and the goddess that she depends on, Aphrodite. Her actions are consonant with what Aphrodite stands for, "the sacred erotic dimension of life" (Dreyfus and Kelly 2011, 62). In other words, the Homeric Greeks do not share into our imaginative resistance (indeed, they presumably would have imaginative resistance to our own condemnation of Helen). Thus, imaginative resistance is sensitive to cultural beliefs. This suggests that it may be variable not only through space but also through time.

Overcoming Imaginative Resistance

So, while evaluative content is subject to imaginative resistance, which suggests that evaluative judgment is resistant to change, there may be variation in evaluative judgments across cultures and times, suggesting the reverse. The ancient Greeks would imaginatively resist judging Helen's actions negatively, while we would imaginatively resist judging them favorably. How is that possible?

The evaluative judgments we produce are justified by our emotions, which, in the case of literary fiction, are dependent on factual beliefs or on factual quasi-beliefs. Among the beliefs that the ancient Greeks had and that led them, combined with the factual quasi-beliefs relative to Helen's conduct outlined above, to a positive feeling and a positive evaluation is the idea that there are links between gods and humans, which constrain human action. Clearly, while we share the factual quasi-beliefs about what Helen did, we do not share this "factual" belief relative to God-driven human action. And this colors our emotions relative to Helen's actions and orients them in the opposite direction to what they would have been if we had shared that belief.

Here, it seems clear that background beliefs of that sort have basically changed throughout the great distance in time that separates us from the ancient Greeks. Religion has undergone major changes and human responsibility has become paramount with the notion of free will. But beyond this specific example, it seems that there are much quicker changes in evaluative judgment which have occurred in the fairly recent past and that, in some cases at least, may have been partly caused by changes in emotions brought by literary fiction. In other words, the idea that emotions triggered by fiction are authentic emotions can explain why fiction can have a role in building our perception of values and in changing our evaluative judgments by allowing us to overcome imaginative resistance.

Here I would like to briefly discuss an example in which changes have occurred within human memory, adultery. While no one would condone adultery or think it the best of possible behaviors, our views toward it have undergone a sea change. From the worst possible thing to do (mostly for woman) after murder, it has become rather a minor error of behavior. And that change of views has been accompanied by changes in law. Adultery has been harshly punished throughout human history and cultures (with much harsher punishment for adulterous wives than for adulterous husbands). Indeed, laws punishing adultery have only been repelled during the second half of the twentieth century in Western countries.[3] The reasons for this major change are complex, but one possible factor is the change in evaluative judgments that were triggered by literary fictions and as an example, I would like to discuss quickly two major novels of the nineteenth century, *Madame Bovary* and *Anna Karenina*.

On the face of it, the two novels tell very similar stories: a woman commits adultery and ends up killing herself. Yet the two women behave quite differently, both in the ways they commit adultery and in their motivations for it, and in the ways they commit suicide and in their motivations for it. Flaubert's Mme Bovary is a fairly unintelligent, rather poorly educated reader of romances, who, faced with marriage to the dull Charles, hunts after what she believes to be her due, i.e., true love. This leads her first in the arms of the rogue Rodolphe, a provincial seducer, and then in those of the mediocre Leon, while her husband looks on in passive ignorance. Indeed, she commits suicide because discovery becomes inevitable, thus crowning her disgraceful behavior with an ultimate act of moral cowardice. If anything, Emma (Mme Bovary) is the reverse of a romantic heroine. She is never truly in love and her egotism, which leads her to contemplate without a qualm abandoning her child, is permanently to the fore.

Anna Karenina, by contrast, is a dutiful woman, cultivated and intelligent, married to an honorable but rigid and boring high civil servant. She has a son that she loves. She meets Vronsky and falls in love with him. In contrast with Emma, she does not hide her adultery and ultimately publicly leaves her husband to live openly with her lover. Her husband refuses to let her take her child with her and to let her see him. She is ostracized by society as an adulterous woman, while Vronsky is not. She commits suicide when it seems obvious to her that Vronsky is falling out of love with her.

While having compassionate feelings for Emma is difficult, having compassionate feelings for Anna is not. Whereas Emma is not only deceiving her husband, but also deceiving herself as to the strength of her feelings for her rather dismal lovers, Anna is deceiving neither her husband, nor herself. She is in love with Vronsky and ready to pay the price for her feelings. The Western literary fiction has given a rich place to romantic love and its afflictions, changing popular feelings toward love-motivated transgressions and overcoming imaginative resistance to notions according to which adultery may be, if not commendable, at least understandable in some circumstances.

Conclusion

Fiction has often been attacked on the grounds that it favors idleness or perverts morals. Thus, young women were forbidden to read novels in the morning (a time set aside for serious activities such as embroidery) and some novels, e.g., *Madame Bovary*, have led to trials for immorality during the nineteenth century and even during the twentieth century (e.g., D. H. Lawrence's *Lady Chatterley's Lover*). Yet, on the other hand, defenders of fiction have often claimed that fiction (and notably literary fiction) has a role to play in moral development, precisely because it allows or reinforces the development of moral values (see Carroll 2002; Sidney 2001).

Let us note that while they have been used on opposite sides, either to attack or defend fiction, these two arguments share a common ground, the idea that fiction can have an influence on our perception of values or, in other words, on the formation of our evaluative judgments.

Evaluative judgments, as we saw, are expressed by evaluative adjectives. The use of these adjectives, to be appropriate, rests on the sequence that goes from perceptual experiences to emotions, through factual beliefs. The emotions can also be triggered by quasi-beliefs drawn from fiction, which justifies the arguments for and against fiction outlined above. What fiction can do is refine emotions, as shown by the comparison between the emotions triggered by two well-known novels, *Anna Karenina* and *Madame Bovary*. They tell *prima facie* very similar stories about very similar women: both are adulterous women that end up by committing suicide. Yet, while Emma's actions by and large trigger negative emotions such as despise or disgust, Anna's trigger sympathy or compassion. What literary fiction allows us to do in such cases is to refine our evaluative judgments by allowing us to develop different emotions relative to apparently similar scenarios: indeed, adultery is not a good deed, but circumstances may tamper somewhat that harsh evaluation and lead to a more compassionate judgment.

In other words, fiction can not only trigger imaginative resistance, but also modify it through a refinement of the emotions that it is causing, either through factual quasi-beliefs or through perception.

Notes

1. I borrow this example from Dreyfus and Kelly (2011, Chapter 3).
2. One clear example has been given above: "Killing girls at birth is a good idea". While in most countries, this would lead to imaginative resistance, there are cultures in which it seems to be a much more acceptable moral view, e.g., in some parts of China or India (see Hvistendahl 2011).
3. They do remain in effect in most non-Western countries.

References

Brady, Michael. 2009. "The Irrationality of Recalcitrant Emotions." *Philosophical Studies* 145, no. 3: 413–30.

Brady, Michael. 2013. *Emotional Insight*. Oxford: Oxford University Press.

Brady, Michael. 2014. "Emotion, Attention, and the Nature of Value." In *Emotion and Value*, edited by Sabine Roeser and Cain Todd, 52–71. Oxford: Oxford University Press.

Carroll, Noel. 2002. "The Wheel of Virtue: Art, Literature, and Moral Knowledge." *Journal of Aesthetics and Art Criticism* 60, no. 1: 3–26.

Deonna, Julien, and Fabrice Teroni. 2014. "In What Sense Are Emotions Evaluations." In *Emotion and Value*, edited by Sabine Roeser and Cain Todd, 15–31. Oxford: Oxford University Press.

Dreyfus, Hubert, and Sean Dorrance Kelly. 2011. *All Things Shining: Reading the Western Classics to Find Meaning in a Secular Age*. New York: Free Press.

Hume, David. 1826. "Essay XXIII. Of the Standard of Taste." In *Philosophical Works of David Hume*, Vol. III, 256–82. Edinburgh: Black, Tait & Tait.

Hvistendahl, Mara. 2011. *Unnatural Selection: Choosing Boys Over Girls, and the Consequences of a World Full of Men*. New York: Public Affairs.

Mulligan, Kevin. 1998. "From Appropriate Emotions to Values." *The Monist* 81, no. 1: 161–88.

Pelser, Adam. 2014. "Emotion, Evaluative Perception, and Epistemic Justification." In *Emotion and Value*, edited by Sabine Roeser and Cain Todd, 107–23. Oxford: Oxford University Press.

Prinz, Jesse J. 2007. *The Emotional Construction of Morals*. New York: Oxford University Press.

Sidney, Sir Philip. 2001. "The Defense of Poesy." In *English Essays: Sidney to Macaulay*, Vol. XXVII, 1909–14. New York: The Harvard Classics, P.F. Collier & Son. Bartleby.com. www.bartleby.com/27/.

Stokes, Dustin. 2006. "The Evaluative Character of Imaginative Resistance." *British Journal of Aesthetics* 46, no. 4: 387–405.

Tappolet, Christine. *Emotions, Values and Agency*. Oxford: Oxford University Press, 2016.

Walton, Kenneth. 1994. "Morals in Fiction and Fictional Morality." *Proceedings of the Aristotelian Society*, Supplementary 68: 27–66.

4 Who is Afraid of Contrary Emotions?

Clotilde Calabi and Marco Santambrogio

The Issue of Contrary Emotions

Are there genuinely contrary emotions and is it irrational to feel them simultaneously? It certainly is irrational to believe that Real Madrid won the 2016 UEFA Champions League Final and simultaneously disbelieve it—i.e., believe that Real Madrid did *not* win the 2016 UEFA Champions League Final. On the other hand, it can happen to everyone to feel pleased to some extent that Real Madrid won the 2016 UEFA Champions League Final and simultaneously displeased with it to some extent. Nothing irrational appears to be involved here.[1]

Some philosophers have concluded that such emotions cannot be genuinely contrary. If they were, so it is argued, it would be hard to understand why they do not constitute an irrational pair. Maybe the objects of these emotions are not one and the same. For instance, one can be pleased with some *aspect* of the outcome of the UEFA Champions League Final and displeased with some *other* aspect of it. Thus, emotional attitudes, such as being pleased and displeased, do not fully parallel cognitive attitudes, such as belief, in so far as their objects are not, or fundamentally not, the propositions referred to by the 'that'-clauses following the attitude verb.

In this paper we take the opposite stance: we argue that emotional attitudes are fundamentally propositional and entirely parallel belief, knowledge and other cognitive attitudes. Moreover, the notion of contrariety is *not* to be understood differently for emotions than for judgments. Thus, some emotions that have the same object *are* genuinely contrary. We provide an account of why this involves no irrationality. Greenspan (1976) suggested that the logic of emotions differs from that of belief. We agree and identify where exactly they diverge.

Conflicts Between Beliefs and Between Emotions

Beliefs go awry when they are false. But false beliefs are not all on a par. If I believe that Tom is at home because Mary told me, but in fact she was wrong, then I believe something that is, as a matter of fact, false. This can be a more or less serious matter, depending on what is at stake, but no one would blame me of irrationality. If I believed that the Earth is flat, contrary to all the evidence available to me, then there would be something more deeply wrong with me. It would be even worse if I believed that Groucho is taller than Chico, Chico is taller than Harpo, and Groucho is not taller than Harpo, since I ought to be able to see by myself that this could not possibly be true. This is a definitely irrational belief. Besides single beliefs, sets of them can also be irrational. For instance, it is irrational to believe that Hesperus is not a planet while also believing that Hesperus is the same as Phosphorus and believing that Phosphorus is a planet.[2] These beliefs are inconsistent and everyone ought to be able to see that they cannot all be true together.

A number of philosophers, poets and laymen have taken emotions to be, unlike beliefs, beyond the pale of reason. In the past decades, however, the thesis that emotions can themselves be assessed as to their rationality has gained much consensus. Emotions can be ascribed to a subject by means of statements of various syntactic forms. We ordinarily say "Tom is afraid of flying", "Mary is pleased with the outcome of the competition" etc., but, in this paper, we are only concerned with emotional states that are ascribed by such statement as "Subject S EMOTES that *p*"—where EMOTES is a placeholder for verbs like *fear, hope, is disgusted, is pleased,* etc., and *that p* is a proposition, such as *that it will rain tomorrow,* that is the *object* of the emotional state, in the following sense. In "Mary fears that Lady Gaga might not show up", which ascribes fear to Mary, the clause "that Lady Gaga might not show up" gives the correct answer to the question "What is it that Mary fears?" Such emotion ascriptions closely parallel belief ascriptions, which fundamentally are of the form "S believes that *p*"—that *p* being the object, in the sense specified above, of S's belief.[3]

There is a general reason for claiming that belief and other cognitive attitudes must have the same objects as emotions. We ordinarily say, for instance,

(1) Sam knows that it is possible that Lady Gaga might not show up and Mary fears it,
(2) Sam believes that Lady Gaga might not show up and Mary hopes the same,
(3) Sam remembers that Lady Gaga did not perform in the past two years and Mary regrets it.

Taken at face value, 1–3 can be true. The most straightforward way of accounting for this is to claim that sameness of their 'that'-clauses shows that propositions can be the objects of both cognitive and emotional attitudes.

Usually, only individual emotional episodes—such as an intense experience of amusement, an excruciating feeling of remorse, a paralyzing fear—are examined for appropriateness and rationality. However, much as whole systems of beliefs, besides individual beliefs, can be rationally assessed, similarly we can also ask which systems of emotions are rational.

Let us call a set of episodes of emotions *inconsistent* if the propositions that are their objects are inconsistent, i.e., cannot all be true together. If emotions and cognitive attitudes such as belief were exactly similar with respect to rationality, then it seems that it should be as irrational to have inconsistent emotions as it is to have inconsistent beliefs. Othello is generally deemed to be out of his mind, i.e., irrational, when he shouts in despair:

> *By the World,*
> *I thinke my Wife be honest, and thinke she is not:*
> *I thinke that thou art iust, and thinke thou art not.*
>
> (Shakespeare, Othello, Act 3, Scene 3)

Is there any kind of irrationality in the following cases involving emotions, however?

(1) Sam and Mary, who are close friends, compete for the same job at a philosophy department. Sam gets the job. Mary is at the same time pleased and displeased that he gets it.[4]

(2) Actress Lola, sitting in the audience at the Emmy Awards' ceremony, fears that Ricky Gervais will mention her on stage and also fears that Ricky Gervais will not mention her.

Mary has two contrary emotions—she is both pleased and displeased—with the same object, referred to by the same 'that'-clause. The contrariety of being pleased to being displeased closely parallels that between belief and disbelief. Lola, on the other hand, is ascribed emotions of the same kind (fear) with two contradictory propositions as objects—that Ricky Gervais will mention her on stage and that he will not.

Cases like these are quite common. If Mary and Lola are irrational to any extent, then there is reason to think that we are all irrational when emotions are involved. A related problem is this: irrespective of how we ordinarily behave emotionally, are we under any obligation to avoid inconsistent emotions, much as we ought to refrain from inconsistent beliefs?[5]

Most philosophers agree that, intuitively, no irrationality is involved in cases (1) and (2). We concur with them, but our account is different, and simpler. Notice, first, that if we judge that there is *something good* about the proposition that p, then not only do we tend to feel pleased—to some extent at least—that p, but we would also be justified in feeling pleased that p.[6] Similarly, if we judge that there is *something not good* about the proposition that p, we tend to be justifiably displeased that p, at least to some extent. Now, it is not just possible, but also quite normal, that for any proposition that p, there is something good about both that proposition and its negation. Moreover, there is no demand on rational agents that, as they evaluate a given situation from any point of view—emotional, aesthetic, moral, etc.—they pass all-things-considered judgments only. Needless to say, partial judgments of the kind "This is good (in one respect—and possibly bad in others)" are perfectly legitimate. This is all we need in order to realize that no irrationality is involved in being simultaneously pleased and displeased that Sam got the job. Incidentally, we brought in the attitude of judging, in this simple piece of reasoning, only to make things more vivid since, if one can rationally judge that the same proposition is both good and bad, then there is surely no inconsistency in feeling both pleased and displeased with it.[7]

Similarly for Lola fearing both that Ricky Gervais will mention her and that he will not mention her. Lola sees some danger for herself in both cases. Notice that this simple argument for the rationality of Mary and Lola is confirmed by accounts of rationality in terms of the ensuing behavior. According to some philosophers, emotions are irrational whenever they cause irrational behavior. Now, no matter how irrational behavior is to be characterized, Mary's emotions are rational. It would be perfectly natural to complete our example as follows: after congratulating Sam, Mary decides to apply for another job. Surely, this is not irrational behavior. The same goes for actress Lola: fearing that *p* and also fearing that *not-p*, she—quite rationally—does nothing, while biting her nails.

Notice—and this is important—that Mary is perfectly aware that Sam's getting the job is the same event as her not getting it. This does not amount to any reason for her not to have the emotions we have ascribed to her. We could even imagine that Mary initially mistakes the job for which Sam successfully applied for a job other than the one for which she herself applied. When she later comes to realize that they are one and the same job, there is no reason for her to change her emotional reactions. In this respect, emotions contrast starkly with beliefs. It can happen to anyone to believe, e.g., that Hesperus is a planet and Phosphorus is not a planet. However, when one realizes that Hesperus and Phosphorus are the same planet, one is bound to change her mind. Now, this difference between emotions and beliefs must be explained somehow. Let us spell out what the contrast we are pointing out—between emotions and beliefs—amounts to in general.

The Rationality Constraint

Our beliefs aim at being true. If we have conclusive evidence that it is true that *p* (and we realize that this is so), then we cannot but believe that *p*. Similarly, if we have conclusive evidence that it is false that *p*, we cannot but disbelieve that *p*—i.e., believe that *not-p*. Truth is all we care about when it comes to believing. Of course, most of the time we do not have conclusive evidence for anything, and we harbor beliefs based on inconclusive evidence. The rationality of our beliefs mainly depends on whether the evidence we rely on is adequate or not. In particular, if we realize that a set of propositions is inconsistent, we have conclusive evidence that they cannot all be true, and it would be irrational to believe them all simultaneously, no matter what additional evidence is available. This accounts for the following *Rationality Constraint for Belief.*

> RATIONALITY CONSTRAINT FOR BELIEF. Let S be a rational sub-
> ject, a and b either proper names or definite descriptions, F a simple,
> one-place predicate.

PART ONE. (3) follows from (1) and (2):

> (1) S believes that $a = b$,
> (2) S believes that $F(a)$,
> (3) S believes that $F(b)$,

PART TWO. If (1) and (2) hold true, then

> (4) S disbelieves that $F(b)$,
>
>   and
>
> (4') S believes that it is not the case that $F(b)$,
>
>   are false. (4) and (4') are equivalent.

For instance, if Tom is rational, and believes that Hesperus = Phosphorus, and believes that Hesperus is a planet, then he must also believe that Phosphorus is a planet, and cannot disbelieve that Phosphorus is a planet—i.e., believe that Phosphorus is not a planet.

The constraint only holds for rational subjects. If one is extremely confused, then one might, perhaps, believe and disbelieve that p (even though it is not clear in such cases whether it makes much sense to ascribe beliefs of any kind.). Normally, we all abide by the Rationality Constraint.[8]

It might be objected that it can happen to anyone to believe, e.g., that on the Gouter route to Mont Blanc rockfall accidents frequently occur, and also that on the normal French route rockfall accidents do not occur, even though one knows full well that the Gouter route is the normal French route to Mont Blanc. This objection can be answered by appealing to the distinction between *dispositional* and *occurrent* belief. It is one thing to be disposed to assert a proposition when it is called for, to use it in inferences and to guide behavior. It is quite another to entertain in one's mind the same proposition, to focus one's mind on it, etc. Thus, it is doubtful that, as one believes that on the Gouter route serious rockfall accidents occur and disbelieves that on the normal French route rockfall accidents occur, one is *occurrently* aware that the Gouter route is the normal French route to Mont Blanc. Even though one has not forgotten it and, if asked which route is the normal French one to Mont Blanc, one can promptly and correctly answer, one is not currently focusing on it. There are more difficult cases where it seems appropriate to say that one cannot put two and two together, or that one believes that p with one part of one's brain—so to speak—and disbelieves that p with another part. In such cases, it is doubtful that we are dealing with one rational subject. It is as if two distinct persons coexisted.[9] As a matter of fact, there is a wide consensus among philosophers that the Constraint holds true.[10]

We pointed out above that Mary and Lola are not irrational: yet Mary is both pleased and displeased that Sam got the job, and Lola both fears that Ricky Gervais will mention her and fears that Ricky Gervais will not mention her. On the contrary, no one could rationally both believe and disbelieve that Sam got the job, etc. This amounts to saying that a Rationality Constraint comparable to that for belief does not hold for (most) emotions. Some explanation of this difference between belief and the emotions is called for, especially in view of the fact that emotions are far from being indifferent to truth, as we now show.

Believing that a state of affairs holds is obviously *not a sufficient* condition for having any emotion directed to that state of affairs. For instance, even if one realizes that Hesperus is a planet, this is no reason for him to have any emotion at all concerning it. In stark contrast to the case of belief, truth is *not* all that matters for a subject to feel emotions. On the other hand, it is a *necessary* condition for a subject S to have any emotion at all that *p*, that S believes either that it is true that *p*, or that it was true that *p*, or that it will possibly be true that *p*. Could Mary be pleased that Sam got the job if she believed that Sam did not get the job? Could Lola fear that Ricky Gervais will mention her if she believed that he will never do so, for whatever reason? Could anyone regret/be pleased, etc., that the Brits voted for Brexit and, yet, that they will be chairing the European Union (which is plainly impossible)? In each case, the answer is No. We feel no emotions whatever towards states of affairs that we believe cannot be actual, for whatever reason. In particular, no one could feel any emotion that *p and not-p*, which is obviously impossible. Clearly, this is not to be confused with the fact that we can *imagine* states of affairs whose occurrence is not impossible, and can also imagine that we would be moved emotionally in some specified way if they did occur. This is also different from saying that emotion reports are *factive* in the sense that, for instance, we cannot properly assert that Mary is pleased that Sam got the job unless it holds true that Sam got the job.

However, even though no one could rationally have any emotion that *p and not-p* (since one is bound to realize that it is impossible that *p and not-p*), we have seen that it is perfectly possible, and rational, to fear that *p* and simultaneously to fear that *not-p*, to be pleased that *p* and, simultaneously, to be displeased that *p*, and so on. Surely, one is bound to realize that the two propositions, that *p* and that *not-p*, are inconsistent. Yet, they can still be the objects of separate, simultaneous and contrary emotions—albeit not of beliefs. How is this possible?

Disbelieving and Being Displeased

As we have seen above, disbelieving that *p* amounts to believing that *not-p*. Most philosophers agree that if one believes that *p* and disbelieves that *q* (i.e., believes that not-*q*), then one also believes that *p* & not-*q*. In other words, they think that the following (&-introduction) rule for belief holds:

S believes that *p*   S disbelieves that *q* (= believes that not-*q*)

S believes that *p* & not-*q*.

Even though not everyone agrees on the general case, the rule still stands a good chance of being reliable, if not universally, at least in most cases. This is to be contrasted with emotional attitudes. Surely, the following rule stands *no* chance of being valid:

S is pleased that *p*   S is displeased that *q* (= pleased that not-*q*)

S is pleased that *p* & not-*q*.

It is easy to see why. Consider the case of Mary again, who is both pleased and displeased that Sam got the job. The premises of the inference are therefore true. The conclusion, however, is obviously false, since no one can be pleased (or displeased, for that matter) about something one knows can never happen, since it is an obvious contradiction.

Does Mary being displeased that *p* amount to her being pleased that not-*p*—i.e., that Sam did not get the job? As we have just seen, Mary can only be pleased with something that she believes either happened in the past—i.e., that Sam got the job—or is happening now, or will happen in the future. That being so, she cannot be pleased that Sam did not get the job — something she knows is not, and will never be, the case. We must conclude that, in general, being displeased that *p* cannot amount simply to being pleased that not-*p*. What does it amount to, then?

Why is Mary displeased that Sam got the job? Because she applied for the job herself and she *would have been pleased had she gotten it*. She is displeased insofar as she was hoping for a different outcome, which did not materialize. Comparing it to the actual outcome, she is unhappy. Here, then, is what it is to be displeased that *p*: S is displeased that *p* if and only if, (1) it happened that *p* and S believes that it did, (2) if it had happened, instead, that not-*p*, and S believed that it did, then S would have been pleased, and (3) S realizes that (2) holds.[11]

One might object: according to this account, anyone who, like Mary, is both pleased and displeased with something, is bound to be pleased no matter how things turn out. A rather pleasant predicament, isn't it? Well, yes and no, for one is also bound to be displeased however things turn out. Also, one can *imagine* how things could have turned out otherwise. Then, comparing the possible outcome with the actual course of affairs, one can consider how much better things could have turned out. We are not claiming that being displeased is *always* a matter of comparing two or more possible states of affairs that cannot both be actual, but this is often the case. It is even possible that one feels terribly displeased as a result of considering alternative courses of events. (This is not the case with our Mary, who is more pleased than displeased that Sam got the job.)

It is now clear why the &-introduction rule for *being pleased* stands no chance of being valid. Disbelieving that q amounts to believing that it is true that not-q—i.e., it is false that q—*in the same world where the disbelieving is taking place*. This fully explains why no one can rationally believe that p and simultaneously disbelieve that p. This also explains why the Rationality Constraint for Belief holds in general. It is quite different with being pleased and displeased that p. In the case of Mary, Sam in fact got the job and Mary is pleased with this. Her pleasure is taking place in the actual world. She is also displeased with it and her displeasure is also taking place in the same world. But her being *pleased* that Sam *did not* get the job takes place in the counterfactual world(s) in which Sam is turned down—not in the actual world. Therefore, one cannot conjoin her being pleased that p with her being pleased that not-p.

Lola's case is different, but only slightly so. As fear concerns the future, factuality is not involved. What she fears are two possible courses of events, namely that Ricky Gervais will mention her and that he will not. Since such courses are incompatible, she cannot fear that Ricky will and will not mention her. Instead, she separately fears both horns of the dilemma. This has no tendency to show that Lola is irrational, since the Consistency Constraint does not hold for fear.

Criticizing Other Accounts

Let us conclude by pointing out the extent to which our account differs from most. The majority of philosophers shun the hard problem of contrariety for emotions by claiming either that conflicting emotions are not really contrary, or that their objects stand in no logical relation. Our strategy is different. We happily admit that Mary and Lola (in different ways) harbor directly contradictory emotional states. We claim that the reason why no inconsistency is involved in their cases is to be found in the inferential properties of emotions, which differ from belief and other cognitive attitudes.

The common strategy, which is not ours, is best exemplified by David Carr, who claims:

> Thus, to the extent that (as Geach observes) one can both love and hate the same objects or states of affairs, love and hate are not—unlike believing and disbelieving—directly contradictory states. One might say that one both loves and hates fish; but once it is appreciated that fish has properties F (appealing taste) and G (annoying bones) and that one loves fish in respect of F but hates it in respect of G, any and all appearance of formal contradiction is dispelled.
>
> (Carr 2009, 36)

It is not altogether clear that the reasons for loving fish cannot be the same as those for hating it, but the reason why Mary is pleased that Sam got the job is definitely not the same as her reason for being displeased that he got it. Still, Mary is both pleased *that Sam got the job* and displeased *that Sam got the job*. Whatever her reasons, the objects of her contrasting emotions, which we take to be propositional, are the same. And, whether or not love and hate are directly contradictory, being pleased and being displeased seem to be. Thus, Carr's strategy as it stands is unsatisfactory.

Similarly, Christine Tappolet imagines a situation in which "you are both afraid of making some steps and attracted to making these three admittedly dangerous steps". She asks, "Does this pattern of ambivalent emotions make for a contradiction? It does not, for your emotions key you in to two compatible aspects of what you are about to do: its danger and its attractiveness" (Tappolet 2005, 230–31). Tappolet is surely right that danger and attractiveness are compatible aspects of any situation. Moreover, the emotions of fear and that of being attracted are clearly not mutually exclusive. This might be sufficient to conclude that no contradiction is involved in her example. But—we ask—are the aspects of what you are about to do the objects (or parts of the objects) of your emotions, or are they merely the reasons for, or causes of, your emotions concerning what you are about to do? Actress Lola fears that Ricky Gervais will mention her and also that Ricky Gervais will not mention her. We have argued that those two 'that'-clauses give the full objects of Lola's fears and they obviously *are* incompatible. Thus, Lola's pattern of ambivalent emotions might make for a contradiction. Similarly, Mary is both pleased and displeased that Sam got the job. The two attitudes of being pleased and displeased apparently are mutually exclusive, and yet they can have the same object. Again, this *might* make for a contradiction. We conclude, therefore, that Tappolet owes us some supplementary argument to show that, contrary to appearance, no contradiction is in fact involved in our examples and in others of the same sort. Even in case Tappolet's aspects are merely the reasons of your emotions, her argument is in need of being supplemented somehow, since situations exist in which contrasting emotions are motivated by the same reason. Consider for instance the following dialogue: Ada and Bertie are talking about food—particularly, cheese.

Ada: "Bertie, do you like Stilton?"
Bertie: "Well, yes and no. I find it very tasty, of course. But I also find it slightly disgusting. So, the correct answer is that I like it and also dislike it."
Ada: "How interesting! Could you please be more precise? Why exactly do you find it delicious?"
Bertie: "Because it is so smelly, of course."
Ada: "And why do you find it disgusting?"
Bertie: "Because it is so smelly, of course."

Michelle Montague's solution to a case similar to that of Mary and Sam consists in appealing to a fine-grained notion of emotional content:

Our emotions are extremely sensitive to how a state of affairs is framed. In the above example, there is one state of affairs at issue—the outcome of the grant application process. But appealing just to this state of affairs cannot account for the emotions involved in the case. How this state of affairs gets framed in part determines one's emotional response. When the state of affairs is framed in terms of Jane's succeeding, she feels joy; when the state of affairs is framed in terms of her competitors failing, she does not, barring nastiness, feel joy.

(Montague 2009, 177)

Her strategy, applied to our example, clearly amounts to showing that the objects of Mary's conflicting emotions are sufficiently fine-grained to be distinct and logically unrelated. Much like Carr and Tappolet, Montague surmises that no real contradiction would thus be involved. However, as we have presented them, Mary's emotional states consist in being pleased *that Sam got the job* and being displeased *that Sam got the job*. It makes little difference whether the propositions referred to are Fregean (hence fine-grained) or Russellian (hence coarse and germane to states of affairs). However Mary herself frames the relevant state of affairs, the reports ascribing contrary emotions to her involve *the same proposition*. As in all puzzles concerning propositional attitudes (notably belief) the problem is not that of reproducing the subject's own perspective on the relevant situations. Rather, the problem is to account for the fact that the reports we naturally tend to give are in fact correct and consistent. In our examples, assuming that Mary is perfectly rational, is it correct to report that she is pleased that Sam got the job and also displeased that Sam got the job? And similarly for Lola. Moreover, if these reports are correct, how can they be coherent, whereas the parallel reports for belief would certainly not be? This is the question we have been trying to answer. Our answer is as simple as it can be, and involves no fiddling with the objects of emotions and their content. We have argued that contrary emotions are nothing of which to be afraid.

Notes

1. We are very grateful to Anita Konzelmann, Christine Tappolet and Fabrice Teroni for their helpful comments and important suggestions. We would like to thank also Carla Bagnoli and Uriah Kriegel for their insightful observations.
2. These are three separate beliefs with simple objects, whereas the one about the Marx brothers is a single belief with a complex object.
3. Much as emotional ascriptions, belief ascriptions can *also* be objectual in their syntactic form, as with "Mary believes Fiona's theory", "Mary believes something implausible", etc. We cannot pause here to argue that the propositional form is more fundamental.
4. This is Greenspan's (1976) original example, discussed by Tappolet (2005), Carr (2009), Montague (2009), and Kristjansson (2010).
5. What kind of *ought* is this? It is not as if we had a choice between believing and abstaining from believing that p and not-p, and we choose the latter if we intend to be rational. Rather, once we realize that p and not-p is inconsistent, we cannot but abstain from believing it.

6. It was pointed out to us in conversation that if being pleased that *p* entailed believing that *p* is good, and being displeased that *p* entailed believing that *p* is not good, then Mary would be inconsistent in being both pleased and displeased that Sam got the job. The formulation given in the text ("there is *something* good") sidesteps this issue altogether.
7. This is not to say that we endorse Greenspan's thesis that emotions are somehow grounded in judgments, even though we sympathize with it (Greenspan 1976).
8. Thus, it is unnecessary to take the notion of belief so constrained as an idealization of the ordinary notion.
9. Stalnaker (1984, Chapter 5).
10. A notable exception here are neo-Russellians, who object to the Rationality Constraint as phrased above. They accept a slightly different form of it, but from the point of view of the present paper, the difference is of no consequence.
11. Clause (3) is necessary for, if Mary did not know how she would react in counterfactual circumstances, as it might easily happen, she could make no comparison with the actual course of events. Bear in mind that being displeased, like being pleased and many other verbal phrases of emotion, is factive.

References

Carr, David. 2009. "Virtue, Mixed Emotions and Moral Ambivalence." *Philosophy* 84: 31–46.

Greenspan, Patricia. 1976. "A Case of Mixed Feelings: Ambivalence and the Logic of Emotions." In *Explaining Emotions*, edited by Amelie Rorty, 223–50. Berkeley: University of California Press.

Kristjánsson, Kristján. 2010. "The Trouble with Ambivalent Emotions." *Philosophy* 85: 485–510.

Montague Michelle. 2009. "The Logic, Intentionality, and Phenomenology of Emotions." *Philosophical Studies* 145, no. 2: 171–92.

Schiffer, Stephen. 1978. "The Basis of Reference." *Erkenntnis* 13: 171–206.

Schiffer, Stephen. 2006. "A Problem for a Direct-Reference Theory of Belief Reports." *Nous* 40, no. 2: 361–68.

Stalnaker, Robert C. 1984. *Inquiry*. Cambridge: MIT Press.

Tappolet, Christine. 2005. "Ambivalent Emotions and the Perceptual Account of Emotions." *Analysis* 65, no. 3: 229–33.

5 Bitter Joys and Sweet Sorrows

Olivier Massin

Consider pleasures understood in a broad sense, encompassing all positive affects: that is, bodily pleasures, but also intellectual pleasures, such as the pleasure of reading a great book, the pleasure of receiving a compliment, of winning the lottery, pleasures in activities such as the pleasure of playing, the pleasure of having a conversation, of hunting and, more generally, every episode of hedonically positive mental states such as joy, proudness, interest, relief, admiration, and so on. I will use "displeasure" as the antonym of "pleasures" understood in this broad sense. "Feelings" will refer to mental episodes which will either be pleasures or displeasures.[1] We sometimes experience pleasures and displeasures simultaneously: whenever we eat *sfogliatelle* while having a headache, whenever we feel pain fading away, whenever we feel guilty pleasure while enjoying listening to Barbara Streisand, whenever we are savoring a particularly hot curry, whenever we enjoy physical endurance in sport, whenever we are touched upon receiving a hideous gift, whenever we are proud of withstanding acute pain, etc. These are examples of what we call "mixed feelings". *Mixed feelings are cases in which one and the same person experiences pleasure and displeasure at the same time.*

Mixed feelings raise two questions: (i) If pleasure and displeasure are contraries, how can mixed feelings be possible? (ii) Does the excess of pleasure (or displeasure) that we feel when experiencing mixed feelings itself constitute a new feeling, that results from the co-occurrence of the first two? I will argue (i) that mixed feelings are possible and that their existence does not threaten the contrariety of pleasure and displeasure, and (ii) that there are no resultant feelings: having a lot of pleasure and a little displeasure does not result in having *additional* mild pleasure. Finally, I will suggest (iii) that although both false, skepticism towards the existence of mixed feelings, as well as the idea according to which resultant feelings exist, are inspired from a single and correct idea: that pleasure and displeasure do *fuse* in some cases.

The Possibility of Mixed Feelings

Many discussions about mixed feelings concern their actual, and more generally possible existence.[2] The main reason why the existence of mixed feelings is considered problematic is because it seems to threaten the relation of contrariety between pleasure and displeasure. The idea is the following: if we can experience pleasure and displeasure at the same time, it must be because pleasure and displeasure are not contraries. According to this idea, the three following propositions are incompatible:

> P1—Mixed feelings consist in the co-occurrence of pleasure and displeasure in a same subject at the same time.
> P2—Pleasure and displeasure are contraries: they cannot be found in a same subject at the same time.
> P3—Mixed feelings are possible.

Given that P1 must be accepted by definition, we are forced to reject either P2 or P3. Faced with this seeming incompatibility between mixed feelings on the one hand, and the contrariety of pleasure and displeasure on the other, some simply choose to give up the contrariety of pleasure and displeasure (P2) in order to save the possibility of mixed feelings. According to them, pleasure and displeasure, instead of constituting a same dimension and of being separated by a null indifference point—as positive and negative temperatures do— are in fact independent dimensions of variations of one's experience—as hue and saturation are dimensions of colors (Diener and Emmons 1984; Watson and Tellegen 1985; Cacioppo and Berntson 1994; Watson 2000, 26–33, 44–54; Larsen et al. 2004; Schimmack 2001, 2005; Rehmke—quoted by Titchener 1908, 56—already writes: "[p]leasure (*Lust*) and unpleasure (*Unlust*) are 'incommensurable dimensions', in the same way as sounds and colours". See Massin (2014) for a critic).

Others, on the contrary, preserve the contrariety of pleasure and displeasure by trying to show that, appearances notwithstanding, mixed feelings do not really exist, as against P3 (Epicure—in Long and Sedley 1987, vol. 1, 115; Titchener 1908, 46–47; Young 1918; Russell and Carroll 1999). Rather than simultaneously experiencing pleasure and displeasure, we would either be merely wavering between the two (Alechsieff 1907), or one of the feelings would only be a pseudo-pleasure or displeasure (Young 1918; Duncker 1941, 410–12). Finally, others opt for an intermediate view according to which only certain pleasures and displeasures are contraries. Pleasures and displeasures *of the same type* would thereby be incompatible, but *not* pleasures *of different types*. For instance, it would be possible to have a bodily pleasure and a spiritual pleasure at the same time, but impossible to have a spiritual pleasure and a spiritual displeasure at the same time (Scheler 1955, 338–39).

I believe by contrast that these three propositions are fully compatible. The alleged incompatibility between them rests upon an equivocal use of the terms "subject" and "in". In P1, "subject" refers to a person, and saying that pleasures and displeasures are *in* a person is equivalent to saying that this person *has* certain pleasures and displeasures. In P2, "subject" refers to the bearer of the property of being a pleasure (or being a displeasure) in such a way that saying that pleasure is *in* a subject amounts to saying that this subject *is* a pleasure (or a displeasure). The subject that *has* a pleasure is a person. The subject that *is* a pleasure is a mental episode. There is no more contradiction in holding that pleasure and displeasure are contraries and that they can occur simultaneously in one and the same person, than in holding that black and white are contraries and that a chessboard can be black and white at the same time. It is just that different parts of the chessboard are black and white and, in the same way, different mental episodes of the person are pleasant and unpleasant. When Paul looks forward to the spring whilst feeling sad about his grandfather's death, his yearning for the spring is a pleasure, and his mourning the death of his grandfather is a displeasure. As soon as we distinguish between the mental episodes of a same person, mixed feelings do not threaten the relation of contrariety between pleasure and displeasure anymore.

For the relation of contrariety to be violated, we would need the very same mental episode to be at once a pleasure and displeasure: this would amount to saying that the same person can take pleasure and displeasure in the same object, under the same aspect, in the same way, at the same time. It is doubtful that such cases really do exist. Greenspan holds that cases such as friendly rivalry are instances of the sort, such as when Paul is both glad and saddened by his friend's success in the competition in which they were both taking part (Greenspan 1980). But this case can be understood as follows: Paul is *intrinsically* glad about his friend's success, a success that saddens him *extrinsically* because it implies that *he*, Paul, has failed—which in turn intrinsically saddens him (for an alternative analysis of ambivalent cases, see Calabi and Santambrogio's contribution to this volume).

The Non-Existence of Resultant Feelings

Let us thus assume that mixed feelings exist and that pleasures and displeasures are indeed contraries. One can still wonder whether the concomitance of pleasures and displeasures yields a total feeling, resulting from their addition. Pleasure sometimes outweighs displeasure, displeasure sometimes outweighs pleasure, and sometimes they exactly compensate for each other. Do such excesses of pleasure or of displeasure constitute new feelings, distinct from the concomitant pleasures and displeasures?

In order to lay down the problem properly, we need to introduce the concept of hedonic balance. The expression *hedonic balance* refers to the algebraic sum of the positive values representing the intensity of all the pleasures and of the negative values representing the intensity of all the displeasures of a person at a time. One problem posed by this widely accepted concept (see, however, Rachels 2004) is this: *is hedonic balance only a theoretical fiction*, which merely reflects the fact that there might be more pleasure than displeasure in one person, *or does it correspond to a new mental episode?* In other words, is there a feeling resulting from the concomitance of pleasures and displeases, that goes beyond those pleasures and displeasures? Suppose Paul has a pleasure of 3 "hedons" and a displeasure of -2 hedons: his hedonic balance is of 1 hedon. Now does Paul have a pleasure of 1 hedon corresponding to that hedonic balance? Those who answer positively believe in resultant feelings.

Wundt (1922, II, sec. 12, §12) is one chief upholder of that view.[3] According to him, all the feelings that are present in the mind at a given time necessarily form a total or resultant feeling (*Totalgefühl*) that is unique and distinct from the partial or component feelings that compose it.[4]

Why should we believe in the existence of resultant feelings on top of component feelings? A first argument in favor of their existence would be that resultant feelings have some phenomenal quality. We can for instance easily answer the question "How are you feeling?", and the question seem to be on how we feel on the whole. Indeed, there seems to be a certain way we feel at a certain time, and no hedonic calculus is needed in order to find out about it. Nevertheless, the way we feel might not correspond to a resultant feeling, instead it could be:

(1) A *general* feeling: we feel tired, relaxed, depressed, energetic, etc. Such "feelings of general condition", as Ryle (1951) calls them, do not necessarily reflect one's hedonic balance. They are themselves component feelings, which are factored in the hedonic balance. They do not necessarily represent the only feelings we may have: we can feel exhausted and happy to have reached a mountain peak, or feel in great shape and be annoyed to have missed our train.

(2) A *salient* feeling: we can feel unwell because of a headache. The hedonic balance of a person may be positive even though the feeling that is attracting her attention is negative. This is what happens, for instance, whenever an intense displeasure is outweighed by many little pleasures. Salient feelings, similarly to feelings of one's general condition, are component feelings that should be summed within the hedonic balance.

Once these two types of feelings are set aside, the existence of a total feeling reflecting our hedonic balance becomes less obvious. In order to answer the question "How are you *overall*, do you have at this very moment more pleasure or more displeasure?" it might be pointless to proceed to an introspective search of the effects of having more pleasure than displeasure. Some hedonic calculus may well be inevitable.

A second argument in favor of resultant feelings proposes that there is an intuitive difference between, on the one hand, an individual's hedonic balance at a given time and, on the other hand, the hedonic balance of multiple individuals at a given time: the former seems less artificial than the latter. Broad (1959, 249) thus argues that the sum of pleasures and displeasures of different individuals does not, in any way, represent an addition *in rerum natura*, contrarily to the sum of pleasures and displeasures of one single individual. Thus, we could say that an individual is happy at a given moment when his hedonic balance is positive.[5] However, as Broad points out, it would be a category mistake to defend that a collection of individuals is happy when its hedonic balance is positive. Without resultant feelings, Broad argues, we would not be able to understand what exactly about the hedonic balance of one individual is more natural than the hedonic balance of several individuals.

This argument is hardly more convincing than the preceding argument from phenomenology. The reason why the hedonic balance of an individual seems more "natural" than the hedonic balance of several individuals might just be that one individual is a more natural entity than a collection of individuals. If the average life expectancy of pangolins seems less artificial than the average life expectancy of pangolins and artichokes, it is because the class of pangolins is less artificial than the class of pangolins and artichokes. It is not because the average life expectancy of pangolins represents some addition *in rerum natura*, contrary to the average life expectancy of pangolins and of artichokes.

Not only are the arguments in favor of resultant feelings inconclusive, the existence of such feelings faces the following dilemma[6]:

(1) Suppose first that a resultant feeling is fully distinct from all the component feelings: it is a new feeling emerging simultaneously on the basis of these component feelings, as Wundt would have it. This leads to a paradox: given that the hedonic balance of a person at a given time sums *all* his pleasures, it should also sum the resultant feeling. Paul has a pleasure of 3 hedons and a displeasure of -2 hedons: his hedonic balance is of 1 hedon. According to the resultant feelings hypothesis, this corresponds to a new pleasure of Paul, distinct from his component pleasures. It follows that Paul's *complete* hedonic balance should take into account this pleasure of 1 hedon. Because Paul has three distinct feelings—his 3 hedons pleasure, his -2 hedons displeasure *and his new 1 hedon resultant pleasure*—Paul's complete hedonic balance will then be of 2 hedons (3–2 + 1). In other words, if resultant feelings are feelings in their own right, distinct from component feelings, they must be taken into account in the hedonic balance. If this is the case, however, the 2 hedons result above is not enough yet. According to the resultant feelings hypothesis, the 2 hedons result corresponds to yet another new pleasure of 2 hedons, which must in its turn be included in the following sum: ((3–2) +1)+2). The hedonic balance is getting out of control.

(2) Suppose now that the resultant feeling is not *fully* distinct from all component feelings: it is either identical to one of the (dis-)pleasures, or part of one of them. But then, *which one?* In the case of Paul who has just *two* component (dis)pleasures, the answer should be obvious: his resultant pleasure corresponds to the *surplus* or *residue* of his component pleasure, that is, to the part of that pleasure which is not counterbalanced by his displeasure.[7] But things become intractable in more complex (and usual) cases. Just consider a case involving three components (dis)pleasures. Julie is listening to Purcell (a pleasure of 5 hedons) whilst taking her bath (another pleasure of 5 hedons) and regretting having missed her train (a

displeasure of -5 hedons). Her hedonic balance shows 5 hedons. Is Julie's resultant pleasure the one she gets out of listening to Purcell? Or the one she gets out of taking a bath? Or a bit of both?

I conclude that the results of hedonic calculus do not represent any new psychological reality.

Fusions of Feelings

An important idea of Scheler (and Wittgenstein) is that false philosophical theses often have some grain of truth (Mulligan 2017). If mixed feelings are so innocuous, why do they seem so baffling? If resultant feelings are so intractable, why do they remain so attractive? Here is a hypothesis. The views that mixed feelings violate the contrariety between pleasure and displeasure and that resultant feelings are real, are two false views motivated by one true thesis: the thesis according to which feelings might *fuse* under certain circumstances. The general idea is that in some contexts pleasure and displeasure behave in the same way as hot water and cold water blended in the same container do (a metaphor backed up by common language which is full of associations between affective episodes and liquids; see Peña Cervel 2001; Kövecses 2003). Take some hot pleasure. Take the same quantity of cold displeasure. Pour it into one person. When some further conditions are met, you get a lukewarm, apathetic individual, who has neither pleasure nor displeasure.

The nature of mixture and fusion is a delicate metaphysical question: one problem is to know whether the ingredients that have been blended are still present in the resulting mixture. If this is the case, in which sense is the mixture homogenous? If it is not, in which sense is it a mixture? In what follows, I want to discuss the case of affective *fusions* only, in contrast to the case of affective *mixtures* I shall not consider here. In affective fusions, the ingredients do not anymore exist alongside in the result: they have fused.[8]

In the same way that, once they have fused, hot and cold water vanishes and give way to lukewarm water (by contrast to a tea with milk where the initial ingredients remain present), in sentimental fusion (by contrast to affective mixtures), blending pleasure with displeasure may yield a single feeling (slight pleasure, slight displeasure, indifference). Given that the product of such a fusion consists either in pleasure, in displeasure or in indifference, and that several ingredients were originally present, some of them at least have been destroyed. As Bain writes:

> Pleasure and pain are opposites in the strongest form of contrariety; like heat and cold, they destroy or neutralize each other.
>
> (Bain 1875, 12–13)

At first, fusions of feelings may seem to support both the views that mixed feelings are impossible, and that resultant feeling are real. First, it might seem that affective fusions support the view that mixed feelings do not exist, for we then end up with one simple feeling. But this is not the case: fusions of feelings actually *entail the existence of* mixed feelings. For pleasure and displeasure to fuse or mutually destroy each other, they must *first* co-exist.

Second, fusions of feelings may seem to support the existence of resultant feeling, for the simple feeling which results from the fusion of different feelings may appear to be exactly the kind of resultant feeling we have been looking after in vain. But again, this is not the case: a fused feeling cannot be a resultant feeling, since the latter would have to exist *at the same time* as the component feelings. The fused feeling begins to exist only after the component feelings have disappeared. The multiplicity of pleasures and displeasures ceases to exist as soon as the fusion of feelings begins to exist.

In no way do fusions of feelings plead against mixed feelings, nor in favor of resultant feelings. Quite the opposite. That being said, there is a grain of truth in the idea according to which mixed feelings are impossible, as well as in the idea that there are resultant feelings, and the theory of fusions of feelings helps pinpointing it. First, some mixed feelings cannot *last* (because pleasure and displeasure fuse). Second, the hedonic balance of an individual with mixed feelings at t sometimes corresponds, at $t+1$, to a unique episode, distinct from pleasures and displeasures produced at t. Although possible, mixed feelings are often *ephemeral*. In such cases, a substitute of a resultant feeling appears as soon as pleasure and displeasure fuse.

What are the conditions under which concomitant pleasure and displeasure will fuse? In the quote above Bain applies the idea of fusion of feelings to *all* cases of concomitant pleasures and displeasures (see also Bain 1859, 441). Others limit affective fusions to some specific co-occurrences of pleasure and displeasure only (Hume 2000, Bk II, Part III, sec. 9; Scheler 1973, 331; Sidgwick 1981, 141; Mulligan 1998, §6). It seems to me that the latter view is right. Julie may feel deep shame when faced with her passion for photo-novels, and Paul can be madly in love with Julie whilst deploring her unrestrained taste for tacky literature. Such feelings do not fuse. The theory of fusion is valid when it comes to certain pleasures and displeasure only. Which ones?

Some feelings have objects, others don't. Julie may be sad about having lost her cat, but she may also be sad *tout court*, without her sadness being directed toward any particular object. My proposal is that *only objectless feelings may fuse*. Indeed, for pleasures and displeasures with an object to be able to fuse, their objects should be able to fuse as well, which is unlikely (Marshall 1889, 533). What would a fusion between Paul's love for Julie and his migraine look like? Nothing indicates that mixed feelings that contain pleasures with an object are doomed to an ephemeral existence, resulting in a fusion of feelings. However, as soon as pleasures and displeasures are set free from their objects, nothing keeps them apart from each other and they start behaving like liquids by spreading into their subject. They then end up mixing together. The theory of fusions of feelings is only valid when it bears on pleasure and displeasure that have no objects.

This necessary condition may not be sufficient though. A deep, objectless state of bliss will not fuse with a pain in one's toe.[9] Scheler (1973, 330–31) proposes that only feelings of a same level/strata/depth will fuse with each other: this arguably constitutes a second necessary condition for affective fusions.

To sum up, pleasure and displeasure may occur at once in the same person. The surplus of pleasure (or of displeasure) which this person has at this moment, is a theoretical fiction that corresponds to no psychological reality. However, when pleasure and displeasure have no object they cannot co-exist durably in the same person. In such case, they may fuse and produce either pure pleasure or pure displeasure, of which the intensity might be equal to the sum of the intensity of previous pleasures and displeasures.[10]

Notes

1. "Affects" would perhaps be a better term than "feelings" to designate pleasures in this broad sense, for not only feelings stricto sensu, but also emotions, moods, sentiments . . . count as pleasures and can be mixed. However, since the debate of interest here has been historically formulated in terms of "mixed feelings", I shall stick with that term here.
2. See Titchener (1908, 45–54), Young (1918), Beebe-Center (1965) and Schimmack and Colcombe (2000) for different reviews of this debate.
3. Contrary to the widespread use that I endorse here, Wundt employs the term "feeling" (*Gefühl*) or "affective tonality" to refer not only to pleasures and displeasures, but to all subjective mental elements—by opposition to sensations, which are their contents. According to Wundt, feelings vary along three main dimensions: pleasure-displeasure, excitement-inhibition and tension-relaxation (Wundt 1922, I, sec. 5–7; See Reisenzein, 2000 for an exposition).
4. Bayne and Chalmers (2003) and Bayne (2010) defend a similar thesis that applies not only to feelings, but also to all conscious episodes. According to them, the different conscious episodes of a subject form a total conscious episode, which is more than their conjunction. Given the all-encompassing use he makes of the term "feeling" (see previous note), Wundt's thesis might not be that different from the unity of consciousness thesis endorsed by Bayne and Chalmers. Moreover, note that Bayne and Chalmers can be correct even if resultant pleasures and displeasures do not exist: it suffices that the conscious episode be neither pleasure nor displeasure.
5. A refined version of such a hedonic conception of happiness is defended by Feldman (2010).
6. Structurally, the same objection holds against the existence of resultant forces qua distinct from component forces (Massin, 2017a, §2.2).
7. See Massin (2017a) for a residualist account of the composition of forces along these lines.
8. On the contrary, when Wundt talks about blends or fusions of feelings, what he has in mind is a concept of blending where the initials ingredients subsist.
9. I here assume that pain, being located, has no object. See Massin (2014, 2017b) for a defense.
10. Most of material of this chapter has been translated from the French by Mélanie Sarzano and Marie van Loon. I am very grateful to Anita Konzelmann, Mélanie Sarzano, Fabrice Teroni, Christine Tappolet and Marie van Loon for their

invaluable comments and suggestions on this chapter. Thanks to Riccardo Braglia, CEO and Managing Director Helsinn Holding SA and the Fondazione Reginaldus (Lugano) for financial support of the work published here.

References

Alechsieff, Nicolaus. 1907. "Die Grundformen der Gefühle." *Psychologische Studien* 3: 156–271.

Bain, Alexander. 1859. *The Emotions and the Will*. London: John W. Parker and Son, West Strand.

Bain, Alexander. 1875. *The Emotions and the Will*. London: Longman.

Bayne, Tim. 2010. *The Unity of Consciousness*. Oxford: Oxford University Press.

Bayne, Tim and David Chalmers. 2003. "What Is the Unity of Consciousness?" *The Unity of Consciousness: Binding, Integration, and Dissociation*, edited by Tim Bayne and David Chalmers, 23–58. New York: Oxford University Press.

Beebe-Center, John Gilbert. 1965. *The Psychology of Pleasantness and Unpleasantness*. New York: Russell & Russell.

Broad, C. D. 1959. *Five Types of Ethical Theory*. Paterson, NJ: Littlefield, Adams.

Cacioppo, John T., and Gary G. Berntson. 1994. "Relationship Between Attitudes and Evaluative Space: A Critical Review, with Emphasis on the Separability of Positive and Negative Substrates." *Psychological Bulletin* 115: 401–23.

Diener, Edward F., and Robert Emmons. 1984. "The Independence of Positive and Negative Affect." *Journal of Personality and Social Psychology* 47: 1105–17.

Duncker, Karl. 1941. "On Pleasure, Emotion, and Striving." *Philosophy and Phenomenological Research* 1: 391–430.

Feldman, Fred. 2010. *What Is This Thing Called Happiness?* Oxford: Oxford University Press.

Greenspan, Patricia. 1980. "Case of Mixed Feelings: Ambivalence and the Logic of Emotion." In *Explaining Emotions*, edited by Amelie Rorty, 223–50. Berkeley: University of California Press.

Hume, David. 2000. *A Treatise of Human Nature*, edited by David F. Norton and Mary J. Norton. Oxford: Oxford University Press.

Kövecses, Zoltán. 2003. *Metaphor and Emotion*. Cambridge: Cambridge University Press.

Larsen, Jeff T., Peter A. McGraw, Barbara A. Mellers, and John T. Cacioppo. 2004. "The Agony of Victory and Thrill of Defeat." *Psychological Science* 15: 325–30.

Long, Anthony Arthur, and David N. Sedley. 1987. *The Hellenistic Philosophers: Translations of the Principal Sources, with Philosophical Commentary*. Cambridge: Cambridge University Press.

Marshall, Henry Rutgers. 1889. "The Classification of Pleasure and Pain." *Mind* 14, no. 56: 511–36.

Massin, Olivier. 2014. "Pleasure and Its Contraries." *Review of Philosophy and Psychology* 5, no. 1: 15–40.

Massin, Olivier. 2017a. "The Composition of Forces." *British Journal for the Philosophy of Science* 68, no. 3: 805–46.

Massin, Olivier. 2017b. "Bad by Nature: An Axiological Theory of Pain." In *The Routledge Handbook for the Philosophy of Pain*, edited by Jennifer Corns, 321–33. New York and London: Routledge.

Mulligan, Kevin. 1998. "The Spectre of Inverted Emotions and the Space of Emotions." *Acta Analytica* 18: 89–105.

Mulligan, Kevin. 2017. "Thrills, Orgasms, Sadness & Hysteria: Austro-German Criticisms of William James." In *Thinking About the Emotions: A Philosophical History*, edited by Alix Cohen and Robert Stern. Oxford: Oxford University Press.

Peña Cervel, Sandra. 2001. "A Cognitive Approach to the Role of Body Parts in the Conceptualization of Emotion Metaphors." *Epos* 17: 245–60.

Reisenzein, Rainer. 2000. "Wundt's Three-Dimensional Theory of Emotion." *Poznan Studies in the Philosophy of the Sciences and the Humanities* 75: 219–50.

Russell, James A., and James M. Carroll, 1999. "On the Bipolarity of Positive and Negative Affect." *Psychological Bulletin* 125, no. 1: 3–30.

Ryle, Gilbert. 1951. "Feelings." *The Philosophical Quarterly* 1: 193–205.

Scheler, Max. 1973. *Formalism in Ethics and Non-Formal Ethics of Value*. Translated by Manfred Frings and Robert L. Funk. Evanston: Northwestern University Press.

Schimmack, Ulrich. 2001. "Pleasure, Displeasure, and Mixed Feelings: Are Semantic Opposites Mutually Exclusive?" *Cognition & Emotion* 15: 81–97.

Schimmack, Ulrich. 2005. "Response Latencies of Pleasure and Displeasure Ratings: Further Evidence for Mixed Feelings." *Cognition & Emotion* 19: 671–91.

Schimmack, Ulrich, and Stan Colcombe. 2000. "Mixed Feelings: Towards a Theory of Pleasure and Displeasure." Unpublished manuscript, www. erin. utoronto. ca/~ w3psyuli/ms/mixed feelings. pdf.

Sidgwick, Henry. 1981. *Methods of Ethics*. Indianapolis, IN: Hacket Publishing Company.

Titchener, Edward B. 1908. *Lectures on the Elementary Psychology of Feeling and Attention*. New York: Palgrave Macmillan.

Watson, David. 2000. *Mood and Temperament*. New York: The Guilford Press.

Watson, David, and Auke Tellegen. 1985. "Toward a Consensual Structure of Mood." *Psychological Bulletin* 98: 219–35.

Wundt, Wilhelm. 1922. *Grundriss der Psychologie*. Stuttgart: Kröner.

Young, Paul Thomas. 1918. "An Experimental Study of Mixed Feelings." *The American Journal of Psychology* 29: 237–71.

6 The Emotion of Being Moved

Julien A. Deonna

Certain sights, scenes, events or works of art "move" us. The birth of a child, the wedding of a friend, the musical performance of one's progeny, the honoring of a deserving hero, a long hoped for victory, are all situations that many of us find, at least on special occasions, "moving". In this article, I try to get a grip on what this affective state in which the negative seem to play an important role consists in.[1] Until very recently, the topic seems to have been overlooked by philosophers and psychologists alike.[2] Perhaps many have thought that when we say of something that it moves us, we are simply reporting the fact that we are experiencing some indeterminate emotion. Or, alternatively, that we experience some determinate emotion that we do not bother or have difficulty specifying.[3] If so, it is unclear that there is an interesting object of study here and it is no surprise that it has been left alone.

If we take a closer look, however, and focus on the examples we started with, the latter suggestions seem superficial. That is at any rate the opinion of many psychologists and philosophers that have been drawn to the topic in the last decade or so (Cova and Deonna 2014; Deonna 2011; Fiske, Schubert and Seibt 2016; Kuehnast et al. 2014; Konečni 2005, 2011; Menninghaus et al. 2015; Tokaji 2003). Although it is true that we sometimes use the expression 'being moved' in the ways just alluded to, more often we are not referring to ordinary emotions, i.e., we are not reporting episodes of shame, anger, fear, jealousy, amusement and hope by saying that we are moved. This may encourage the idea, as I will soon argue in more detail, that a central use of the expression denotes a specific affective phenomenon. These semantic observations merely offer a point of departure for an investigation of a fully metaphysical nature which will argue that we are dealing here with a distinct emotion that deserves a place alongside the others that we have just mentioned (shame, anger, fear, etc.).[4] In what follows, I introduce and briefly defend my own version of what being moved consists in, an account elaborated in collaboration with Florian Cova (Cova and Deonna 2014). The comparison of this account to its rivals I leave for another day and a more suitable setting.

What are the reasons to think that an expression relating to affective phenomena constitutes the name of a specific type of emotion? Philosophers and psychologists alike tend to think that fulfilling the following five criteria constitute a good indication that we are dealing with an emotion: all of its instances (i) are directed at objects, (ii) have the same formal object or core relational theme, (iii) have the same distinct phenomenology, (iv) have the same type of action tendencies and (v) the same general function.[5] Now whether or not 'being moved' satisfies the five criteria—all of which will be explained in due time—is a question that might be answered either by the philosopher reflecting on the concept or by the psychologist conducting an empirical investigation into how people use the term. The approach in this paper uses both avenues since people's claims about how they use the term—which is what our empirical approach taps into—is best accompanied by the philosopher's own careful navigation of the semantic (mine)field.[6]

The first and second criteria for positing a cohesive emotion-type go hand in hand and concern the *intentionality* of mental states, that is, their being directed at things outside themselves. Emotions, like most or all mental states, are intentional, but they are so on two counts: not only are they directed at, or about, certain *particular objects* (persons, events, states, processes, properties, etc.), they also have *formal objects*, i.e., a value in the light of which this particular object is apprehended.[7] Different instances of a given emotion-type will have different *particular* objects (I may be angry at my partner, at the government, at my boss, etc.), but the *formal* object will stay constant (I apprehend these different objects in the light of their *offensiveness*). In anger, then, you take something to be offensive and this is why it makes sense to think of anger as a distinct kind of *evaluative* attitude. Note in passing that it is in virtue of subjects *focusing* on certain properties of the particular objects (say the distracted attitude of the husband, the spending habits of the government, the promotion policies of the boss, etc.) that the affective evaluation will be triggered. So when thinking of the particular object, it is useful to further distinguish *target* from *focus* (de Sousa 1987), i.e., the object *simpliciter* from those properties of it that are responsible for triggering the emotional response.

If we generalize this picture, we can say that various episodes of fear, sadness, guilt, and so on, will be about, or directed at, a rich variety of things, but that fear always presents itself as an apprehension of danger, sadness of a loss, guilt of a wrongful act. It is an essential feature of each emotion-type, then, that subjects construe the particular object of the emotion in an evaluative way specific to that emotion-type. Hence, the formal object both sheds light on the essence of an emotion-type and constitutes a feature in virtue of which it is possible to evaluate the intelligibility and the appropriateness of such emotions. For instance, we would say that an instance of fear directed at something that seems quite harmless and innocuous is barely intelligible and inappropriate.

Now, how does our double criterion apply to the case at hand? Does it make sense to suppose that being moved has varying particular objects that share a general feature that is always salient for the subject when she is moved? Only if we answer this question affirmatively will we be in a position to say with confidence that "being moved" refers to something that amounts to an emotion in its own right.

As our initial examples testify, it is clearly true of being moved that it is typically directed at particular objects. Recall that we may be moved by the birth of a child, the wedding of a good friend, the music performance of one's progeny, the honoring of a deserving hero, the long hoped for good news, but also by an unexpectedly kind gesture, a flag being hoisted, a reconciliation between two estranged friends, the sacrifice of a soldier, a medal ceremony, a surprise party in one's honor, the first words of a child, the last words of a dying mother to her children, a reunion between long-lost relatives, a range of mountains at sunset, etc.

This list of paradigmatic cases immediately invites the following qualifications and observations. First, it is not suggested that we are all systematically moved by these scenes or events. Still, when we are moved, such cases will be typical triggers. Second, what moves us may concern us personally (I am the recipient of the unexpected kindness, it is my child who finally arrives), but it need not (the recipient is a random stranger, the child is that of a third party). Third, what moves us may be real or fictional, and in fact fictional contexts appear especially prone to move us. Of course, each of these points would deserve extensive development, but I have to limit myself to stressing the following regarding the particular objects of being moved. It is a striking feature of all these cases that they exemplify one (or more) of the following core positive values: love, brotherhood, solidarity, abnegation, peace, health, beauty, sacrifice, friendship, community, virtuosity, etc. This is no accident. Indeed, if the examples given are the *targets* of being moved, it makes a lot of sense to think of the positive core values that they exemplify as their *foci*. In short, I claim that the particular objects of being moved are distinct core positive values[8] exemplified by certain situations and events.

If then the particular object of our candidate emotion is always one of a variety of possible core positive values, what about its formal object? Recall that the answer is constrained in the following way: the formal object has to be a value and it has to be the same across all instances of the emotion in question. In this light, the formal object of being moved can only be one thing, namely, goodness. This grandiose sounding claim, then, which I hope the rest of this paper will make plausible, is that we are moved when we are struck by the positivity or goodness of a specific core positive value's presence.[9] In being moved, we are not only sensitive to the presence of some specific positive value, we are sensitive to how good it is that it is present. Being moved is a very special emotion in that it is an overall positive evaluation of the presence of some specific positive value. Here are some illustrations suggesting that this picture is faithful to the phenomenon.

An appropriate emotional response to generosity is gratitude. An appropriate response to success is joy. Sometimes, in special circumstances that we shall soon try to systematize, gratitude because of a generous act or joy at successful performance brings it about that we are moved by the generous act or the successful performance. What happens in these situations, I claim, is that the subject gets to gradually disengage herself from the direct appreciation of the generosity of the act (disengaged from her gratitude) or the successful act (disengaged from her joy) and finds herself engaged in the appreciation of the overall goodness that these specific values actually turned out to be exemplified. Proper attention to the phenomenology of being moved, I will soon suggest, should reinforce this idea that being moved is an overall positive response to some specific positive situation occurring. The same can be said about the triggering conditions of being moved to which I now turn.

If we look again at our examples, three patterns can be singled out as favorable conditions for our candidate emotion. The first consists in positive values made salient on a background of negative values. Solidarity, courage, resilience, kindness, health, fraternity or life itself emerging *from within* or *despite* difficult circumstances constitute a favorable terrain for our candidate emotion. The soldier's sacrifice, the reconciliation of old estranged friends and the reunion of the long-lost family members are just a few instances of this pattern. Second, we have positive value put forward by more or less elaborated *staging*. Weddings, baptisms, staged performances of ability, prize and medal ceremonies and surprise parties in one's honor are all examples of core positive values being artfully showcased. Finally, we have the cases in which the circumstances of the positive value are so exceptional or extraordinary that their mere presence is sufficient to move us. The birth of one's child, the sudden appearance of the majesty of a mountain panorama might be cases at hand. In the three configurations discussed, a core positive value stands out or is made into a spectacle in such a way that it is more likely to be noted for what it is, i.e., a real good thing. And recognition of *this* is what being moved consists in.

Let us now turn to our third criterion: phenomenology. Does our candidate emotion have its own characteristic phenomenology? In other words, is there something about 'what it is like' to have this kind of experience that is peculiar to it? It is difficult to come up with good descriptions of the phenomenology of affective states in general, but being moved by the sorts of cases discussed above is so experientially salient and distinctive that perhaps descriptions are not unattainable.

A subject who feels very moved feels not only an acceleration of her breathing and heartbeat, but also a tightening of her throat, heaving as well as warmth in her chest, maybe some trembling of her lips and above all she will start tearing up. This, at any rate, is the pattern transpiring from subjects' reports when focusing on localized bodily phenomenology (Cova and Deonna 2014, 455–57). But it is interesting to move away from this disjointed picture of emotional phenomenology and look at it from the perspective of the overall experience that the subject undergoes. Frijda, when trying to capture the phenomenon, speaks of a bodily posture that is both "knocked over" and "deferential", a global state that leads one to "weep silently" (Frijda 2007, 38–39). This, as an account of the onset and endpoint of the experience, is clearly on the right track; but let me dare go a bit further. From the first-person perspective, the major increase in overall arousal is indeed initially experienced as a shock, a feeling of being quite unexpectedly but surely overwhelmed by what is happening.[10] Yet, this unsettling loss of control is also experienced as the recognition that something important, profound or meaningful is occurring, something one is privileged to witness. The experience of privilege is accompanied by considerable relief or even gratitude at receiving the privilege. Although the attended specific good might be accruing to you, part of the depth of the feeling seems to come from its triggering being independent of any foreseeable personal benefit. The result is a momentary suspension of ordinary engagement with the world, a state that can be described as a contemplative and deferent sort of contentment.

Some closing remarks about the phenomenology of being moved. First, although being moved seems to involve a sense of being taken by force, it does not always have this intensity. What I have just described is being moved at its experiential apex.[11] Second, while this phenomenology strongly resembles that of sadness and while it is by nature quite disruptive, it will be unpleasant (if at all) only superficially or locally. As just seen, from the standpoint of the overall experience, it is a form of contentment even if it is one that is devoid of pleasure (at least sensory pleasure). For this reason, unless it is neither the place nor the time, we like to be moved.

Let us now return to the two last related criteria which serve to evaluate whether or not being moved amounts to a separate and distinct emotion: does it have a distinctive function, and does it have distinctive action tendencies? The two are related insofar as the function of an emotion is generally manifested in its action tendencies. Trying to see how the phenomenon of being moved measures up against this double criterion by focusing on the "disturbance" that is involved in experiencing it could easily lead us, as it did Claparède (1930), to a negative conclusion. It is "entirely unclear what adaptive relation might exist between the situation felt to be 'moving' and the behaviour of the "pure emotion", or how the behaviour adjusts the subject to the circumstances that moved him".[12] Such a verdict is natural if we compare being moved to fear or anger. These emotions immediately prepare us to negotiate the situations which typically trigger them and so fulfill the function for which evolution has selected them. In the case of being moved, no such observation can be made. The bodily disturbance typical of this state seems rather to produce shock and blissful paralysis instead of any discernible adaptive action.

But this conclusion is somewhat hasty. Other standard emotions face the same issue regarding function and action tendencies. Shame and sadness, for instance, are characterized by a certain passivity, a turning inward, and so it is hard to associate them to any definite action tendencies. But that does not in and of itself make them non-adaptive. Although shame, for example, initially fosters hiding and isolation, there are good reasons for thinking that in the long run it contributes in a more diffuse manner to changes in the self that are beneficial to the collective (Deonna, Rodogno and Teroni 2011). It is not difficult to draw a parallel with the phenomenon of being moved. Just like shame, and in fact like most positive emotions, it is characterized by a distancing without any discernible immediate action tendencies but with beneficial features that are more diffuse and delayed.[13] A proponent of evolutionary explanations might then claim that this emotion helps reinforce the links that tie a community together by signaling to its members the importance that the subject attaches to the most fundamental values that sustain it. If this social bonding function is a feature of other emotions, it is perhaps all the more central to this particular emotion, which more than any other touches on our fragile humanity. From the first-person point of view, which has been our focus hitherto, being moved is firstly a reminder, or often a discovery, of the values that we hold most dear. It is also above all an experience in which we discover those values exemplified where we did not expect them, or had stopped expecting them. Lastly, being moved is an experience with a particularly strong tendency to move us, in a more literal sense. The gratitude that is at the heart of the experience and the hope that ensues can infuse our every value with new life and enlighten our every action.

Before I conclude, I wish to consider an important apparent counter-example to the suggested account. Is it really true that we are only moved by events that we construe positively? Are we not sometimes moved by events construed in a negative way? Are we not sometimes moved when we see someone suffering? Certain cases of compassion, sympathy or commiseration in particular would then constitute counter-examples to the hypothesis.

Here is what can be said about these "negative cases" in the limited space at my disposal. The first thing is to distinguish between two categories of "negative cases" where the label "being moved" is used (both in ordinary discourse and in our subjects' reports). In the first category, we find the "purely negative cases" that seem completely at odd with my analysis, examples such as a cat ran over by a bus or an old man almost incapable of getting about. In the second category, we find tales of suffering in which recovery or redemption are not far away—these are the "semi-negative cases". The two categories deserve separate treatments.

Purely negative cases are simply cases of sadness or sorrow. They are the opposite of being moved in that they constitute the registering that a positive value (what is dear to us) has been vanquished by a negative value. Sadness is the experience of the loss or ruin of positive values. Why then do some people think of those as cases of being moved? The answer to this is that the two experiences are, as we have seen, very similar to one another,[14] and it is thus no surprise that they would occasionally be thought of in that way. Now, whether we think of these reports as involving linguistic errors (it is just a mistake to label these cases "being moved") or as a manifestation of the expression's polysemy ("being moved" is an ambiguous expression), there is no reason to doubt that there is a distinct phenomenon I am uncovering.

The explanation is different for what I have called the "semi-negative cases". It is true that we often report cases of compassion or sympathy by saying that we are moved by this or that person's suffering. The reason for this is that circumstances that tend to cause compassion are also often circumstances that move us. Plight and suffering is often taking place against a background of resistance, resilience, solidarity, humanity, dignity, etc. These are typically occasions in which core positive values are made salient on the background of negative values, the sort of configuration which I said is fertile terrain for being moved. While we then sympathize with the plight of an individual or a collective, we are *also* likely to be moved by the positive value that succeeds, if only temporarily, in making a stand despite the adverse circumstances. Far from constituting counter-examples, the cases at hand satisfy to the letter the idea of being moved as experiences of core positive values.

We have considered the five commonly used criteria to evaluate whether an affective phenomenon qualifies as an emotion in its own right. I have tried to show that being moved meets these criteria and that the emotion in question is an unsettling yet soothing form of pleasureless contentment brought about by the contemplation of a specific core positive value making a stand. This idea raises a series of very diverse questions that I have only barely broached and which I cannot answer here: what is the link between this emotion and joy, awe, elevation and other so-called transcendental emotions (Algoe and Haidt 2009; Cova, Deonna and Sander 2016)? Does the hypothesis advanced here apply more generally to aesthetic experience, in particular to music, the quintessential object of the phenomenon of being moved? Provided we assess this emotion for appropriateness like we do other emotions, what is the relation between inappropriate episodes of this emotion and sentimentality? What is the function of tears in general and in the phenomenon of being moved in particular? Finally, what is the link between being moved and happiness? The beginning of some promising answers can be found in the literature (Cova and Deonna 2014; Hanich et al. 2014; Rottenberg and Vingerhoets 2012; Vingerhoets 2013), but for the most, these questions are still awaiting proper elaboration and responses.

Notes

1. Although the phenomenology, the triggering circumstances and behavioral manifestations typically involve very negative features, I shall be showing that being moved is an essentially positive emotion.
2. One notable exception is the Genevan psychologist Claparède in his 1930 "L'émotion « pure »". Although Claparède believes that being moved constitutes a distinct type of experience, he regards it as a form of affective disturbance that has no adaptive value. As we will see, I take this view to be mistaken.
3. If one consults the Webster, Collins or Oxford English dictionaries concerning the meaning of the words "move" or "moving", one will find "stirring the passions or affections (usually tender)", or "having an effect on your emotions and causing you to feel sadness or sympathy for another person", both to be understood in one of the two outlined senses.
4. The claim that will be defended is made more plausible by the fact that corresponding expressions in other languages (e.g., "je suis ému", "sono commosso", "Ich bin gerührt", "ik ben ontroerd", "Estoy conmovido") behave in very similar ways.

5. For a defense of these criteria, see Deonna and Scherer (2010) and Deonna and Teroni (2012).
6. The present short paper focuses on the conceptual canvassing of the type of emotion that being moved is. I will refer when appropriate to the empirical data—a thorough internet-based survey we ran on English-speaking participants living in the US and recruited through Amazon Mechanical Turk—that can all be found in Cova and Deonna (2014).
7. For the role of formal objects in the philosophical theory of emotions and their relation to values, see in particular Teroni (2007).
8. We need an account of what a *core* positive value is and why some of them (humor? respect?) are less likely than others to move us. For present purposes, an intuitive understanding of the notion is sufficient. For some initial characterization, see Cova and Deonna (2014, 454).
9. I have been guided towards this claim by Kevin Mulligan who makes a slightly different use of it in Mulligan (2016).
10. The idea that being moved involves an initial shock may seem difficult to reconcile with the fact that we keep being moved by events or scenes already encountered many times. Although I would not want to deny that these cases put interesting pressure on the account, I find it that even in these cases I am moved precisely to the extent that the events or scenes in question keep succeeding in catching me unaware.
11. It is plausible to regard the expression "I am touched" as designating an attenuated form of the phenomenon of being moved.
12. Claparède (1930, 347).
13. Regarding positive emotions, the "broaden-and-build" theory has emphasized the fact that they lack distinct action tendencies insofar as they tend to generally broaden our "thought-action repertoire", i.e., serve to build enduring personal resources such as new dispositions to act or new values (Fredrickson 2001).
14. There is one crucial difference between the two types of experience though. It is possible to show that people do not report "warmth or pleasure in the chest" in purely negative cases. This I take as evidence that people are reporting sadness and not being moved in these cases.

References

Algoe, Sara, and Jonathan D. Haidt. 2009. "Witnessing Excellence in Action: The 'other-praising' Emotions of Elevation, Gratitude, and Admiration." *The Journal of Positive Psychology* 4: 105–27.

Claparède, Édouard. 1930. "L'émotion 'pure'." *Archives de Psychologie* 22: 333–47.

Cova, Florian, and Julien Deonna A. 2014. "Being Moved." *Philosophical Studies* 169: 447–66.

Cova, Florian, Julien Deonna A., and David Sander. 2016. *Is Elevation Just a Way of Being Moved?* Unpublished manuscript, University of Geneva.

Deonna, Julien A. 2011. "Être ému [Being moved]." In *Les ombres de l'âme: Penser les émotions négatives* edited by Christine Tappolet, Fabrice Teroni, and Anita Konzelmann Ziv, 111–30. Geneva, Switzerland: Markus Haller.

Deonna, Julien A., Raffaele Rodogno, and Fabrice Teroni. 2011. *In Defense of Shame: The Faces of an Emotion.* New York: Oxford University Press.

Deonna, Julien A., and Klaus R. Scherer. 2010. "The Case of the Disappearing Intentional Object: Constraints on a Definition of Emotion." *Emotion Review* 2: 44–52.

Deonna, Julien A., and Fabrice Teroni. 2012. *The Emotions: A Philosophical Introduction*. New York: Routledge.

de Sousa, Ronald. 1987. *The Rationality of Emotions*. Cambridge: MIT Press.

Fiske, Alan, Thomas Schubert, and Beate Seibt. 2016. "'Kama Muta' or 'Being Moved by Love': A Bootstrapping Approach to the Ontology and Epistemology of an Emotion." In *Universalism Without Uniformity: Explorations in Mind and Culture*, edited by Julia Cassaniti and Usha Menon, 79–100. Chicago: Chicago University Press.

Fredrickson, Barbara L. 2001. "The Role of Positive Emotions in Positive Psychology: The Broaden-and-Build Theory of Positive Emotions." *American Psychologist* 56: 218–26.

Frijda, Nico H. 2007. *The Laws of Emotion*. Mahwah, NJ: Lawrence Erlbaum Associates.

Hanich, Julian, Valentin Wagner, Mira Shah, Thomas Jacobsen, and Winfried Menninghaus. 2014. "Why We Like to Watch Sad Films. The Pleasure of Being Moved in Aesthetic Experiences." *Psychology of Aesthetics, Creativity, and the Arts* 8, no. 2: 130–43.

Konečni, Vladimir. 2005. "The Aesthetic Trinity: Awe, Being Moved, Thrills." *Bulletin of Psychology and the Arts* 5: 27–44.

Konečni, Vladimir. 2011. "Aesthetic Trinity Theory and the Sublime." *Philosophy Today* 55: 64–73.

Kuehnast, Milena, Valentin Wagner, Eugen Wassiliwizky, Thomas Jacobsen, and Winfried Menninghaus. 2014. "Being Moved: Linguistic Representation and Conceptual Structure." *Frontiers in Psychology* 5.

Menninghaus, Winfried, Valentin Wagner, Julian Hanich, Eugen Wassiliwizky, Milena Kuehnast, and Thomas Jacobsen. 2015. "Towards a Psychological Construct of Being Moved." *PLoS One* 10, no. 6, e0128451.

Mulligan, Kevin. 2016. "Happiness, Luck and Satisfaction." *Argumenta* 1, no. 2: 133–45.

Rottenberg, Jonathan, and Ad J. J. M. Vingerhoets. 2012. "Crying: Call for a Lifespan Approach." *Social and Personality Psychology Compass* 6, no. 3: 217–27.

Teroni, Fabrice. 2007. "Emotions and Formal Objects." *Dialectica* 61: 395–415.

Tokaji, Akihiko. 2003. "Research for Determinant Factors and Features of Emotional Responses of 'kandoh' (the State of Being Emotionally Moved)." *Japanese Psychological Research* 45, no. 4: 235–49.

Vingerhoets, Ad J. J. M. 2013. *Why Only Humans Weep: Unraveling the Mysteries of Tears*. New York: Oxford University Press.

7 The Uncanny and Other Negative Existential Feelings

Jérôme Dokic

The Feeling of Uncanniness

In his famous essay on *The Uncanny*, Freud ([1919] 2003) explores a peculiar existential feeling. A situation can strike us as being not quite familiar, and thus novel in some respects, but the feeling of uncanniness involves more than a failure of familiarity; it concerns the strangeness of what, in our environment, should be familiar to us. For instance, the perception of a wax figure or a human-like automaton answers some of our expectations about the presence of an animate being, while other expectations, having to do with its dynamics and its capacity to interact with us, are manifestly not met. The result may be a state of slight discomfort which is characteristic of the feeling in which Freud is interested.

The feeling of uncanniness is a negative feeling; it belongs to the category of unpleasant affective experiences. Freud goes further and associates it with the frightening, but given the examples he himself offers, it is not obvious that this feeling should necessarily involve fear and dread, even though it typically brings to the subject uneasiness or even palpable anxiety.

As Freud observes, the Uncanny has been widely exploited in the domain of fiction. However, if the feeling of uncanniness may evoke the Kantian category of the sublime, it is not intrinsically aesthetic, but concerns human life in all its normal and pathological variations.

The feeling of uncanniness is existential in the sense that it somehow alters our sensory, affective, practical and cognitive relationship to the external world. Matthew Ratcliffe defines existential feelings in terms of two characteristics. First, they are (often subtle) bodily states of which we are at least partly conscious. Second, they are not intentionally directed towards specific objects or situations but are "background orientations through which experience as a whole is structured" (Ratcliffe 2008, 2). Although this definition is of course schematic, it fits the various forms the feeling of uncanniness can take. Freud himself describes this feeling as a type of "emotional impulses", characterized by the fact that they are "restrained, inhibited in their aims and dependent on numerous attended circumstances" (Freud [1919] 2003, 123). On the one hand, following Williams James's metaphor, feelings of uncanniness belong to the "fringes" or "margins" of bodily consciousness (James [1890] 1980). On the phenomenological level, they have an "indistinct, spreading, blurred quality" and "seem to actively resist attempts to focus attention directly on them" (Mangan 2001). On the other hand, the feeling of uncanniness does not always target well-identified aspects of the perceived situation. We are often at a loss if we are to explain exactly what in the relevant situation is familiar or not, and to select the appropriate response. In general, existential feelings, like other kinds of feelings (such as the feeling of "déjà vu"), generate a form of cognitive and motivational opacity which sets them apart from ordinary cases of emotions such as fear.[1]

Extraordinary Feelings

Even though existential feelings are ubiquitous in ordinary life, they also occur, often in spectacular forms, in many psychiatric cases. For instance, patients with the Cotard delusion, which is associated with a severe form of depression, have feelings of derealisation and depersonalisation. Nothing seems real or concrete to them, including their own bodies. Some of them hold that they are dead or disembodied, or declare "I do not exist", flying in the face of a well-entrenched Cartesian way of thinking.

Another pathological case is the Capgras delusion. Capgras patients firmly hold that a close family member has been replaced by an identical-looking impostor, sometimes considered as malicious. For instance, in the presence of his wife, one patient coldly declares "This person is not my wife", throwing disarray into his family, as we can easily understand. The warm glow of familiarity formerly associated with perceptual and practical acquaintance with his wife seems to have wholly disappeared. The patient visually recognizes his wife's face, but he describes it as unreal, as if the person in front of him were wearing a wax mask.[2]

Cotard and Capgras delusions involve negative existential feelings that are especially salient and seem to explain, at least partly, why the patients develop delusions ("I am dead", "This is not my wife", etc.). These feelings reveal a pathological failure of affective experience. This is obvious in the case of the Cotard delusion, where the patients seem to lack positive affective experiences altogether. The Capgras delusion too is tied to a failure of affective experience, albeit more circumscribed. Electrodermal studies have revealed that the patients do not have the physiological responses that we ordinarily show in the presence of close family members. On a plausible neuroanatomical hypothesis, the patients' so-called "visuo-affective pathway" is dysfunctional. The visuo-affective pathway enables swift connections between sensory stimulations and the limbic system, in parallel with the slower "visuo-semantic" pathway, which underlies conscious sensory experience and recognition (see, e.g., Young 1998).

Familiarity and Strangeness

The analysis of the Capgras delusion should help to clarify the nature of the feeling of strangeness or non-familiarity, which is a key component of the kind of affective experience discussed by Freud.³ It is true that the patients do not feel any feeling of familiarity in front of their relatives. Should we conclude that the absence of such feeling provides an exhaustive description of their affective experience? If the answer is positive, there is no feeling of strangeness or non-familiarity, but only the absence of a feeling of familiarity. In other words, the feeling of familiarity would not have a polar opposite—in the case in point, a distinctive feeling of strangeness or non-familiarity. In this respect, it would be different from many emotions that have polar opposites, such as happiness and sadness, love and hate or admiration and contempt (see Mulligan 1998).

The claim that the feeling of familiarity lacks a polar opposite would certainly deserve more discussion, but I am inclined to reject it since an important consideration seems to me to support the opposite claim. Some subjects have a visuo-affective deficit analogous to that of patients with the Capgras delusion, but in contrast to Capgras patients, they do not develop the delusive belief that one of their relatives has been replaced by an impostor (see Tranel, Damasio, and Damasio 1995). These subjects believe (indeed know) that the person in front of them is the familiar person whose face they can recognize, but report that their visual experience is strange, flat, that it is *as if* the person were somebody else.

Two theoretical options are available at this point. The first option is the claim that non-delusive subjects have the same types of feelings as Capgras patients. An additional factor, other than affective experience, must then be invoked to explain the formation of delusive beliefs in the pathological case. This factor is typically identified as a deficit tied to the mechanisms underlying belief revision. The patients form a highly implausible belief based on abnormal affective experience, but maintain this belief in the face of background knowledge to the contrary, which should lead them to revise the extravagant interpretation which they give to their feelings.⁴

The second option is the claim that the affective experiences of the two groups are quite different. While non-delusive subjects have merely lost the positive feeling of familiarity that we experience in front of a family member, Capgras patients have in addition a negative feeling of strangeness, which is so strong that they cannot refrain from forming the belief that the person with their relative's face must in fact be an impostor.

The latter option strikes me as more plausible. The former option is not very elegant from an explanatory point of view, since it assumes that the delusion arises from two factors that seem to be conceptually independent, namely abnormal affective experience and undermined capacity to revise one's beliefs. In contrast, the second option offers a unified explanation, but it entails that the feeling of familiarity has a polar opposite after all, namely the feeling of strangeness.

The Doxastic Analysis of Feelings

Feelings of familiarity or strangeness are often tied to perception, but they do not seem to correspond to perceived qualities on a par with color, form or orientation. There is indeed a tendency to describe the feeling of familiarity as if an aura or halo surrounded the familiar person ("the warm glow of familiarity"), but such descriptions are arguably metaphorical. As Mangan observes, the feeling of familiarity "is not a color, not an aroma, not a taste, not a sound. It is possible for the feeling of familiarity to merge with, or be absent from, virtually any sensory content found on any sensory dimension" (Mangan 2001, Introduction). The feeling of familiarity, like other kinds of feelings, is not the experience of a manifest property in the world.

On the assumption that feelings are not intentional experiences like sensory experiences, how should we understand their relationship to the formation of some of our beliefs about the world? To answer this question, let us turn to the doxastic analysis of feelings once offered by William Alston:[5]

A subject S feels that $p =_{df}$ S is in a conscious, non-cognitive state such that by virtue of being in this state:

(1) S has a *prima facie* tendency to believe that *p*.
(2) S has a *prima facie* warrant for this belief.

Clause (1) of this definition is psychological. What is a tendency or inclination to form the belief (or judgment) that *p* (whether *p* is a true or false proposition)? The subject who feels that *p* does not merely have the disposition to believe that *p*, of which she might be unaware. Rather, the subject feels an "inner force" that pushes her to form this belief. In many cases, the relevant tendency is *prima facie* in the sense that the subject may not actually form the belief that *p*. With more or less effort, she can resist this tendency. For instance, I feel that an unknown person is familiar, but I do not form the judgment that she is familiar, because I realize that my feeling of familiarity is due to the fact that the person vaguely looks like a friend of mine.

The question arises as to the sense of the phrase "non-cognitive" in the *definiens*. Alston is not fully explicit on this point, but I would like to suggest the following interpretation.[6] On a plausible model, the content of a perceptual judgment *derives* from the content of the underlying sensory experience. For instance, I judge that the cup in front of me is full of coffee at least partly because this is what I see (or seem to see). In contrast, the content of a feeling is not independent from the belief that it inclines the subject to form. In this case, the content of the feeling derives from the content of the belief. In other words, feelings, but not sensory experiences, are *mere* (felt) doxastic inclinations. Following Alston's happy metaphor, feelings only provide "seeds of cognition". They do not constitute grounding experiences or evidential bases for our beliefs.

The analysis of feelings as involving doxastic inclinations provides a coherent account of what Sartre calls "perception of absence" (Sartre [1943] 2001). In his famous example, I perceive Pierre's absence in his usual café. Of course, one might wonder how the absence of anything can literally figure in the sensory content of our experience. In this respect, the introduction of the feeling of absence is salutary. Such feeling is constitutively tied to the inclina-tion to believe that Pierre is not to be seen in his usual café. In general, the occurrence of a feeling results from rapid parallel information processing at the subpersonal level. Thus, I can have the feeling that Pierre is absent even before I have consciously identified the persons actually present in the café.[7]

Clause (2) of Alston's definition is epistemological. Feeling-based beliefs are spontaneous and do not rest on independent evidence, but they can still have some justificatory value or epistemic authority. If I feel that a person is familiar, I have a reason to believe that the person is indeed familiar to me. However, my reason is *prima facie* in the sense that it can be defeated by other, more important rational considerations.[8]

The doxastic analysis also applies to existential feelings. What character-izes existential feelings is their doxastic "depth", so to speak, that is, the fact that they can spontaneously generate beliefs that are background orienta-tions or frames of reference for many other beliefs. The more an existential feeling is doxastically deep, the more the subject's inclination to form the corresponding beliefs is irresistible and difficult to revise. This may explain that in pathological cases, patients maintain their delusive beliefs in con-tradiction to common sense. For instance, Capgras patients do not merely experience a local feeling of strangeness about a person who looks like a family member, but their delusive beliefs reflect a pathological frame of refer-ence, according to which the relative has disappeared from the *visible* world in general. Nothing *counts* anymore as a genuine visible encounter with the lost relative.

Arguably, the depth of existential feelings puts pressure on clause (2) of Alston's definition. In line with Wittgenstein's terminology in *On Certainty* (Wittgenstein 1969), we might say that they give rise to subjective certainties rather than beliefs. Certainties are what the subject takes for granted; they do not play the role of ordinary empirical beliefs in inquiry. Thus, they are not justified and do not justify (even *prima facie*), but their epistemic authority derives from the fact that they are hinges of our epistemic practice.

Negative Existential Feelings and the Sense of Reality

The last issue that I would like to raise concerns the role of negative existen-tial feelings in the constitution of the "sense of reality" or the lived relation-ship of "being in the world". Whether the context is normal or pathological, the presence of a negative existential feeling reflects a significant change in the lived relationship between oneself and the rest of the world. The question is what influence such a change bears on the subject's sense of reality or being in the world.

According to Ratcliffe, some existential feelings suffice to upset or shake the subject's sense of reality. He writes that such feelings "often seem to be insepa-rable from distortions and diminutions of a sense of reality and of belonging to a world" (Ratcliffe 2008, 3). Ratcliffe adds that in pathological cases, the patients' delusions are less beliefs conceived as propositional attitudes than *expressions* of a fragmented sense of reality.

I would like to suggest a slightly different perspective from Ratcliffe's. First, I do not see any obstacle to considering at least some delusions as beliefs with (often not very specific) propositional contents.[9] These beliefs result from negative existential feelings which, like other kinds of feelings to be found in non-pathological cases, constitutively involve doxastic inclinations.

Second, I dispute the claim that negative existential feelings always generate a disorder of the sense of reality. Such a disorder has to do with the impression of a *failure of coherence* among the subject's feelings, sensory experiences and cognitive background (her beliefs and knowledge). The subject does not feel "being in the world" when she has difficulties in coping with reality in a coherent way, because of more or less persistent cognitive dissonances.

Obviously, many psychiatric disorders involve a deficient sense of reality. For instance, in schizophrenia, the absence of coherence among different sources of information (sensory, affective and cognitive) at the subject's disposal is lived with difficulty, and pertains to her recurrent impression of being detached from the world and derealized. In this respect, the status of the Capgras delusion is less clear. At least some of the patients do not seem to experience a failure of internal coherence which would motivate them to revise some of their beliefs. On the contrary, they seem to have restored some pseudo-coherence by re-interpreting their visual experiences: "This person looks like my wife, but she is not my wife". Roughly, schizophrenia makes the subject oscillate between different experiential frames of reference, whereas the Capgras delusion seems to force the substitution of the ordinary experiential frame by another experiential frame according to which, as suggested above, the patient's relative is not part of the visible world anymore.

The impression of a cognitive dissonance can be considered as a kind of negative existential feeling. When the subject has such an impression, her sense of reality or being in the world is altered, and can produce, in extreme cases, delusive beliefs. However, delusive beliefs can also result from negative existential feelings, such as feelings of strangeness, in the absence of cognitive dissonance, as I have just suggested with respect to the Capgras delusion.

Moreover, an impression of cognitive dissonance can also result from a *positive* existential feeling. Patients with the Fregoli delusion declare that they often encounter in various places familiar persons (their wife, their father, etc.) who are cunningly disguised. As in the Capgras delusion, it is plausible that one of the key components of the Fregoli delusion is a disorder of the mechanisms underlying perceptual identification. Fregoli patients have an *exaggerated* affective response to unknown faces. In itself, this response is best conceived as a positive existential feeling. If there is an additional negative affective element, it can only come from a higher-level impression, namely that of a dissonance between the patient's feeling of hyper-familiarity, her visual experience and her background beliefs and knowledge. Such cognitive dissonance might still be experienced by less delusive patients, but it is arguable that once the delusion is fully in place, some pseudo-coherence is restored and no cognitive dissonance arises anymore.

Freud's feeling of uncanniness clearly results from a cognitive dissonance which can shake our sense of reality. When we feel the anxiety-inducing strangeness of a human-like automaton or a wax figure, our sense of reality may break down for one moment, albeit without separating into fragments. To the extent that the feeling of uncanniness is tied to a cognitive dissonance involving familiarity, it is so to speak an existential "meta-feeling". It results from the impression of a cognitive dissonance between a feeling of strangeness and implicit expectations about the presence of a familiar thing or situation.

Conclusion

Our discussion has targeted a negative existential feeling due to a failure of familiarity, namely the feeling of uncanniness highlighted by Freud. I have analyzed a central component of such a feeling, namely experienced strangeness, and shown that it is a distinctive phenomenological experience, which does not reduce to a mere absence of familiarity (even if the subject is aware of it). I have emphasized the constitutive role of feelings, especially existential feelings, in the fundamental organization of our beliefs and behavior. Finally, I have argued that the feeling of uncanniness is best conceived as an existential meta-feeling, which results from a cognitive dissonance between expected familiarity and actual strangeness of the relevant situation.[10]

Notes

1. As is well known, Freud tried to explain the opacity of the feeling of uncanniness in terms of his theory of psychological repression, nowadays largely discredited.
2. On these delusions and others, see Coltheart and Davies (2000).
3. The question of whether the strangeness experienced by Capgras patients belongs to the Uncanny in Freud's sense will be tackled later (section 5); my answer will be negative.
4. For a defense of the two-factor explanation, see Max Coltheart and Martin Davies's contribution to Coltheart and Davies (2000).
5. See Alston (1969, 25). Alston's analysis, which concerns what he calls "adjectival feelings" (such as the feeling reported by "I feel tired"), is here transposed to feelings whose contents can be specified by propositions.
6. Here is Alston's own elucidation of the phrase: "In the Hegelian tradition feeling is taken to be noncognitive because it contains no 'subject-object distinction'. It is a seamless whole, though it contains within it seeds of knowledge that will flower when its implicit content is brought to light" (Alston 1969, 24, fn. 16).
7. For further discussion of the perception of absence, see Martin and Dokic (2013).
8. Obviously, this clause deserves more discussion. It may only apply to feelings that are reliable indicators of some underlying facts. For instance, my feeling that a face is familiar reflects that my brain is used to process this face, which in turn is a reliable indicator of its familiarity. On externalist assumptions, my feeling can then be taken as a *prima facie* reason to form the belief that I know this face, even before I can identify it. For further discussion, see Dokic (2012).

9. A defense of this claim can be found in Bayne and Pacherie (2004).
10. I would like to thank the Editors for penetrating comments about a previous version of this essay. I have tried to take at least some of them into account here.

References

Alston, William P. 1969. "Feelings." *The Philosophical Review* 78, no. 1: 3–34.

Bayne, Tim, and Élisabeth Pacherie. 2004. "Bottom-Up or Top-Down? Campbell's Rationalist Account of Monothematic Delusions." *Philosophy, Psychiatry, & Psychology* 11, no. 1: 1–11.

Coltheart, Max, and Martin Davies eds. 2000. *Pathologies of Belief*. Oxford: Blackwell.

Dokic, Jérôme. 2012. "Seeds of Knowledge: Noetic Feelings and Metacognition." In *Foundations of Metacognition*, edited by Michael J. Beran, Johannes L. Brandl, Josef Perner, and Joëlle Proust, 302–20. Oxford: Oxford University Press.

Freud, Sigmund. [1919] 2003. *The Uncanny*. Translated by David McLintock. London: Penguin.

James, William. [1890] 1980. *Principles of Psychology*. New York: Holt.

Mangan, Bruce. 2001. "Sensation's Ghost. The Non-Sensory 'Fringe' of Consciousness." *PSYCHE* 7, no. 18.

Martin, Jean-Rémy, and Jérôme Dokic. 2013. "Seeing Absence or Absence of Seeing?." *Thought: A philosophical Journal* 2, no. 2: 85–177.

Mulligan, Kevin. 1998. "The Spectre of Inverted Emotions and the Space of Emotions." *Acta Analytica*, 89–105. Original French version: 1995 "Le spectre de l'affect inverti et l'espace des émotions", *La Couleur des pensées*, edited by Patricia Paperman and Ruwen Ogien, 65–83. Paris: Editions de l'EHESS (*Raisons Pratiques* 6).

Ratcliffe, Matthew J. 2008. *Feelings of Being. Phenomenology, Psychiatry and the Sense of Reality*. Oxford: Oxford University Press.

Sartre, Jean-Paul. [1943] 2001. *Being and Nothingness: An Essay in Phenomenological Ontology*. New York: Citadel Press.

Tranel, Daniel, Hanna Damasio, and Antonio R. Damasio. 1995. "Double Dissociation Between Overt and Covert Face Recognition." *Journal of Cognitive Neuroscience* 7, no. 4: 425–32.

Wittgenstein, Ludwig. 1969. *On Certainty*, edited by Elizabeth M. Anscombe and Georg H. von Wright, translated by Denis Paul and Elizabeth M. Anscombe. Oxford: Blackwell.

Young, Andrew. 1998. *Face and Mind*. Oxford: Oxford University Press.

8   Disgustingly Handsome

Nausea in the Face of Physical Beauty

Anita Konzelmann Ziv

"Oh yes, disgustingly handsome," muses Solal as he contemplates himself in the boudoir mirror of Ariane, the woman he loves and the woman whose soul he is going to put to the test. This thought, strange as it is, contains in a nutshell the theme of Albert Cohen's great Genevan novel "*Belle du Seigneur*", in which he depicts the horror and the beauty of attempting to live a perfect love.

The thought "disgustingly handsome"[1] evokes curiosity and tension, not only because of its apparent contradiction in terms but also because it seems to conflict with our experience of beauty. Whether natural or man-made, beautiful things generally arouse pleasant experiences, don't they? Far from arousing disgust or nausea, beauty usually fills us with joy and delight. It brightens up our life. Physical beauty is not an exception: the beauty of a child, a woman or a man often suffices for us to be caught in admiration and enchantment. Even the affective blend of admiration and resentment that a person physically less fortunate might feel in the presence of extraordinary human beauty is still far from feeling disgust.

Disgust, in contrast, essentially "contains an element of plain 'resistance', and this is first of all the vehement *rejection of a presumption*" (Kolnai 2004, 65). According to most theories of disgust, "the disgusting" is closely related to putrefaction and its manifestations, such as bad smell or the unpleasant characteristic consistency of decomposing organic matter. Accordingly, a subject's typical response to her perception of the disgusting, be it by the sense of smell, touch or vision, is nausea. Inasmuch as this reaction drives the subject to avoid or expel harmful substances, disgust is supposed to be a defense against potential contamination (Mizrahi, this volume; McGinn 2011; Rozin, Haidt and McCauley 2008; Demmerling and Landweer 2007; Kolnai 2004; Miller 1997). Now, beauty is far off from putrefaction. We certainly do not perceive it by smelling bad odors or by touching or seeing something execrable. Beauty does not repel but attracts. Thus, beauty does not seem apt to be the object of nausea or disgust. And even if it is widely recognized that the disgusting can exert a certain power of attraction, there is no comparable consensus concerning an alleged power of repulsion exerted by the beautiful. Hence, to consider beauty as apt to generate nausea is to invoke a profound ambivalence: an ambivalence that needs to be explained.

The object of the self-reflexive thought "disgustingly handsome" is, we are told, endowed with exceptional masculine beauty. Solal de Solal, the princely hero of Cohen's novel, is introduced as a tall man with "narrow hips, flat stomach, broad chest and, under the tanned skin, muscles like intertwining serpents" (Cohen 1995, 6–7). His hair is abundant and his smile splendid due to a perfect set of teeth. His beauty and his elegance mark him out for being admired and loved by women. So why, gazing at his reflection in the mirror of Ariane, should he consider himself as "*disgustingly* handsome"?

Mediated Disgust

First of all, we need to consider that the expression "disgustingly handsome" could be understood in terms of a simple rhetorical figure which, by means of semantic contrast, reinforces the main qualification "handsome". Such oxymorons are common: Swiss German speakers, for example, use the expression "woefully beautiful" in the face of outstanding beauty, whereas the Venezuelans qualify an attractive woman as "*podrida de buena*", literally meaning "rottenly good". In these cases, the function of the negative qualification is to emphasize the abundance of beauty or goodness: the achievement of a perfection that goes beyond what the words "beautiful" or "good" are supposed to communicate. Given the importance of the topic of disgust in *Belle du Seigneur* we would be ill-advised, however, to understand the thought "disgustingly beautiful" by which Solal introduces himself to the reader in this manner. In order to seize the whole scope of the hero's initial self-evaluation, we should take it literally.

Solal's elliptic utterance "disgustingly handsome" is not so much describing his physical appearance as it is expressing the affective state by which he assesses the value of his beauty. In view of the circumstances, his felt disgust cannot be understood in terms of nausea caused by the vision or touch of something execrable or by a strong stench. Rather, it seems to be the aesthetic analog to what is often described as "moral disgust", an emotion directed to what repels us morally such as lying and cruelty. As philosophical theories of disgust emphasize, this kind of disgust is not immediately elicited by sense perception but mediated through certain attitudes, e.g., beliefs. There is, however, a functional parallel between immediate and cognitively mediated disgust. Lying, for example, is supposed to elicit disgust because one knows that it is destructive, in that it "tends to erase the primary functional character of the act of judging (acknowledging truth)" (Calabi 1999, 517). Given its tendency to undermine a primary function of human life, lying is considered analogous to putrefaction, which equally tends to "get the upper hand on the functional organization of the organism and aims at its extinction" (Calabi 1999, 517).

Let us stress, however, that mediated disgust does not necessarily invoke a moral object, i.e., it is not necessarily moral disgust. When a person feels disgusted at a certain "lascivious intellectualism"—"that kind of subjective, irresponsible, and opulent, overrefined and sometimes bombastic reveling in thought itself and in its exhibition" (Kolnai 2004, 67)—they thereby invoke a non-moral value. Likewise, aesthetic disgust provoked, say, by the ugliness of a piece of furniture does not imply any moral value. What these forms of mediated disgust have in common is to signal an offense at our personal set of values. We might say, then, that through her feelings of disgust a person learns to which values she is attached.

Claiming that the primary function of mediated disgust is to point out our personal values has the advantage of suspending the controversy about the moral status of disgust (Kelly 2011, 137–52). Our personal set of values undoubtedly contains both moral and non-moral values. Disgust can be triggered by either of them. Solal's disgust, for instance, is clearly not moral disgust since its object is not a reprehensible action or attitude. His beauty is not the result of wrongfully depriving anybody of theirs. Yet even if mediated disgust does not necessarily reveal moral faults, its close relation to personal values at least suggests that morality is somehow entangled in our feeling disgusted. One way to cash out the nature of this involvement is to invoke reflexivity. A person's morality hinges on her faculty to "bend back" on her attitudes, her actions and reactions. Reconsidering what one felt, thought and did in given circumstances is the condition of assessing one's path in life. By way of self-evaluation we not only gauge our moral standards but also continually calibrate and recalibrate them. Within this framework, feeling disgusted at something that is not linked to stench and putrefaction can play a morally relevant role in that it provokes reflection on the attitudes that mediate the feeling. It might force us to identify the values at stake and to discern whether our attitudes, in this light, are justified or not. Reflecting and re-calibrating elements of one's normative system in this way will arguably affect one's moral competences and development.

Satiation, Envy and Resentment

Undoubtedly, the disgust felt by Solal towards his physical beauty is a form of mediated disgust. But which personal values could possibly be revealed through his disgust? Which beliefs and other attitudes could serve as its mediators? At first sight, the theories of disgust seem to allow only one option to explain the deep tension that is present in feeling disgust at beauty, namely "disgust of satiation" (Kolnai 2004, 63–65). This explanation rests on a well-established psychological truth: in order to maintain their positive valence, the causes of pleasant sensations need to remain within certain limits of quantity, intensity and duration. While caresses, chocolate or music are widely valued pleasant things, one can grow tired of a surplus of music, just like one grows tired of a surplus of chocolate or caresses. This "downward reevaluation" is susceptible of passing from weariness to disgust. William Miller takes this kind of disgust to function like punishment, or more simply like a barrier that indicates when "enough has been enough" (Miller 1997, 110).

Can satiety with its potential for disgust be applied to enjoying beauty? Can beauty fatigue us? According to the aesthetic theories of German enlightenment, the answer is affirmative. These theories indeed qualify pure or perfect beauty as disgusting. Mendelssohn, Lessing and Kant claim that saturated beauty, for its lack of internal tension, cannot remain interesting and inevitably leads to weariness and disgust. The only efficient antidote, according to their theories, is to corrupt beauty in making it less perfect: inasmuch as it thus conserves the possibility of indefinite growth, beauty can perpetuate its aesthetic attraction (Menninghaus 2003). This explanation of feeling disgust towards beautiful works of art seems, however, inapt to explain disgust towards natural beauty. Granted that certain reproductions of a beautiful landscape, due to an overdoing of beauty, might indeed evoke repulsive feelings, the beautiful landscape itself hardly elicits such a response. One can take delight in a beautiful view for a lifetime, or revel in the beauty of a child without this ever generating any kind of disgust.

It is true, though, that excessive human beauty can intimidate to the extent of seeming unbearable: a person's inclination to move back from the beauty of a model and to settle for a lesser degree of perfection shares indeed with disgust the tendency to avoid its object and to put a distance between them. This similarity in behavior, however, ought not to make us forget that the overawed retreat from the "too beautiful" is phenomenally different from disgust. The same is true of the psychosomatic trouble known as "Stendhal syndrome", experienced by certain persons when exposed to a profusion of beauty. Causing a variety of bodily disorders, the syndrome is best described in terms of being literally awestruck. While the feeling that causes overawed retreat seems approximately characterized in terms of a blend of humbleness and shame, the Stendhal feeling rather merges admiration with devotion. In contrast to these responses to beauty, reactions phenomenally close to loathing or disgust are sometimes elicited by the tendency to pursue beauty at any price. In the realm of physical beauty, this tendency reveals itself in practices whose results are often questionable. Think of bodies molded by anabolic steroids, or faces congealed after repeated contact with the scalpel of plastic surgery. Going too far in this respect risks ending up in factitious beauty which is apt at soliciting disapproving sentiments.

Inasmuch as it is neither the result of artificial shaping nor artistic production, Solal's beauty is neither apt to arouse disgust of satiation nor the kind of disgust responding to exaggerated efforts at achieving physical perfection. It is true, however, that the topic of satiety is predominant in Cohen's novel in which the attempt to live a perfectly beautiful love is pushed to an almost absurd degree. In the opening scene, however, this topic is not yet directly addressed. In order to explain the disgust Solal expresses there, we need to determine the intermediate attitudes from which it arises. One could think, for example, that disgust towards the beautiful is a secondary emotion arising from negative primary emotions such as jealousy and resentment. Honestly, don't we sometimes feel the sting of envy in the face of a very handsome person? And isn't it true that contempt might then smoothly blend with our admiration so that we perceive the person's beauty as somehow undeserved? Don't we easily give in to the temptation to belittle someone's beauty by linking it to a lack of "internal values" or intelligence?

Granted, such phenomena exist. Yet we still need to explain how disgust might emerge from them. Supposing that the envy of those less privileged by nature thickens to the point of disgust at physical beauty, or that the resentment of the spurned lover evolves into nausea at the beauty of the beloved, conflicts with the essentially repulsive character of disgust. Envy and resentment, for their part, are not repulsive emotions: the envious person is not repelled but rather "stung" by the object of her envy, and resenting implies that the belittled item exerts a certain seduction. Therefore, both envy and resentment seem ill-suited to ground disgust towards the beautiful. Moreover, Solal's disgust is directed to his own beauty and is, as such, reflexive. Were it essentially underpinned by another negative emotion, the latter had better be reflexive too. Envy and resentment, however, are not reflexive: one cannot envy oneself nor feel resentment towards oneself. The aversive emotions that allow reflexivity—e.g., hatred, anger, contempt—do not seem more relevant in the circumstances. Solal does not show any hate for himself or his beauty, and he is not in an angry state. Since his disgust is directed to the value of beauty, contempt neither seems a likely candidate for it to proceed from. Generally, contempt aims at actions rather than properties and is known to lack this "intimacy of feeling, of sensing or perceiving", the tonalities and shades of values which make disgust "invaluable for the consolidation of an ethical orientation in concrete affairs" in the domain of value ethics (Kolnai 2004, 83).

The Bottom Line of Explanation

What I want to suggest is that the profound tension in disgust towards one's own beauty can be explained only by resorting to a complex cognitive base. Within the framework of the novel *Belle du Seigneur*, this base is shaped by the play of three interlocking key themes: narcissism, *vanitas* and the exploration of love. Since physical beauty plays a central role in this age-old game, settling its role will help to better understand what grounds Solal's disgust.

Narcissism

The scene in which the thought "disgustingly handsome" is formed bears the imprint of a typical narcissistic scenario. The handsome man taking pleasure in admiring his own beauty reflected by a mirror is indeed a classic of affective reflexive evaluation. Often related to an overestimation of the value or the degree of beauty, narcissism is traditionally linked to the vice of vanity. The narcissistic person is supposed to suffer from a form of egocentrism that makes her insensitive to others' needs as well as from a mistaken self-evaluation. What is relevant for our analysis of disgust towards the physically beautiful is the entirely contemplative character of the narcissistic scene. When Solal contemplates his appearance in the psyche of Ariane, he comprehends the whole of his physical traits as underlying his beauty, a value arousing admiration and enchantment. There is nothing in the reflected appearance that would call for any modification of the evaluative thought "Beautiful". The latter is not a descriptive judgment but the expression of an affective state through which the presence of beauty reveals itself to consciousness. Disgust towards the beautiful requires that beauty is apprehended as such, and apprehending beauty requires being attracted by it. This requirement being satisfied in narcissism, let's now turn our attention to the aspects that motivate aversion to the beautiful.

Vanitas

The importance of the motif of *vanitas* imposes itself on every reader of *Belle du Seigneur*. The evanescence of human life and personal assets, as expressed in the famous words of Ecclesiastes "All is vanity", has found many an artistic expression throughout the ages. Here, *vanitas* enters the scene by way of a surprising variant of the *memento mori*. Surrounded by the symbols of material and cultural richness—a book by Bergson, chocolate fondant, Schuman's *Scenes from Childhood*—Cohen's hero, handsome and in the prime of life, purposefully disguises himself as a toothless old man. Solal slips on an "old faded greatcoat" and puts a "moth-eaten fur hat on his head", smears "his noble cheeks with some sort of shiny gum" and affixes a white beard. To complete the metamorphosis, he sticks "two strips of black tape . . . over his front teeth, except for one on the right and one on the left, so that his mouth looked like an empty space flanked by two gleaming canines" (Cohen 1995, 23). This stage setting manifests, on the one hand, Solal's obsession with the evanescent character of life and the goods it provides and prepares, and on the other hand, the test of love which he intends for Ariane to pass. Solal seems to think that the loss of illusions on the character of love constitutes the ultimate revelation of the futilities that justify the judgment "All is vanity". Even if the *vanitas* motif provides an explanation of the disgust generated by physical beauty, it is only in relation to questioning the value of love that this kind of disgust fully reveals itself.

In the disguise section of the novel, Solal's knowledge of future ugliness overlaps with his apprehension of present beauty. The passage from the narcissistic episode to the episode of his disguise takes shape in the thought: "So beautiful, yet such beauty   destined for the graveyard, to be tinged with green here and yellow there, consigned to a coffin split by the damp earth" (Cohen 1995, 7). Thus, one could think that Solal's disgust towards his own beauty is justifiable by these conceptual elements that suggest decomposition and putrefaction. For it is known that imagining a scene susceptible of eliciting a certain emotion often suffices to actually generate the emotion. Through its suggestive force, the scene encompassing the narcissistic episode and the episode of disguise allows the overlapping of two contrary affective responses: the admiration of intact beauty and the disgust towards the fallen beauty that will reside "silent and stiff" in its coffin.

If physical beauty elicits both admiration and repulsion in such a way, the conditions for ambivalence in disgust seem to be satisfied. In superposing the image of fallen beauty with the apprehension of existent beauty, Cohen exhibits in the introductory scene of his novel a pattern well known in visual arts. Impressive examples of this practice are some of Egon Schiele's self-portraits, where the painter combines the motif of the doppelganger with that of the soothsayer, representing himself as young and old, living and dead, beautiful and ugly at the same time. In the novel, the pattern reappears in Solal's obsession to conceive of his fellow beings, when he observes them aspiring to go from rags to riches, as "these future corpses" (Cohen 1995, 33).

Exploration of Love

An even more relevant motive for disgust towards the beautiful emerges when love is explored against the background of the set of attitudes determining the value of physical beauty. Solal's disguise as an old toothless man is preparation for his attempt to probe the soul of Ariane, the woman he does not yet know personally but whom he "loved at first sight" when his "soul flew out and clung to her long curved lashes" (Cohen 1995, 35). Having climbed the balcony of the residence where she lives, Solal breaks into her room to "attempt the impossible" (Cohen 1995, 7): winning the love of a woman by offering her nothing more than his love. His offer, now shorn of all seductive artifice, reduces to a mere speech of love:

> No man will love you or know you as I love and know you, nor could another honour you with such love. Two teeth only, but I give them to you with my love. Will you receive this love of mine?
>
> (Cohen 1995, 37)

In this way, he challenges the idea (dear to all idealists) that love is the ultimate stronghold of the noble soul, the witness of its very essence that aims at nothing than the other's soul. Solal hopes for a positive outcome that will glorify God and the idealist truth, "for here is she who redeemeth all women. Behold the first woman!" (Cohen 1995, 37).

Not surprisingly, the attempt is a failure. Beautiful Ariane, horrified by the ugliness of this wretched old man talking to her about passionate love, backs away "with a coarse yelp, a yelp of fear and hate" (Cohen 1995, 37). Sloughing off now his disguise, Solal announces to Ariane that they are evicted from the paradise of ideal love where "we would have ridden away for ever side by side, young, with all our teeth." When they meet again, so he declares, he will vilely seduce her in two hours "in ways that women love and cannot resist, foul and filthy ways", and she will come away with him "in doe-eyed ecstasy". In this way, he intends to "avenge the old and the ugly and all the poor innocents" who don't know how to win the love of women. The foul and filthy ways of this revenge, likely to generate a foolish love, naturally involve the deployment of all the attributes at the disposal of the beautiful male (Cohen 1995, 38). There is no need to mention that this new attempt succeeds.

In Solal's eyes, what actually confers physical beauty a repulsive character is its inevitable involvement in every attempt to establish a romantic relationship: love, sung of and defended by the poets, is to that extent foolish and ugly. To see this divine passion depends on the presence of thirty-two bonelets in a mouth, or an ideal mass of flesh on a skeleton: this is loathsome. It forces us to conclude that love, even for those who attempt to break with this logic, is nothing more than the worship of the will and strength to kill. Solal's disgust is a response to the seductive power of physical beauty, a power which does not depend on any other value, as well as to the pretense that beauty can generate a noble passion. In his case, disgust at the beautiful seems to be fueled by good attitudes: the wish to understand the true nature of love, the modesty forbidding the handsome person to abuse his gifts or even the sorrow for those inevitably gravitating towards the beautiful. Nevertheless, these good attitudes are inextricably linked to a deep pessimism with regard to love and the worth of human life in general. Such pessimism, however, is not a universal truth, and neither is the slogan "All is vanity" on which it may be grounded. Nobody can be morally obliged to subscribe to either of them or derive their moral values from them. In this perspective, Solal's disgust towards the beautiful appears as a rather idiosyncratic emotion which, even if appropriate in a given value-system, cannot claim universal validity.

That being said, disgust towards physical beauty definitely has a normative scope. By way of conclusion, let's consider the idea that through our feelings we are "struck" by values. It has been suggested that, when a value strikes us affectively, we apprehend our "vocations", that is the internal norms constitutive of the person we are and determining our ways of acting (Mulligan 2009). How might we apply this idea to disgust towards the beautiful? Generally speaking, one could think that ambivalent disgust of this kind allows the subject to apprehend the fact that her vocation consists in cultivating personal values transcending the pleasure generated by simple physical beauty. In the case of Solal, his reflexive disgust leads him to understand that he runs a risk of boasting about his beauty, and he needs to balance it with the values of tact and finesse in order not to betray noble love. From another perspective, the strong negative reaction he undergoes in view of his beauty could lead him to contemplate the rightness of the values that he holds. In particular, his ambivalent disgust calls into question the idealist vision of love he fosters, suggesting that beauty and physical attraction should find their place in it in a more nuanced way than by means of a simplistic "all or nothing". Solal's extended reflections on the role of beauty in love, as well as his constant arguments with Ariane, bear witness to his efforts in this direction. But the confrontation between pessimism and hope remains for him a zero-sum game. When he tells her in a provocative way that she wouldn't love him if he were ugly, bald and toothless, Ariane responds:

> Listen Sol, it's not because you're handsome that I love you, though I'm glad you are. It would be sad if you ever got ugly, but, good-looking or hideous, you'll always be my dearest love . . . Because I have given you my heart, because you are who you are, because you are capable of asking all these crazy questions, because you are my fretting child, my ailing boy.

Solal is touched by this avowal and his pessimism seems to dwindle. Shortly after, however, he comes to believe that Ariane must lie without knowing it, and that she simply believes that she would love him even if he were hideous. For at this moment, he is handsome. "Disgustingly handsome" (Cohen 1995, 759f).

Note

I would like to thank Fabrice Teroni and Christine Tappolet for their substantial comments. I also thank Richard Dub for his precious linguistic support.

1. The original French expression *"beau à vomir"* literally even means "nauseatingly/ sickeningly beautiful".

References

Calabi, Clotilde. 1999. "Le dégoûtant". *Critique* 55: 512–21.
Cohen, Albert. [1968] 1995. *Belle du Seigneur*. Translated by David Coward. Harmondsworth: Viking Penguin Books.
Demmerling, Christoph, and Hilge Landweer. 2007. "Ekel". In *Philosophie der Gefühle. Von Achtung bis Zorn*, edited by Demmerling, Christoph and Hilge Landweer, 93–110. Stuttgart, Weimar: Metzler.
Kelly, Daniel. 2011. *Yuck! The Nature and Moral Significance of Disgust*. Cambridge: MIT Press.
Kolnai, Aurel. [1929] 2004. *On Disgust*. Translated and edited by Carolyn Korsmeyer and Barry Smith. Chicago: Open Court.
McGinn, Colin. 2011. *The Meaning of Disgust*. Oxford and New York: Oxford University Press.
Menninghaus, Winfried. [1999] 2003. "The Beautiful as Vomitive." In *Disgust: The Theory and History of a Strong Sensation*. Translated by Howard Eiland and Joel Golb, 26–31. New York: State University of New York Press.
Miller, William I. 1997. *The Anatomy of Disgust*. Cambridge, MA: Harvard University Press.
Mulligan, Kevin. 2009. "On Being Struck by Value—Exclamations, Motivations and Vocations." In *Leben mit Gefühlen: Emotionen, Werte und ihre Kritik*, edited by Barbara Merker, 141–61. Paderborn: Mentis.
Rozin, Paul, Jonathan Haidt, and Clark McCauley. 2008. "Disgust." In *Handbook of Emotions*, edited by Michael Lewis and Jeannette M. Haviland-Jones, 757–76. New York: The Guilford Press.

9   Stench and Olfactory Disgust[1]

Vivian Mizrahi

The Janus-Faced Nature of Stench

Stench seems inextricably linked to certain persistent smells, such as rotten eggs, stink bombs or certain rubbish bins on very warm days. Given to us through olfactory experiences, it appears as a sensible quality of certain objects or substances that can be detected by any subject equipped with a working olfactory system. However, although stench seems at first sight to be an objective property that characterizes particular objects or substances, it can equally appear as a subjective property dependent on the psychological and behavioral responses of the perceiving subject. Certain smells indeed appear as nauseating only to certain people. Such is the case, for example, with the durian, a fruit greatly appreciated by Asian gourmets but whose smell was described by an American traveler as "pig shit, turpentine and onions garnished with a dirty gym sock" (Sterling 2000, 134). Although olfactory preferences can be anchored in culture and linked in particular to alimentary practices, they can also vary among members of the same group as well as for individuals over time.

Like Janus, therefore, the notion of stench appears to have two faces. On one side, it seems to belong to the world that surrounds us. This is the case, for example, when we say that the smell of sewers is unbearable or that curdled milk stinks. On the other side, it seems more closely linked to our psychological dispositions. The variations observed in people's preferences for certain smells suggest that the attribution of stench to certain objects or substances strongly relies on the way subjects react to certain smells.

One could object, however, that the two-faced nature of the notion of stench stems from a conflation between smells perceived, on the one hand, and the stench experienced, on the other. It could be argued, for example, that the smell of Camembert or durian is objectively given, but that the appreciation of smells relies on subjective preferences. Thus, a Frenchman would be more inclined to appreciate the odor of Camembert than to appreciate that of durian, whereas the reverse would probably hold true for an Indonesian. According to this view, an odor, such as that of Camembert or durian, is an objective property accessible through olfaction, whereas stench corresponds to an essentially different aspect of the psychological life of the perceiving subject. Separating stench from smell is promising to the extent that it allows for an explanation of both the objective and subjective components of our olfactory experiences. It omits, however, to take into account that smell and stench seem inseparable from the phenomenological point of view. Could one, for example, dissociate the smell of rotting meat from its stench or imagine the smell of jasmine to be fetid?

In this chapter, I suggest that stench has to be understood in emotional rather than strictly perceptual terms by arguing that stench is the object of olfactory disgust. This approach will lead me to claim that there are no intrinsically unpleasant smells, but only smells associated with unpleasant emotions. To defend these theses, I will first give a brief sketch of olfactory disgust and explain the specific nature of the relation between smell and stench. This analysis will allow me to critically approach the notion of the hedonic value of smells and to propose a non-polar-opposition view of olfactory pleasantness.

Smell and Olfactory Disgust

Certain bad smells are sufficiently powerful to trigger a reaction of aversion in the subjects confronted with them and force them to move away from their source. Such a reaction is often accompanied by a characteristic grimace and a feeling of discomfort that can go as far as a sickening feeling of nausea. Characteristic of disgust, this avoidance behavior and bodily reaction seem to indicate that stench and disgust are tied to each other. Disgust can be directed to the smell of durian, but it can bear on the entire range of sensible qualities, such as the taste of Brussels sprouts, the consistency of beef brains, or the presence of maggots in the cupboard.

My approach to disgust here is rather circumscribed, because my goal is to shed some light on the notion of stench and not to consider the notion of disgust as a whole. I will therefore focus on the notion of olfactory disgust and examine the relation between this particular form of disgust and smells. A straightforward way to account for the particular relation between smell and stench is to analyze it in causal terms. According to this view, stench would be the object of olfactory disgust, whereas certain smells would be the cause of stench. This view could take the form, for example, of a dispositionalist theory of stench by identifying stench with a capacity of certain smells to cause nausea in certain subjects. Following this analysis, stench would depend on the disposition of a subject to feel, or not to feel, disgust for certain smells. Thus, if the smell of durian is repulsive for a Frenchman but not for an Indonesian, this is because Indonesians are not disposed to experience disgust over the smell of durian. As for the other emotions, different psychological dispositions (temperament, character, beliefs, etc.) explain why an identical stimulus (a smell) can be correlated with different emotional responses (disgust, nostalgia, etc.) (Deonna and Teroni 2009). By placing stench on the emotional level and smell on the perceptual level, the dispositionalist model seems to offer an elegant solution to the apparent ambiguity of the notion of stench. However, this approach is not entirely satisfactory, because it doesn't properly account for the phenomenology of stench. Indeed, if smell and stench can be confused, it is not because we mistake the true causal nature of stench but because stench appears as phenomenologically inseparable from the smell with which it is associated. The fact that stench is related to certain smells and not others does not simply result from the fact that we are disposed to feel a certain emotion in the presence of certain smells, but rather from the fact that we localize stench exactly where we detect these smells. In brief, from a phenomenological point of view, smell and stench seem to form a whole that is hard to capture with a dispositionalist account of stench.

Let us take, by way of comparison, the case of pain. When I prick myself with a rose, it is plausible to assert that the thorn is the cause of the pain that I feel at the tip of my finger, because I can dissociate my pain from its cause. It is indeed possible to claim that I have two almost simultaneous experiences: a tactile experience directed to the thorn and an experience of pain directed to the tip of my finger. The pain caused by the thorn can persist even after it has been removed. In contrast, when my nose detects curdled milk at the back of my fridge, the stench and the smell constitute a whole, in the sense that it is impossible to distinguish the olfactory qualities of the curdled milk from its stench.

To sum up, separating stench from smell is promising insofar as it allows for an account of intersubjective variations in smell appreciation. It has, however, the unfortunate consequence of taking stench out of the domain of smelling, consequently betraying our phenomenological intuitions regarding the olfactory character of stench.

From Molecules to Emotions

Beauty is in the eye of the beholder, Oscar Wilde said. Should one say that stench is in the nose (or the brain) of the one who smells? Should one concede, for example, that there is no objective criterion justifying the attribution of stench to some smells rather than others? In order to answer these different questions and deepen our understanding of what links stench to smell, we have to return to the nature of smells and olfactory disgust.

It is important to understand that smell is a chemical sense; that is, olfactory receptor cells are stimulated by chemical molecules rather than physical stimuli. In order to be smelled, an odorant must have certain characteristics, such as volatility (the molecules in question must be able to enter into the nose!), a degree of solubility in water, weak polarity, a high-lipophilic character and vapor pressure. These characteristics are important because they help to explain why some molecules have an odor and others do not. Sugar, for example, which is nonvolatile at ambient temperatures, does not smell, but heating will free certain volatile molecules that constitute the typical smell of caramel. However, the chemical properties of a molecule are not sufficient to explain the odors we smell, because olfaction requires a perceptual apparatus able to detect them. Contrary to its reputation, human olfaction is far from being impoverished. Recent psychophysical studies suggest that the human olfactory system is in fact capable of distinguishing one trillion smells, outperforming "the other senses in the number of physically different stimuli it can discriminate" (Bushdid et al. 2014, 1370).

Smells can drive our behavior by providing information about objects and substances, such as the ripeness of a melon or the cleanliness of a restroom, but they are also intimately linked to our emotions. The hedonic appreciation of odors (their pleasantness or unpleasantness), for example, is recognized as the most salient characteristic of our olfactory judgments (Schiffman 1974) and therefore constitutes a central concern of intercultural studies of smells. As illustrated by the famous madeleine of Proust, the evocative power of smells is also supposed to underline the strongly emotional character of olfactory memories. But what is the emotional or hedonic dimension of a smell? Does stench correspond to the negative side of the hedonic dimension of smells? In that case, what would be its positive side? To address these questions, I now turn to the nature of olfactory disgust.

According to some biologists and psychologists, disgust constitutes a primitive and visceral response aimed at staying away from and preventing the ingestion of toxic or pathogenic substances. If we follow Rozin (1990), disgust stems from the "omnivore's dilemma," that is, the search for alimentary variety, on the one hand, and the potential danger associated with ingesting new foodstuffs, on the other. Insofar as he can adapt to very different surroundings, the omnivore possesses a selective advantage in comparison to species whose diet is more restrictive. This advantage comes, however, with a major difficulty: choice. Indeed, the omnivore has to both select food that will provide essential nutrients and avoid those that might be harmful. In this regard, disgust seems to constitute an effective solution, because it allows the omnivore to avoid eating food that could be fatal to him. In a more general way, Curtis and Biran (2001) suggest that disgust constitutes a trait selected by competition between parasites and their hosts. In the same way that human bodies have evolved to resist infectious agents, certain behavioral traits have been selected to avoid potential sources of infection. According to Curtis and Biran's evolutionary explanation, aversion to and systematic avoidance of certain substances experienced as disgusting function as an effective defense against infectious agents that are potentially lethal to the organism and the genes it shelters.

For several reasons, the analysis of disgust in terms of the avoidance of potentially noxious substances appears to be a particularly good fit for the case of olfactory disgust. First, even if there are interpersonal and cultural differences in the way people appreciate odors, there seems to be a strong intercultural convergence regarding the smells considered repulsive, such as putrefaction, bodily odors (sweat, excrement), and the smell of decomposing matter (Schaal et al. 1997). Second, although foul odors are not the direct cause of the spread of diseases, there is a strong correlation between repulsive smells and the risk of the transmission of disease from their source. Third, although molecules that are perceived as foul do not share particular chemical characteristics, the analysis of stench in terms of noxiousness explains what these different chemical components have in common. Lastly, this analysis offers an original solution to the two-sided (olfactory and emotional) nature of stench, because the molecules detected by the olfactory apparatus are directly linked to the risks of contamination that the object of disgust constitutes.

Perceptual experiences are often the basis for our emotions. Thus, seeing a bear can cause fear, or hearing particular words can cause sadness. The case of olfactory disgust is no different in this sense, because it is the perceiving of certain smells that causes a certain aversion in us. What is unique to the case of stench is that stench, the object of olfactory disgust, can be *identified* with the object of the olfactory experience. The smell that is constituted by chemical molecules detected by the olfactory apparatus is directly linked to the chemical components that constitute the potential danger to the organism.[2] By contrast, fear can be an emotion appropriate to the sighting of a bear, but the same is not true for the visual properties themselves. Thus, the fact that the bear is brown, that it is on the right side of my visual field, and that its silhouette is set against a blue background is not directly relevant to the evaluation of its dangerousness. What is relevant, however, is that these visual properties are exemplified by a bear and not a cow. If the chemical properties that constitute a smell can be identified with the chemical properties potentially toxic to the smeller, it is plausible to maintain that olfactory properties themselves exemplify the immediate object of olfactory disgust. As it happens, most of the smells that we consider pestilential are chemical components resulting from the activity of bacteria. When these molecules come into contact with the olfactory apparatus, the contact is sufficient to indicate the presence of bacteria, or toxins produced by bacteria, that are potentially pathogenic for the organism.[3]

Pleasant and Unpleasant Smells

If the analysis of stench presented here is on the right track, one could say that the unpleasant character of a smell is not perceptual but derives from the unpleasant character of the emotion (disgust) associated with the smell. I suggest that the hedonic character of a given emotion is determined by "what it is like" to experience this emotion and not by its object. For example, it is the joy or sadness felt as a result of the outcome of a tennis match, and not its score, that constitutes the pleasure or displeasure felt, respectively, by the winner and loser of the match. Following this analysis, there are no intrinsically pleasant or unpleasant smells, but only emotions endowed with a certain hedonic value. Should we say, therefore, that the unpleasant character that we attribute to certain smells is both illusory and subjective?

Certainly not. First of all, being the object of an emotion does not render stench illusory or unreal. Like danger or jollity, stench is real even if it refers to our affective life rather than a "colder" aspect of cognition. In fact, the ontological status of stench depends directly on the general theory of emotion defended. If emotions are considered to be perceptions of value (Tappolet 2016), stench could be defined as the value of olfactory disgust. If, on the other hand, emotions are identified with bodily sensations (James 1884), one would be inclined to assimilate stench to the elements that trigger such sensations. Moreover, the characterization of disgust in terms of an avoidance of substances potentially noxious to the organism helps explaining the correctness conditions of olfactory disgust. It allows us, for example, to consider as appropriate the reaction of disgust caused by putrefying matter, but as inappropriate the aversion felt by people suffering from parosmia[4] when they perceive the scent of a rose. The danger of bacteriological contamination involved in putrefaction is indeed real, whereas it is inexistent as far as roses are concerned.[5]

Does this mean that interpersonal differences are always a matter of emotional error or illusion? Probably not. To begin with, the intensity and occurrence of olfactory disgust, as for all emotions, depends as much on the circumstances as on certain characteristics of the subject himself. In this way, olfactory changes that occur in pregnant women (Cameron 2007) during the first weeks of pregnancy could be derived from an evolutionary mechanism aimed at protecting the fetus from poisons. But such a protective mechanism—which is well adapted to conditions in which available food presents an acute risk of contamination and to conditions in which hygiene standards are lacking—becomes an embarrassing handicap in an environment where such risks do not exist. Interpersonal and intercultural variations can also be explained by learning processes influencing isolated individuals or human groups. Even if certain aversive reactions can be considered innate, the avoidance of toxins will not be efficacious unless it can adapt to new environments. For example, the aversion to a particular food acquired after ingesting a poisonous substance constitutes an important advantage if this acquired aversion prevents the organism from ingesting the same toxin in the future. The disgust developed in such circumstances results from an emotional conditioning that is comparable, for example, to a fear of dogs developed after having been bitten by one. Another major source of emotional conditioning is the behavior of fellow humans. To avoid a particular food, we don't need to have become ill after ingesting it. The facial expression characteristic of olfactory disgust is indeed a very effective warning to other members of a group of the nauseous smell of a substance (Wicker et al. 2003). It is quite obvious, moreover, that the alimentary and hygienic habits of a group help to reinforce or attenuate individual predispositions to the experience of olfactory disgust. Rejection or avoidance attitudes toward cheese, for example, differ according to eating habits. However, as I will show below, emotional variations such as those related to cheese are not necessarily accompanied by a disagreement regarding its stench.

Exquisite Stench

Numerous studies in psychophysics classify smells on the basis of a hedonic spectrum that ranges from pleasantness to aversiveness However, if my analysis of stench is correct, the disagreeable character attributed to certain smells derives from the negative valence of an emotion—disgust—and not from some salient phenomenological property of odors experienced through olfaction. If this is the case, judgments of agreeability regarding smells are problematic, because the meaning of "pleasant" and "unpleasant" expressed in these judgments is not well established. Unlike sounds, which are phenomenologically high or low and can be ordered according to their pitch, and unlike thermal properties, which vary from cold to hot, there is no obvious way to classify odors on the basis of opposite valences. Indeed, if stench corresponds to the negative valence of a hedonic dimension of smells, what would the positive valence be? There certainly are smells that are pleasant to us, but can they be opposed to smells for which we feel an aversion?

Unlike most studies that order smells on a scale of pleasantness, I believe there is no hedonic dimension shared by all smells. If certain smells appear pleasant to us (and others unpleasant), it is not because these smells share a dimension of pleasantness (or unpleasantness) but because different smells can be the object of emotions with different hedonic values. Nauseating smells can be compared with one another. The emotion of disgust related to a particular smell can be more or less strong in the same way that there are more or less frightening situations and more or less admirable persons. Yet the opposition between stench and pleasant smells does not really make sense, because olfactory disgust does not have an opposite emotion. A smell can be pleasant because it awakens our appetite, evokes cleanliness, or even corresponds to aesthetic appreciation. But no positive olfactory emotion is strictly the opposite of olfactory disgust.

Most of the cultural divergences that characterize smells result, I believe, from the richness of olfactory emotions. The pleasure experienced by a gourmet when eating Maroilles,[6] for example, does not indicate that he is insensitive to its stench; rather, it implies that smelling and tasting Maroilles can be a source of positive emotions for him. Moreover, if the extreme richness of the olfactory world can explain the variety of emotions associated with it, it can also explain why the appreciation of smells is not always immediate and often requires some training. Smells around us are sources of pleasure, displeasure and sometimes a combination of both, but it is in the art of perfume that the whole panoply of our olfactory emotions is revealed. Instead of ignoring stench, perfumers track it down in its various guises and integrate it into their most subtle compositions. If so many masterpieces of this art are French, this is, according to Luca Turin, because the French, more than anybody else, have an intimate relation with stench. To the question, "Why are so many great perfumes French?" he answers as follows:

To understand this, one has to make a gastronomic detour. It is in the kitchen that this nation of alchemists has known, better than any other, how to exploit fermentation and putrefaction, and venerates without shame such pestilential creations as Munster. Likewise, the closest viti-cultural creation to perfume, a white liquor-like Bordeaux, so sunny in appearance, owes its existence to a mushroom whose name itself captures the sensual genius of the French: noble rot.

What does this have to do with perfume? Very simply that these lat-ter would be terminally boring if only pleasant smells would enter into their make-up, and that they only become truly beautiful when repugnant ingredients are included.

It suffices to have smelt the civet, the castoreum or indole, to realize that the ways of perfume are less impenetrable for an eater of Camembert than for a drinker of yoghurt.

(Turin 1994, 3)

Notes

1. I would like to thank Markus Haller, Emma Tieffenbach, Victoria Tschumi and the editors of this book for their comments and suggestions.
2. According to the theory of smell presented in Mizrahi (2014), odors are properties of stuffs rather than of individuals. This theory would therefore identify the object of olfaction and the object of olfactory disgust with properties of stuffs rather than individuals like molecules or some determinate portion of stuff. This approach seems very plausible when considering certain common objects of disgust, such as bodily secretions and excretions, and certain typical qualities of stuffs, such as being slimy, viscous, festering or sticky.
3. The theory of stench proposed here can be interpreted as a revival of the theory of miasma, which originated in the Middle Ages and held that diseases were caused by decaying organic matter, or miasma, contained in foul air (see Demaitre 2004). Unlike its medieval ancestor, however, this theory does not claim that foul air is the direct cause of diseases, but only that it is a reliable indication of danger. See also n. 5.
4. Parosmia is an olfactory disorder characterized by erroneous olfactory experiences, most often unpleasant ones, in the presence of certain scents.
5. There is no strict equivalence between stinking substances and infectious substances. Numerous pestilential smells emanate from substances that present no health risk: stink bombs, cheeses, etc. It is nevertheless likely that all stinking substances share chemical properties with the substances that do present such a risk.
6. Maroilles is a French cheese with a particularly strong odor. One of its varieties is in fact known as "soaked stink" and "Stinker from Lille."

References

Bushdid, Caroline, Marcelo O. Magnasco, Leslie B. Vosshall, and Andreas Keller. 2014. "Humans Can Discriminate More Than 1 Trillion Olfactory Stimuli Science." *Science* 343: 1370–72.

Cameron, Leslie E. 2007. "Measures of Human Olfactory Perception During Preg-nancy." *Chemical Senses* 32: 775–82.

Curtis, Valérie, and Adam Biran. 2001 "Dirt, Disgust, and Disease: Is Hygiene in Our Genes?" *Perspectives in Biology and Medicine* 44: 17–31.

Demaitre, Luke. 2004. "Air, miasma and contagion—Epidemics in antiquity and the Middle Ages." *Bulletin of the History of Medicine* 78, no. 2: 466–68.

Deonna, Julien et Fabrice Teroni. 2009. "Taking Affective Explanations to Heart." *Social Science Information* 48, no. 3: 359–77.

James, William. 1884. "What Is an Emotion?" *Mind* 9: 188–205.

Mizrahi, Vivian. 2014. "Sniff, Smell and Stuff." *Philosophical Studies* 171: 233–50.

Rozin, Paul. 1990. "Development in the Food Domain." *Developmental Psychology* 26: 555–62.

Schaal, B., et al. 1997. "Variability and Invariants in Early Odour Preferences: Comparative Data from Children Belonging to Three Cultures." *Chemical Senses* 22: 212.

Schiffman, Susan S. 1974. "Physicochemical Correlates of Olfactory Quality." *Science* 185: 112–17.

Sterling, Richard. 2000. *World Food: Vietnam*. Hawthorn, Victoria: Lonely Planet Publication.

Tappolet, Christine. 2016. *Emotions, Value, and Agency*. Oxford, UK: Oxford University Press.

Turin, Luca. 1994. *Parfums: le Guide*. Paris: Hermé.

Wicker, Bruno, Christian Keysers, Jane Plailly, Jean-Pierre Royet, Vittorio Gallese, and Giacomo Rizzolatti. 2003. "Both of Us Disgusted in My Insula: The Common Neural Basis of Seeing and Feeling Disgust." *Neuron* 40, no. 3: 655–64.

10 Anxiety

A Case Study on the Value of Negative Emotion

Charlie Kurth

Why do we feel bad—angry, anxious, afraid, what have you? Are negative emotions like these ever valuable? Does feeling bad ever do good? Among both philosophers and folk, a common response is *no*: negative emotions are things it would be better not to experience. For instance, the Stoic philosopher Seneca maintains that anger "changes all things from the best and justest condition in to the opposite" (1995, 18). Immanuel Kant helps flesh out this worry. As he sees it, in order for an individual to be virtuous, he must "bring all his capacities and inclinations under his (reason's) control" (1996, 536). In this respect, emotions—especially negative emotions—are problematic insofar as they make reflection "impossible or more difficult" (535); the "true strength of virtue is a *tranquil mind*"—for it "is the state of *health* in the moral life" (536, original emphasis). The picture that emerges from all this is not flattering: negative emotions lack value because they are pernicious, inherently unpleasant and inconsistent with human virtue.

I reject this skepticism. As a slogan: negative emotions matter. Not only can they help us manage risks, dangers and threats, they are also central elements of what a good or virtuous character consists in. Negative emotions, that is, have both instrumental and aretaic value. To draw this out, I take anxiety as a case study. I show that contrary to much folk and philosophical wisdom, anxiety can be very valuable—both for our ability to successfully navigate the complexities of social life and as a central dimension of being virtuous. Along the way, we will also draw some conclusions about the value of other negative emotions—particularly, anger and fear.

A Primer on Emotion and Anxiety

For the discussion that follows, it will be helpful for me to say a little about how I'm understanding emotions in general and anxiety in particular. Speaking at a high level, emotions are responses to perceived threats and opportunities. And so to experience a given emotion is to respond to a particular threat/opportunity with a distinctive combination of feelings, thoughts and actions. To see this, consider some familiar emotions.

Joy: A response to progress or success that tends to bring associated thoughts ("I've done well", "That was nice"), positively valenced feelings, and a motivational tendency to affirm one's efforts or stay the course.

Fear: A response to imminent threats or dangers that tends to bring associated thoughts ("Oh no!"), negatively valenced feelings, and a motivational tendency to avoid or escape the threat/danger at hand.

Anger: A response to affronts or slights from others that tends to bring associated thoughts ("How dare you!", "That's out of line"), negatively valenced feelings, and a motivational tendency to defend oneself or one's interests.[1]

Understanding emotions in this way draws out that they function as distinctive forms of evaluative awareness. To fear the dog is to see the dog *as dangerous*—as something to be avoided; to be a happy about the talk you just gave is to see the talk *as a success*—as a commendable performance.

Moreover, if emotions are evaluative responses of this sort, then they have accuracy conditions—they are things that can be (un)fitting in virtue of (mis)representing the evaluative content of their targets. Consider: it's fitting to fear the dog when the dog *really is* dangerous, and it's fitting to be happy about your presentation when the presentation *actually was* a success. Recognizing that emotions can be (un)fitting is significant for two reasons. First, it reveals that when we are considering whether a particular emotion has value, we are (typically) asking whether *fitting* instances of that emotion are valuable. That is, we're interested in questions like whether it's helpful to fear the (vicious, snarling) dog when the dog is, in fact, dangerous. Second, just because an emotion is fitting in this (technical) sense doesn't automatically mean that it's useful: your fear of the dog, though fitting, may nonetheless provoke it to attack.

With this background in hand, we can turn to anxiety. Anxiety is a response to uncertainty about a possible threat or challenge.[2] More specifically, when one feels anxious, one sees one's situation as involving a threat or challenge whose potential is unpredictable, uncontrollable or otherwise open to question. Anxiety of this sort typically brings thoughts about one's predicament ("I'm worried", "What should I do?"), negatively valenced feelings of unease and concern, and a motivational tendency to be cautious toward the uncertain threat or challenge one faces. Moreover, how one responds will turn on one's perception of the difficulty at hand. For instance, if one sees one's situation as involving a potential physical harm (e.g., the large man approaching in the dark parking lot) or social threat (e.g., criticism from peers about one's debate performance), one will tend to respond *defensively*—tendencies toward avoidance, withdrawal, appeasement and other risk minimizing behaviors. By contrast, if one's anxiety results from uncertainty about the correctness of one's beliefs or choices (e.g., a decision about what to do in a novel situation; concerns about how best to respond to a difficult objection to one's views), one will tend more toward *epistemic behaviors*—reflection, investigation, deliberation and the like. This suggests anxiety has (at least) two dimensions: a defensive response that's directed toward protecting oneself against physical or social threats, and a more epistemically oriented response that's concerned with (good or accurate) decision making (Kurth 2016). With this initial picture of emotion and anxiety in hand, we can turn to the central project: determining whether a negative emotion like anxiety is valuable, and if so, in what way.

Is Anxiety Instrumentally Valuable?

As we noted, when asking about the instrumental value of an emotion, we're typically asking whether *fitting* instances of that emotion are useful. On this front, the quotes from the introduction suggest that negative emotions are unhelpful because they interfere with judgment and action. This worry can be fleshed out in a couple of ways. First, there's the charge that negative emotions will rarely, if ever, be fitting—much less instrumentally valuable—because they're too likely to generate false-positives and false-negatives: we regularly fear things like the murderer in the horror movie that pose no danger; and we routinely fail to fear things like handguns and climate change that do. Second, even when negative emotions are fitting (i.e., when they're not systematically misfiring), they can still distort our understanding of our situations and so motivate us to act in problematic ways. Anger, for instance, can get us to lash out at others in ways that are disproportionate (e.g., the offense was minor) or misdirected (e.g., they were merely a bystander to a genuine offense).[3]

Along both these dimensions, anxiety seems to be in big trouble. With regard to misfires, Woody Allen is a wonderful case in point—he not only finds occasion for anxiety *everywhere* but he's a hopeless mess as a result. However, even if we just focus on fitting anxiety, there's no shortage of examples of it leading to disaster. Consider, for instance, what we find in Scott Stossel's recent memoir *My Age of Anxiety* (2013). He gets anxious whenever he needs to speak before a large group—a fitting response given the potential for a negative reaction from his audience. However, his anxiety about public speaking brings such intense cycles of dread, nausea and sweating that he must resort to Xanax and vodka to prevent himself from running out on the talk he's supposed to give. Hardly a picture of anxiety contributing to health and well-being—much less one's career prospects.

But while these examples of anxiety run amok provide a rhetorically powerful way to raise concerns about the fittingness and instrumental value of anxiety, we should pause to ask whether they really make for a convincing case. Are individuals who have anxiety disorders like Allen and Stossel really good examples of how anxiety *generally* functions, or merely anxiety when it happens to *go awry*? Notice as well that it's not difficult to find examples of fitting and instrumentally valuable anxiety. Consider Henry Marsh, one of the world's most accomplished neurosurgeons. Though he's performed over 400 brain surgeries, these procedures still make him anxious. However, he doesn't see his anxiety as unfitting or problematic. Rather, he sees it as the manifestation of his accumulated surgical expertise. For instance, when trying to figure out whether to remove more of a tumor—at the risk of damaging healthy brain tissue—he's guided by his anxiety. As he explains, "you stop when you start getting more anxious. That's experience" (Knausgaard 2015).

Recognizing all this reveals that the real question is not *whether* fitting anxiety is helpful, but rather whether there's anything interesting we can say about *when* and *why* it can be useful. This is obviously a huge empirical question—one that psychologists, cognitive scientists and emotion researchers are only just starting to understand. But for the beginnings of an answer, we can turn to research on a common technique used in public health and safety advertisements. These ads make use of graphic images, audio and text in order to elicit anxiety and related emotions (worry, unease, distress) in an effort to curb smoking, drunk driving and other harmful behaviors. For our purposes, this research is important in several ways. First, because these campaigns present individuals with information and images about potential threats, the anxiety they trigger will (typically) be *fitting*. Moreover, the research on the effectiveness of these campaigns helps us understand the conditions under which fitting anxiety can bring (health, safety) benefits. Generally speaking, these ad campaigns are better able to reduce the targeted harmful behaviors when the anxiety they provoke (i) conveys the sense that the viewer is *vulnerable* to being harmed by the risky behavior and (ii) instills the feeling that they *can do something* to avoid those harms (Lewis et al. 2007; cf., Brader 2006).

Extending these findings to more general questions about (fitting) anxiety's usefulness suggests that anxiety will be helpful on occasions where it doesn't just make potential threats and challenges more salient, but also helps one identify potential solutions or otherwise leaves one feeling empowered. By contrast, anxiety is likely to bring trouble when it elicits feelings of vulnerability and undermines one's sense of efficacy. Moreover, notice that these findings fit nicely with what we see in Stossel and Marsh. Stossel is an occasional public speaker with (by his own account) a track record of unfortunate performances. His history of flubbed talks thus leaves him feeling not just vulnerable, but also unable to prevent another embarrassing episode—hence all the vodka and Xanax (Stossel 2013). Marsh, by comparison, is an accomplished neurosurgeon with decades of training and experience. So while he both feels unease during a surgery and is well aware of the damage that a poor judgment on his part can bring, his anxiety doesn't leave him feeling unnerved or distracted. Rather, he sees it as a corrective for potentially disastrous overconfidence (Marsh 2014).

Stepping back, viewing the examples of Stossel and Marsh in light of the research on public safety campaigns suggests a negative emotion like anxiety is more useful to the extent that it's experienced not just at the *right time* but also in the *right way*. That is, we don't just want our anxiety to *fit* the situation, but to also be *well-regulated*—we want its intensity to be appropriately calibrated to the challenge at hand. Moreover, if we focus on the Marsh example, two further insights emerge. First, we see that the tendency to experience anxiety at the right time and in the right way isn't just instrumentally beneficial, but also valuable in a deeper sense. Marsh's anxiety doesn't just help him be a more effective surgeon. It also reveals something important about his character: his anxiety demonstrates an admirable emotional attunement—a sensitivity to the surgical risks and uncertainty at hand. Second, Marsh's remark that his anxiety is a product of his experience suggests that effective emotion regulation is skill-like: it's something we can get better at through practice and learning. In the next two sections, we'll look more closely at these two ideas. Doing this will further enrich our understanding of the value that negative emotions can have.

Anxiety, Anger and Virtuous Character

Let's start with the idea that anxiety is more than just instrumentally valuable—in particular, the suggestion from above that anxiety is a component of virtuous character (i.e., that it has what philosophers call *aretaic value*). To do this, it will be helpful to say a little about virtue more generally. As standardly understood, virtues are excellences of character in the sense that they are comprised of integrated packages of beliefs, motivations and feelings.[4] The underlying idea here is that virtues must involve more than just occasions where one's actions or habits happen to bring (morally) good outcomes. Rather, a virtue like benevolence is an excellence of character that has cognitive, conative and affective dimensions. So, for example, instances of benevolence aren't merely cases where one is prompted to help another in need. Rather, they're situations where the assistance one provides is undergirded by both the belief that the person needs help and a feeling of sympathy for her plight. The belief is necessary because we do not (typically) admire those who blindly manage to do good. The affective component is also necessary: to not give to someone in need from a feeling of sympathy (or, worse, to resent giving assistance) would be indicative of a deficient character—you would be emotionally out of tune with what's happening.

With this general picture of virtue in hand, we can turn to the distinctive *moral concern* that virtuous individuals display. Doing this will help draw out the deeper value that negative emotions like anxiety and anger can have. To begin, notice that virtuous individuals are persons who stand up for what's right and good in the sense that they'll *defend* what they see as valuable when it is in danger (Aristotle 1998, 96–8). Virtuous individuals are also *sensitive to uncertainty* in the sense that they appreciate the limits of their knowledge and the extent of their fallibility (e.g., Stohr 2003). Admirable character traits like these form the core of the virtue I'm calling "moral concern."[5]

Now since moral concern is a virtue, its characteristic behaviors—namely, to defend what's valuable and to be sensitive to uncertainty—are (as we saw above) undergirded by a distinctive combination of beliefs, motivations and feelings. It's here that anxiety and anger enter the picture. They are the emotions that comprise the feeling dimension of moral concern. To flesh this out, first consider anger. As we saw in the first section, anger has a distinctive phenomenology and functional role: it's a response to affronts and slights that brings negatively valenced feelings and a motivational tendency to defend oneself, one's interests or one's standing. So we have a nice fit: our understanding of anger meshes with the dimension of moral concern that involves the defense of what one sees as valuable. To further draw out this fit, consider a person who discovers that she has been lied to by someone she trusts, but who isn't at all angry about it. An individual like this strikes us not just as odd, but deficient—she fails to appreciate the violation of her moral worth that has occurred. Moreover, recognizing anger as a constitutive feature of the defense-dimension of moral concern explains our reactions to an unperturbed individual like this. Anger not only helps one stand up for oneself as an individual who has value and merits respect; it is also an *expression* of the moral significance that one takes oneself to have. To not be angry in the face of betrayal is to evince a lack of emotional and evaluative attunement to what matters.

We find something similar for anxiety—especially in its epistemically oriented form (first section). It is, as we've seen, an emotion that's concerned with uncertainty and that prompts a combination of caution and inquiry (information gathering, deliberation, reflection, etc.). Thus, anxiety of this sort fits nicely with the dimension of moral concern that involves a sensitivity and responsiveness to the possibility that one's choice might be mistaken. To draw this out, consider some difficult moral decisions: (i) it's becoming hard for you to care for your Alzheimer's-stricken mother. Her doctors have suggested it's time to put her in a nursing home, but you know she's terrified of those places. What should do you do? (ii) Your colleague has again been mistreated by your mutual boss. Should you stand up for her even though you know it will come at a (significant) cost to your career? (iii) You're a senior professor and have a talented graduate student looking for a job. You've written her a very strong recommendation. But should you do more—say, contact departments where she's applying to try and give them a nudge? Or would that be to take advantage of the system?

In situations like these, you face a decision that involves complex and potentially competing considerations. Worse, these cases are ones where the existing (moral, professional) norms and your own prior experiences provide insufficient guidance about what to do. To be unfazed—to not feel uneasy or uncomfortable about decisions like these—strikes us not just as odd, but deficient. Such an individual would be troublingly disconnected from the significance and complexity of her choice. Seeing anxiety as constitutive of a virtuous moral concern helps explain this. Anxiety doesn't just bring a sensitivity to the problematic uncertainty we find in cases like these; it is also an *expression* of one's appreciation of the complexity of the decision at hand. It evinces one's emotional and evaluative attunement.

If these reflections are on point, they suggest not just that anxiety and anger are essential elements of moral concern, but that they are valuable because of what they say about one's emotional attunement. Importantly, the value here isn't (merely) instrumental in nature. Rather, it's value grounded in the contribution these emotions make to one's *character*: to have the virtue of moral concern is to be a person who feels angry when what they care about is threatened and who feels anxious in the face of a difficult or novel choice.

But one might be skeptical that anxiety (or anger) is aretaically valuable—that it's important beyond the instrumental benefits it brings. To give this worry more substance, consider the following possibility. Suppose you could take a pill—a new version of Xanax, say—that would bring the instrumental benefits associated with anxiety (e.g., caution and reflection) but without the felt unpleasantness and unease. If you had such a pill, would you take it? If you answer yes, it suggests you think there's nothing aretaically valuable in anxiety. It's only valuable in virtue of the moral concern it helps bring about.

For anyone who has battled with anxiety, I suspect the pill has appeal. But to draw out that there's something amiss in this thought, we should consider a case where although anxiety is neither fitting nor instrumentally beneficial, we nonetheless deem it valuable. Such a case, after all, would be an example of a situation where anxiety has aretaic value. So consider again your Alzheimer's-stricken mother. Her disease has now run its course and, tragically, each day only brings her more pain and suffering. You promised her that when this moment came, you would give her a euthanizing dose of morphine. So you must now decide whether to keep that promise. You are anxious—is this the morally correct thing to do?—and, as a result, think hard about both your promise and your mother's condition.[6] After much reflection, you conclude that you ought to do what you promised. And you do. But days later, you're still anxious. Though you keep rethinking your decision, you keep coming to the same conclusion: it was the right thing to do. Yet your anxiety about the choice remains.

What can we say about your anxiety? First, given that it's anxiety about a difficult decision that prompts reflection and reassessment, we can see that we are dealing with the epistemically oriented form of anxiety. This, in turn, helps us understand when your anxiety is (un)fitting. More specifically, your anxiety is clearly *fitting* as you contemplate whether to keep the promise: you face a difficult choice and have reason to reflect and reassess. However, it's less clear—doubtful even—that your anxiety *remains* fitting after you have administered the morphine: since you no longer face a hard choice and since the choice you made cannot be reversed, you have no reason to revisit or reassess it. Moreover, your post-decision anxiety doesn't just seem unfitting, it also seems to *lack instrumental value*: not only is your lingering anxiety unpleasant, but the reflection it prompts does nothing to change either your conclusion or enrich your understanding of what was at stake—each new round of anxiety-induced reflection leads you back to the same considerations and the same conclusion.

However, your persisting anxiety—though unfitting and void of instrumental value—still *reflects well on you*. It is the manifestation of your admirable sensitivity to the difficult choice you faced (cf., Williams 1976). We'd find someone who had no lingering unease in a situation like yours disconcerting; a quick transition back to an anxiety-free demeanor would prompt worries about their *character*. It would suggest they hadn't really appreciated the gravity of their choice. But notice what this means: it means we are again seeing that anxiety has aretaic value—it is an integral part of what we admire about you and the concern you demonstrate in this awful situation.

Stepping back, this case reveals that the aretaic value of anxiety is independent of its fittingness or instrumental contributions. Anxiety is important not just because of the benefits it can bring, but also because of what it says about the character of the individual who experiences it. Moreover, given that negative emotions like anxiety (and anger) are central to human agency, they are features of our (moral) psychology that, if eliminated by popping some special pill, would come at real cost to how we understand and assess ourselves and others. So while the Xanax objection might have initially seemed to cause trouble for our claims about the aretaic value of anxiety, its plausibility fades on closer examination.

Cultivating More Valuable Anxiety

Turn now to the second suggestion that emerged from our discussion of Henry Marsh—namely, that learning to effectively regulate negative emotions like anxiety is much like developing a skill: it's something we can get better at through learning and experience. More specifically, if emotions are forms of evaluative awareness whereby we see (aspects of) our situation in an evaluatively loaded manner (first section), then becoming better emotionally attuned will involve developing a better understanding of what sorts of features merit a given response. This thought has been taken up by philosophers, especially those working in the Aristotelian tradition. Nancy Sherman, for instance, explains that "[c]ultivating the dispositional capacities to feel fear, anger, goodwill, compassion, or pity appropriately will be bound up with learning how to discern the circumstances that warrant these responses" (1989, 167; also Annas 2011). And she argues that we develop such an understanding via a combination of our individual experiences and our interactions with others who help us recognize the particular features of a situation that make a given emotion (in)appropriate.

While these observations about how to cultivate emotions have a breezy plausibility to them, one might reasonably wonder whether they're correct: can we *really* cultivate our emotional capacities in the same way that we develop a skill? On this front, research on cognitive-behavioral therapy (CBT) may offer some answers. CBT is used to treat individuals with (e.g.) severe anxiety, phobias and depression. Its driving premise is that these emotional disorders are sustained by cognitive factors (e.g., minimizing the positive aspects of a situation, catastrophizing, overgeneralizing) and so can be effectively treated by helping individuals develop skills that allow them to both better identify situations that trigger the problematic emotional response, and engage strategies that can help correct the distorting thoughts/attitudes.

In the present context, CBT is interesting for two reasons. First, the techniques at the heart of CBT are of the very sort that Aristotelians like Sherman point to as the core tools for effective emotion cultivation—namely, working with others to better understand when and why an emotional response is (not) appropriate. Thus, it provides us with a concrete model for thinking about how best to regulate and cultivate emotions. Second, research indicates that CBT is quite effective. For instance, a recent meta-analysis found "strong support for the efficacy of CBT" as a treatment for anxiety disorders (Hofmann and Smits 2008). To be clear, the suggestion here is not that we should sign ourselves and our children up for psychiatry appointments! Rather, the point is that research on CBT's effectiveness suggests that the techniques it emphasizes provide support and substance to the Aristotelian suggestion that cultivating emotions is much like developing a skill.

Conclusion

Recognizing the essential place that negative emotions have in our understanding of human agency helps us see what is wrong with Kant's claims about the incompatibility of virtue and negative emotion. Recall that on Kant's picture, virtue is understood in terms of rational self-control: virtue is "the moral strength of a human being's *will* in fulfilling his duty" (1996, 533) and thus the virtuous agent is one for whom "reason holds the reins of government in its own hands" (536). So understood, the problem with feeling negative emotions is that it represents a failure of self-control: emotion—not reason— determines one's behavior. But what Kant seems to have missed is the essential role that negative emotions like anxiety play in *promoting* self-control. Recall the Marsh example. The anxiety he experiences in surgery doesn't represent a failure of self-control, but rather the manifestation of it. It's *because* he feels anxious and it's *because* this anxiety is unpleasant, that it can bring the focus and caution that it does. That gets missed, however, if one focuses—as Kant (and Seneca) seems to—on cases where anxiety, anger or other negative emotions manifest in extreme or clinical forms. But once we set these atypical cases aside, we can see the value—instrumental and aretaic—that negative emotions can have.

Notes

1. These sketches are not intended as a substantive account of what emotions are— that's a thorny issue that I don't want (or need) to take a stand on. Rather, my aim is to give an intuitive picture of how I'm thinking about emotions.
2. The term "anxiety" as used in ordinary speech, philosophy and psychology refers to a range of phenomena that are unlikely to have a common core. So here I focus on an important dimension of what we refer to as "anxiety"—namely, an emotion that

concerns *uncertainty* about what to do in the face of a potential threat/challenge. For further discussion, see Kurth (2018).

3. Seneca's concerns about anger's value are, at least in part, driven by observations like these.

4. While the claim that virtues are constituted by integrated combinations of beliefs, motivations, and feelings is contested by some, it is the received view about virtue. See, for instance, Aristotle (1998) and Annas (2011). David Hume (1975) and Kant (1996) are prominent dissenting voices (but on Kant, see Baxley 2010, Chapter 4).

5. Here I'm using "moral" in the broad sense typical of virtue theory: it refers not just to (e.g.) right and wrong behavior but to the more encompassing "practical wisdom" that virtuous individuals display.

6. Clearly, in a situation like this, anxiety is unlikely to be the only emotion you feel. Anger, sadness and frustration are other likely possibilities. Here I focus just on anxiety to help draw out the aretaic dimension of its value.

References

Annas, Julia. 2011. *Intelligent Virtue*. Oxford: Oxford University Press.

Aristotle. 1998. *Nicomachean Ethics*. Translated by David Ross. Oxford: Oxford University Press.

Baxley, Anne M. 2010. *Kant's Theory of Virtue*. Cambridge: Cambridge University Press.

Brader, Ted. 2006. *Campaigning for Hearts and Minds*. Chicago: University of Chicago Press.

Hofmann, Stefan G., and Jasper A. J. Smits. 2008. "Cognitive-Behavioral Therapy for Adult Anxiety Disorders." *Journal of Clinical Psychiatry* 69: 621–32.

Hume, David. 1975. *A Treatise on Human Nature*. Edited by L. A. Selby-Bigge. Oxford: Oxford University Press.

Kant, Immanuel. 1996. "Metaphysics of Morals." In *Practical Philosophy*, edited by Mary J. Gregor and Allen W. Wood. Cambridge: Cambridge University Press.

Knausgaard, Karl. 2015. "The Terrible Beauty of Brain Surgery." *New York Times Magazine*. www.nytimes.com/2016/01/03/magazine/karl-ove-knausgaard-on-the-terrible-beauty-of-brain-surgery.html. Accessed 17 January 2016.

Kurth, Charlie. 2016. "Anxiety, Normative Uncertainty, and Social Regulation." *Biology & Philosophy* 31: 1–21.

Kurth, Charlie. 2018. *The Anxious Mind*. Cambridge, MA: MIT Press.

Lewis, Ioni, Barry Watson, Richard Tay, and Katherine M. White. 2007. "The Role of Fear Appeals in Improving Driver Safety." *International Journal of Behavioral Consultation and Therapy* 3: 203–22.

Marsh, Henry. 2014. *Do No Harm*. New York: St. Martin Press.

Seneca. 1995. *Moral and Political Essays*. Edited by John M. Cooper and J. F. Procope. Cambridge: Cambridge University Press.

Sherman, Nancy. 1989. *The Fabric of Character*. Oxford: Oxford University Press.

Stohr, Karen E. 2003. "Moral Cacophony: When Continence Is a Virtue," *Journal of Ethics* 7: 339–63.

Stossel, Scott. 2013. *My Age of Anxiety*. New York: Knopf.

Williams, Bernard. [1976] 1981. "Moral Luck." In *Moral Luck*. Cambridge: Cambridge University Press.

11 Grief

Carolyn Price

For most people, loving relationships with family and friends are a principal source of happiness and meaning. Yet, these relationships inevitably carry
the risk of bereavement and grief. In this chapter, I want to consider how we
should understand the place of grief in our lives. Is grief best thought of as a
kind of *wound*—a mental injury that we should seek to heal as quickly and
painlessly as possible? Does grief arise from a failure to come to terms with
what has happened and move on—an exercise in pointless self-torment? Or
should we think of grief in a more positive light, as a process through which
people acknowledge and reflect on what they have lost?

To put the question in its starkest terms, suppose that medical scientists
were to find a *cure* for grief—a pill, perhaps, or some kind of talking therapy
that can quickly sooth grief away. The cure, let us suppose, has no obvious
side effects: it does not interfere with people's capacity to feel deeply about
other events in their lives; it does not leave them feeling groggy or confused.
Instead, those who take it find only that they can now remember their lost
friend or family member fondly, without distress. If this were to happen, should
we celebrate the fact that medical science has found another way to eliminate
pointless pain from people's lives? Or should we worry that something of value
has been lost?

Alongside this controversy about the value of grief, there is also room for
disagreement about what grief is *like*. On the face of it, grief takes different,
even contradictory forms. On the one hand, grief sometimes seems to be a
restless, anguished state, in which the griever protests at what has happened
and yearns for what has been lost. On the other hand, grief sometimes seems
to be a state of inactivity and withdrawal, in which the griever hopelessly
ruminates on their loss. Before we decide what to say about grief's value, we
may first need to say more about what kind of state grief is. For the time being,
I shall set this second question to one side; but I shall return to it at the end.

My discussion is divided into three sections. In the first, I shall say more
about the charges that have been laid against grief, both by ancient philosophers and by more recent theorists. In the second, I shall consider a possible
response to those charges. Although I am sympathetic to this response, I shall
suggest that it does not go far enough. In the final section, I shall offer an

alternative view. As we shall see, this third view turns on the claim that grief is a complex response, which has different phases, and which involves different kinds of sorrow. As a result, my answer to the question about grief's value will also be complex.

Although I shall not offer a detailed account of what grief is until the end, I shall start from some (relatively uncontroversial) assumptions: grief, I shall assume, is a painful emotional response to a serious and irreversible loss.[1] Grief is sometimes viewed as a distinctive form of sorrow; however, many psychologists take it to be a rather complex emotional response, which can involve several types of emotion. These include sorrow, but also anger, despair, anxiety, guilt and shame (Izard 1991, 205). Grief can be elicited by the permanent loss of anything that we love or treasure. Someone might grieve, for example, after a divorce or after losing their job. Here, though, I shall focus on cases involving the death of someone one loves.

The Case Against Grief

In the *Republic*, Plato sets out to defend the view that people should try to bear misfortune as quietly as possible:

> A man should take thought . . . on what has come to pass, and as we regulate our play by the fall of the dice, so he should regulate his affairs in the light of what has fallen out, as reason ordains. . . . We should not be like children who, when they have stumbled, go on holding the affected part and shrieking, but should always accustom [ourselves] to turn as quickly as possible to healing and restoring what is fallen and diseased, making lamentation disappear before medicine.
>
> (Plato 1992, 297–98)

Underlying Plato's comments is the thought that grief is not merely painful and disruptive: it involves a kind of *irrationality*—a refusal to face up to the situation as it is. Hence, the "medicine" he mentions consists of thinking clearly and rationally about the situation. Moreover, Plato seems to be hinting that prolonged and public grief implies a somewhat childish weakness in the face of misfortune. Admittedly, in an earlier passage, Plato concedes that a good person will inevitably feel some sorrow after a bereavement (Plato 1992, 297). Nevertheless, he insists, they will pick themselves up as quickly as possible; they will refuse to dwell on their loss or upset other people by lamenting in public.

Stoic philosophers, such as Epictetus and Seneca, agreed with Plato that grief is irrational; and like Plato, they held that grief is irrational, in part, because it is futile—a pointless protest against a verdict that cannot now be overturned. The Stoics developed a range of philosophical "therapies"—arguments designed to counter the mistaken beliefs and irrational ways of thinking that they took grief to involve. Seneca authored several works of consolation, addressed to bereaved friends who, he thought, had become trapped in grief. His aim was to coax them out of their misery, using a mix of argument and gentle admonition. In contrast, when he sent his condolences to Lucilius—a friend who shared his commitment to philosophy—his advice is rather more direct:

> You have buried one whom you loved; look about for someone to love. It is better to replace your friend than to weep for him.
>
> (Gummere 1917, 435)

The message here is the same as Plato's: the rational response to bereavement is to accept one's loss and move on as quickly as possible.

More recently, Donald Gustafson (1989) has also argued that grief involves a kind of confusion or irrationality. Gustafson's argument turns on the claim that grief characteristically involves a particular desire—the desire that the person whom we have lost should be returned to us. This desire, he thinks, is not is not merely an idle wish—as when one wishes one could fly or that summer could last forever. Rather, he thinks, it is an active longing or seeking after what has been lost. Gustafson's claim finds some support in the way grieving people sometimes behave: cradling a photograph of the beloved, caressing their clothes, and so on—actions that seem to reflect a frustrated desire for contact with the person who has died (Goldie 2000, 129–36). The inevitable frustration of this desire, Gustafson thinks, helps to explain the pain and turmoil of grief. But this desire, he insists, is *irrational*: it is irrational to continue actively seeking after something that you know you cannot have (Gustafson 1989, 467–68).

Gustafson, then, echoes Plato's view that grief is irrational because it is futile: it is futile in the sense that it involves a desire that cannot be satisfied. However, he does not share Plato's view that prolonged grief implies a kind of weakness. Rather, his point is that we cannot *make sense* of grief from the griever's point of view: their beliefs and desires do not fit together in an intelligible way. In the end, he concludes, grief is best viewed as an automatic, programmed response, outside the griever's control—a product of our evolutionary history (Gustafson 1989, 470). This leaves us with a question though: why should our evolutionary history have left us with propensity to respond to bereavement in this confused and pointless way?

Some theorists have offered a rather different reason for holding that grief is something we would be better off without: the claim is that it is an unhealthy emotion, perhaps even a kind of illness or injury in its own right. Stephen Wilkinson (2000), for example, appeals to the painful and disruptive character of grief to argue that it is a type of short-lived psychological disorder.[2] The thought behind this view seems to be that the experience of bereavement is so damaging and disorientating that the griever's usual psychological resources are temporarily overwhelmed, leaving them distressed and unable to cope with the normal demands of life. On this view, grief might be compared to other psychological disorders caused by harmful and life-changing events, such as reactive depression or post-traumatic stress disorder. This view need not imply that grief requires medical intervention: in the vast majority of cases, perhaps, grief is best left to heal by itself. Still, the swifter the recovery, the better: if there were a cure for grief then, on this view, we would have good reason to take it.

Grief as Recognition

In the last section, I identified two charges that have been laid against grief. First, grief has been viewed as a futile and irrational response to loss. Second, it has been characterized as a kind of psychological injury or disorder. In this section, I shall consider a possible response to these charges. I shall start by looking again at the claim that grief is a type of psychological disorder.

As I mentioned earlier, Wilkinson (2000) supports this claim by appealing to the pain and disruption that it entails. This, though, is not a decisive argument. After all, it is not hard to think of painful and disruptive conditions— psychological or physical—that are not disorders. The process of childbirth, for example, is painful and debilitating, but childbirth is not a disorder. We could make the same point about other types of negative emotion. Consider, for example, someone (call her Kay) who has long resented some serious and long-standing injustice (racial discrimination, say) that she has suffered. Her resentment is itself a painful emotion; moreover, it interferes with her ability to get on with her life—for example, by moving her to protest about her treatment, harming her job prospects and her relationships with her neighbors. If Kay were simply to overlook the injustice, accepting it as the normal order of things, she might find life easier and happier. However, none of this implies that Kay's resentment is a psychological disorder. What has gone *wrong* in this case is not Kay's response to injustice, but the injustice itself. Her resentment is appropriate, given the injustice she has suffered; in producing this response, her psychological mechanisms are working just as they should. Hence, to show that some psychological state is painful and disruptive does not by itself establish that it is a disorder. We also need to show that the pain and disruption result from some psychological *dysfunction*. This is not true of Kay's resentment. And it is at least not obvious that it is true of grief.

What about the other charge laid against grief: that it is an irrational response? One common response to this charge is that the pain of grief is not simply meaningless distress: rather it is a form of *recognition* or *perception* that something very bad has happened. It is the perception that something has gone seriously wrong in one's life: one has lost someone one loved. Moreover, in recognizing this, the griever thereby recognizes the value of what they have lost—how much their friend or family member meant to them. On this view, Plato gets things precisely the wrong way round: far from being a failure to face up to the reality of what has happened, grief is a painful recognition of that reality. As Troy Jollimore puts it:

A failure to grieve, where grieving is appropriate, indicates a misunderstanding of the nature of the world one lives in; it signals a failure to comprehend the magnitude and significance of the loss that has occurred.

(Jollimore 2004, 340)[3]

Understood in this way, grief is not simply a regrettable side-effect of love: rather, it is the *continuation* of love—the continuation of our loving appreciation of our relative or friend, and the relationship we shared with them. Similarly, in expressing our grief in acts of mourning, we are not simply making a pointless fuss, as Plato seems to imply: rather, we are publicly acknowledging and honoring the value of the life that has ended. Moreover, as well as challenging the claim that grief is irrational, this response might also help to counter the charge that grief is a psychological disorder. The point is that grief is not the result of some psychological dysfunction: rather, it is a clear-eyed recognition of the griever's loss.

I am sympathetic to this defense of grief. It is not clear, though, that it goes far enough. There are at least two ways in which it might be questioned. First, it might be pointed out that grief is not *only* a recognition that something bad has occurred. It also involves particular ways of thinking and behaving, not to mention bodily symptoms such as loss of appetite, lethargy and so on. The worry is, then, that someone might concede that grief includes an appropriate recognition of loss, while insisting that it also includes *other* elements that are irrational or harmful. In particular, we might recall Gustafson's worry that grief involves an irrational desire to recover what has been lost. This desire, in his view, makes no sense, given that the griever recognizes that their loss cannot be undone. If grief were a wholly rational state, he might argue, it would take a different form. The griever would recognize their loss (and perhaps this recognition would be painful); but they would not be tortured by futile longings for what they have lost. Perhaps they would only wish that things were different.

Second, it might be argued that there are other, less distressing ways of appreciating and commemorating the value of somebody's life. We might remember them with joy and gratitude; we might come together to celebrate, rather commemorate, their lives.[4] If so, should we not try to encourage people to remember the dead with joy, rather than sorrow?

The Complexity of Grief

I want to end by suggesting that the answer to the question I have raised may not be simple. This is because grief itself is not a simple response.[5]

To explain this, I need to return to a point that I made at the start. Grief itself seems to be a rather contradictory phenomenon. Sometimes, it seems to be an agitated response—an anguished, restless craving for the beloved; at others, it seems to be a state of inactivity and withdrawal, in which the griever hopelessly ruminates on their loss. This points towards the possibility that grief is a rather complex response. As I mentioned earlier, psychologists standardly suppose that grief involves several different types of emotion, including sorrow, anger, despair, anxiety, guilt and shame (Izard 1991, 205). Moreover, some psychologists hold that grief involves different stages or phases: John Bowlby (1998, 85), for example, suggests that grief involves an initial stage of numbness, followed by a searching phase—in which the griever seems to be looking for the person they have lost—and a phase of despair, characterized by withdrawal and lethargy.[6] This would certainly explain why grief seems to take such different forms. In what follows, I am going to assume that Bowlby's distinction between searching and despairing grief is correct. This raises the possibility that, when we consider the place of grief in our lives, the answer will be different, depending on which type or phase of grief we have in mind.

Consider, first, an example of searching grief, as Bowlby (1980, 86–95) characterizes it. Suppose that someone (call him Jay) has recently lost his partner Jo. In some ways, Jay continues to act and feel as if Jo were still alive. When the telephone rings, his first thought is that it might be her. Now and then, he even seems to see her out of the corner of his eye. He longs to see and talk to Jo again, and often has an urge to look at old photographs. He feels restless and torn. When a friend tries to persuade him to take some of Jo's things to a charity shop, he initially resists—as if Jo might return to claim them. Indeed Bowlby (1980, 87) characterizes this phase of grief as a state of "disbelief". The term "disbelief" though, seems too strong: after all, if Jay were asked, he would surely say that he knows that Jo has died. Rather, it looks as if his *feelings* have not yet caught up with the situation: emotionally, he is responding to the situation as if Jo were inexplicably missing, rather than dead. Hence, he is moved to try to find her, and is unconsciously looking out for signs of her.

If this is right, then this restless, anguished phase of grief does seem open to some of the criticisms of grief made by Plato and Gustafson: Jay's feelings, I have suggested, are out of step with reality. Moreover, his anguished longing to find Jo seems to be in tension with his belief that she is gone for good. In this sense, perhaps, Jay's emotional response might be viewed as irrational. Still, even if this is right, the irrationality involved does not seem to be of a particularly puzzling or troubling kind. After all, it is not uncommon for people's emotions to lag behind their beliefs, especially when they have experienced some significant and unexpected change in their lives. People who experience some significant *success* (winning an Olympic medal, say) commonly report that it takes time for the news to sink in. What they mean, presumably, is not that they do not believe that they won, but that their emotions have not yet caught up with the situation. If so, there is no cause to think that Jay's response is irrational in any very deep or puzzling sense, or that it arises from some dysfunction in his psychological mechanisms. Still, perhaps it would be best for him to move through this phase of grief as swiftly as possible. Arguably, one function of mourning rituals is to bring home to mourners the reality of their loss.

What should we say about despairing or desolate grief? Bowlby characterizes this phase of grief primarily as one of withdrawal and lethargy. However, he also mentions another feature: the griever's urge to reflect or ruminate on their loss (Bowlby 1980, 93–94). If we imagine Jay in this phase of grief, we might picture him sitting quietly alone, turning over in his mind all the many ways in which Jo's death was a terrible thing. His desolate sadness implies that he has recognized that Jo has gone for good: hence in this phase of grief, there is no reason to think that his feelings are out of step with reality. Nevertheless, it might be suggested that his *behavior* is irrational. In particular, we might imagine his friends telling him that in ruminating over Jo's death, he is merely torturing himself to no purpose.

I want to suggest, though, that Jay's ruminations may not be pointless. Rather, these painful reflections function to take him beyond his initial, painful recognition that he has lost Jo, to delve deeper into what has happened and why. As he explores his memories, he has an opportunity to develop a fuller and clearer appreciation of what she meant to him, of the value of the relationship they shared and of what is now missing in his life. He may ask himself why this has happened and whether he could have acted differently—whether he might have spent more time with her, asked the awkward questions, and so on. Some of the questions Jay asks may well be difficult and troubling: hence, it is not clear that these insights could be gained without distress. Still, it need not be pointless: it is possible that when it is over, Jay will be in a better position to begin his life again.[7]

Admittedly, this may not always be the case: grievers may sometimes draw harmful or false conclusions from their reflections—for example, deciding to cut themselves off from future relationships, or blaming themselves unfairly. Sometimes, there may be no good conclusions to draw. I am suggesting only that the process of desolate reflection can *sometimes* help the griever to cope with their situation—for example, by motivating them to make the most of their remaining relationships. If so, it would not be right to characterize desolate rumination as futile self-torture or as an irrational refusal to move on: rather, it is what the griever needs to do in order to move on.

In this final section, I have suggested that grief is a complex response, which involves several emotions, including more than one type of sorrow. In the case of anguished, searching grief, the griever's feelings have not yet caught up with the situation. In the case of desolate, despairing grief, in contrast, the griever's emotions may well be wholly in tune with reality. Moreover, the desolate rumination characteristic of this phase of grief may well have an important role to play in helping grievers to move on from their loss. Hence, even if we would do best to recover from anguished grief as quickly as possible, it is not clear that the same applies to desolate grief: after a great loss, we may need to spend time in the shadows.

Notes

1. In some cases, grievers may hope that they will be reunited with their loved ones in the afterlife; nevertheless, they may grieve for the relationship that they shared with them in this life.

2. Some psychologists, too, have characterized grief as a type of disease or disorder. For discussion, see Kopelman (1994).
3. Similar views are offered by Nussbaum (2001, 19–88) and Roberts (2003, 235–40).
4. Indeed, people are sometimes encouraged to wear bright clothes to funerals and to think of the event as a celebration of a life, rather than an act of mourning.
5. In this section, I draw heavily on the account of grief I presented in Price (2010).
6. Bowlby does not want us to take the terms "stage" or "phase" too literally: he thinks that people tend to move back and forth between these different phases.
7. Compare Kopelman (1994); McCracken (2005); Price (2010).

References

Bowlby, John. 1998. *Attachment and Loss*, Vol. 3 (*Loss: Sadness and Depression*). London: Pimlico.

Goldie, Peter. 2000. *The Emotions: A Philosophical Exploration*. Oxford: Oxford University Press.

Gummere, Richard, trans. 1917. *Seneca: Epistles 1–65*. Loeb Classical Library. Cambridge, MA: Harvard University Press.

Gustafson, Donald. 1989. "Grief." *Noûs* 23: 457–79.

Izard, Carol. 1991. *The Psychology of Emotions*. New York: Plenum Press.

Jollimore, Troy. 2004. "Meaningless Happiness and Meaningful Suffering." *The Southern Journal of Philosophy* 42: 333–47.

Kopelman, Loretta. 1994. "Normal Grief. Good or Bad? Health or Disease?" *Philosophy, Psychiatry and Psychology* 1, no. 4: 209–20.

McCracken, Janet. 2005. "Falsely, Sanely, Shallowly: Reflections on the Special Character of Grief." *International Journal of Applied Philosophy* 19, no. 1: 139–56.

Nussbaum, Martha. 2001. *Upheavals of Thought: The Intelligence of Emotions*. Cambridge: Cambridge University Press.

Plato. 1992. *The Republic*. Translated by Alexander D. Lindsay. London: J.M. Dent and Sons

Price, Carolyn. 2010. "The Rationality of Grief." *Inquiry* 53, no. 1: 20–40.

Roberts, Robert C. 2003. *Emotions: An Essay in Aid of Moral Psychology*. Cambridge: Cambridge University Press.

Wilkinson, Stephen. (2000) "Is 'Normal Grief' a Mental Disorder?" *The Philosophical Quarterly* 50, no. 200: 289–304.

12 The Moral Shadows of Shame and Contempt

Raffaele Rodogno

Emotions are often understood as positive or negative in hedonistic terms, that is, in connection with the pleasant or unpleasant feelings that they involve (see Teroni, this volume). Whatever its cogency, however, this is not the only criterion employed in philosophy or in everyday practice to draw the line between positive and negative emotions. We do standardly understand certain emotions as positive or negative also in regard to their moral status. In many religious circles, for example, children are raised with the idea that envy is a bad emotion, something negative and to be avoided. One may think that the hedonic criterion is still at work here, for, after all, envy is an unpleasant emotion. The educators, however, do not place their emphasis on the unpleasant way envy feels, but on what being envious would do to you and say about you as a person. A good person would not feel envy, or so are these children taught to think and feel.

The disconnection between the hedonic character of emotions and their moral status is best illustrated by emotions such as *schadenfreude* and compassion. Hence, while involving pleasure, *schadenfreude* is often deemed a morally bad or negative emotion. Similarly, while failing to be pleasant, compassion is often considered a morally positive emotion. If there is no clear connection between the way emotions (hedonically) feel and their positive or negative moral status, what does the latter consist in? What kinds of considerations determine whether an emotion is positive or negative from a moral point of view? Are these considerations *morally substantive*, i.e., do they involve specific moral views about what is good and bad, virtuous and vicious or right and wrong? Or are they rather *structural* considerations involving claims about the role of specific emotions within morality?

In this chapter, I will review some of the most important answers that have been given to these questions. At the most general level, there are two distinct, though connected, ways of understanding the idea of an emotion's moral status. In the next section, I shall discuss each one of these senses in turn. In the final section, I will then illustrate these answers by referring to the cases of shame and contempt, two emotions whose morality, both private and public, has been heavily debated in the recent literature.

Immoral and Non-Moral Emotions

Emotions involve, among other things, evaluations and action tendencies. Fear, for example, involves the evaluation, whether right or wrong, that something is dangerous, and the dispositions to flee or fight. With this point in mind, let me introduce the first and most straightforward sense in which emotions can be understood in positive or negative moral terms: the moral status of an emotion is determined by reference to the moral or immoral nature of the evaluations and action tendencies involved in the emotion. It is important to note that determining the moral or immoral nature of an emotion can only be done against the background of a substantive moral view, be it Kantian, consequentialist, virtue ethical or religious. Hence, for example, one may focus on the action tendencies of a certain emotion, say, anger or shame and realize that they are related to violence and aggression. We may then judge that violence and aggression are morally bad because, for example, their deployment always violates moral imperatives not to treat persons in certain ways, or again, because they tend to bring about suboptimal results in terms of well-being. On this basis, we then conclude that these emotions are morally bad, objectionable or immoral. Alternatively, one may start from the evaluation (rather than the action tendencies) involved by the emotion and realize that these evaluations are not in line with those of a virtuous person, or that entertaining such evaluations will in fact contribute to eroding one's virtue, as in the case of the religious views of envy mention above.

Note that when in the business of determining the moral status of an emotion, one may have different aspects of an emotion in mind. In particular, while so far I have focused on the evaluations and action tendencies of discrete *episodes* of an emotion, one may also focus on the value of developing a *character trait* of appropriate forms of that emotion. For example, while a number of feminist writers have highlighted the morally positive value of anger episodes as a way for women to protest oppressive norms or to gain distinct kinds of knowledge (Bell 2009, 168), others have emphasized that focusing on anger *qua* enduring motivational state brings to light otherwise neglected positive and negative effects of anger on an (oppressed) individual's character (Bell 2009, 169–80).

The substantive moral outlooks that ground the moral status of an emotion as discussed in this section have direct normative implications, i.e., implications on what we ought not to feel and do, what is permissible to feel and do, and what there is reason to feel and do. Hence, if on the basis of a Kantian moral outlook, we conclude that a given emotion involves evaluations and/or action tendencies that violate a moral imperative, it follows that we ought not to feel this emotion, or at least that we ought to use whatever strategies we may have to avoid feeling it. Similarly, on a virtue ethical moral outlook, we might have reason to cultivate certain emotional dispositions while avoiding others, if that can be shown to lead to flourishing or a good life

While the distinction between moral and *immoral* emotions in the sense of "morally good" or "morally bad" just discussed is both common and straight-forward, it fails by itself to exhaust the question of the morality of the emotions. The other important distinction is that between moral and *non-moral* emotions, i.e., between emotions that belong to the moral domain and those that are outside it. Unlike the first, this second distinction is not directly connected to substantive moral outlooks. Yet, as I am about to show, to say that an emotion is moral in this second sense may mean that it plays a crucial role in our moral interactions, irrespective of the morality or immorality of individual episodes of the emotion. In cases such as these, our assessment of these emotions' positive or negative moral status is indeed a rather nuanced affair. Matters are further complicated by the fact that the moral/non-moral distinction can be understood in at least three distinct ways, to which I now turn.

An emotion may be considered moral as opposed to non-moral because it essentially involves moral concepts (Rawls 2003, 421). Some people maintain for instance that indignation is a moral emotion (in this sense) because it is a reaction to a perceived injustice, and "injustice" is a moral concept. In short, indignation essentially involves a moral concept and to that extent it is a moral emotion. Beside indignation, some believe that guilt is moral in this sense, as it involves the evaluation that one is responsible for an action that violates a moral norm.

The second view focuses on the evaluative aspect of the emotions and stipulates that an emotion counts as moral only when the evaluations it embodies satisfy some key structural constraints of moral discourse. Let us unpack this view a little. Many agree that moral evaluations are conducted in terms of moral reasons. Whatever substantive moral reasons one takes there to be (avoiding harm, maximizing utility, honesty, respecting humanity, etc.), current moral discourse is said to exclude from this category those reasons that are not autonomously held by the agent. Hence, a reason cannot count as moral if it is imposed on an agent from the outside and is in fact one that the agent is not prepared to endorse. What is more, to the extent that she acts autonomously, the agent is held responsible for the consequences of her actions. Autonomy and moral responsibility, then, are considered to be structural constraints of our moral evaluations. Emotions which involve evaluations that violate such constraints will fall outside the moral domain. As shown in the next section, many believe that shame is a non-moral emotion precisely because it fails to meet these constraints.

Stated in these terms, however, these two views suggest that (or are at least compatible with) the idea that wrongs and injustices have a life of their own independent of those emotions that just happen to involve them essentially. Many of those interested in understanding the connection between morality and the emotions, however, will reject this picture, as they maintain that emotions are more actively involved in the determination, or in the perception, of the morality or immorality of an action or a character trait.

The third view can be envisaged in this vein. The idea is that an emotion belongs to the moral domain if it is in some sense constitutive of our moral interactions. In the contemporary discussion, this view has its origin in Peter Strawson (1962) who claimed that the "reactive attitudes" are constitutive of the practice of holding responsible: we hold others morally responsible, say, just in case we experience resentment, indignation or (in the self-regarding case) guilt as a response to their actions (or, at least, when we judge that such responses would be appropriate) (Wallace 1994). These emotions are essentially implicated in the stance we take up when we hold others (or ourselves) responsible.

To sum up, we can either assess emotions as being morally good or bad against the background of a substantive moral outlook, or, more structurally, assess whether an emotion involves central elements of our moral discourse and practice. With these distinctions in hand, it is now time to turn to shame and contempt and their morality.

The Moral Shadows of Shame and Contempt

Many understand shame and contempt as counterpart emotions. Both emotions involve specific negative evaluations of a self, but while the shameful subject evaluates her own self, the contemptuous subject evaluates another's. In this section, I delineate the moral shadows of shame and contempt in turn, starting with the former.

Shame is often understood as an emotion of self-evaluation and in particular as involving the painful perception that one has failed to live up to certain standards, norms or ideals. Not everybody accepts this characterization (Velleman 2001) and even among those who do accept it, there is disagreement about (i) how to understand the nature of the failure: is it a blow to self-esteem, self-respect or self-relevant values? (Taylor 1985; Rawls 2003; Deonna, Rodogno, and Teroni 2012); (ii) how to understand the nature of the standards: are they the agent's own or can the agent feel shame for standards she fails to accept? (Calhoun 2004); and (iii) the moral status of shame (Nussbaum 2004; Kekes 1988; Thomason 2015).

The discussion surrounding the last point, i.e., the moral status of shame, has been conducted in terms of both its immorality and its non-morality. As for the former, it will be enough to mention the work of social psychologist June Tangney and her affiliates (Tangney and Dearing 2002) who have written abundantly about the moral status of guilt and shame. According to this body of work, shame is a morally bad if not "ugly" emotion due to the action tendencies associated with its episodes and to the other emotional conditions that accompany it. More particularly, the claim is that shame-prone individuals, i.e., those individuals who display a distinctive tendency to undergo shame more often and more intensely than others, as well as those undergoing episodes of shame are more likely (i) to hide as opposed to engage in fruitful interactions with others; (ii) to experience diminished levels of empathy; (iii) to be angry (shame-prone individuals are more prone to blame others overtly and to be angered at them and more likely to manage and express their anger in a destructive fashion than others); and (iv) to be depressed (and experience high levels of social anxiety and low levels of self-esteem).

As argued in the last section, we can assess an emotion as being morally good or bad only against the background of a substantive moral view. But what is the view in question here? In the relevant psychological literature, the morally good/bad distinction is implicitly taken to overlap with the pro-social/anti-social distinction, while the meaning of the latter is often left unclear. One can safely assume, however, that "pro-social" is understood in terms of what advances the interests of the group, possibly altruistically (i.e., by promoting the interests of others). Surely, even understood in these terms, pro-sociality is not necessarily a morally good thing (and anti-sociality a bad one). After all, much depends on the nature of the interests that the emotion is said altruistically to favor. The feminist remarks on anger mentioned above may be considered here as an extension of this line of criticism. Even if shame were indeed linked to anger, there may be positive moral value in anger episodes, including shame-derived ones, as, for example, a way for individuals to protest oppressive norms or gaining distinct kinds of knowledge (Bell 2009, 168). More radically, however, one may challenge the import of these empirical results on the basis of doubts about the methodology employed in arriving at them. There are three such sets of doubts.

First, there are doubts about the psychometric instruments employed by Tangney and affiliates. Some, for example, have claimed that the scale used to measure shame taps only the "maladaptive" features of shame (Luyten, Fontaine, and Corveleyn 2002; Rodogno 2008) and neglects whatever adaptive features shame may have. Second, empirical approaches focus uniquely on shame episodes and so-called shame-proneness, a tendency likely to be rooted in the subject's specific circumstances and history. What this body of research leaves unaddressed, however, is what one may call an individual's *sense of shame*. This may be understood as a disposition that enables us to be sensitive to distinct aspects of our environment. Consider, by way of analogy, the case of fear. Someone who lacks any sensitivity to danger will be fearless and will likely find herself in dangerous situations. Similarly, someone who is too sensitive to danger in connection to, say, aspects of her health, is hypochondriac and will be motivated to avoid whatever situations she mistakenly thinks are dangerous to her health. Similarly, someone who lacks any sensitivity to self-worth, self-respect or the minimal satisfaction of self-relevant values is described as shameless and will likely find herself in situations that many of us would perceive as shameful. Individuals that do have a sense of shame, however, will be motivated to avoid such situations. Note also that, as opposed to shamelessness, a sense of shame is typically understood as a morally positive thing and this is indeed in sharp contrast with the assessment made by Tangney and affiliates. Third, and as illustrated by the last point, while empirical psychology has prominently focused on the *short-term* action tendencies of shame, there is no reason to ignore the possibility that shame episodes may reinforce more positive *long-term* action tendencies. In particular, our sense of shame may well motivate us to self-reform by focusing our attention prospectively on strategies aimed at avoiding shameful situations.

Elsewhere (Deonna, Rodogno, and Teroni 2012), my co-authors and I have provided an extensive discussion of the three-prong defense of shame just sketched. Our conclusion, however, is not to the effect that shame is a morally good emotion. It is the rather more cautious one that shame is a force for the good insofar as the standards, norms and values that are constitutive of it enjoy the right connection to morality and that in individuals with the right values or attachments shame may be a tool for self-reformation. Even then, however, we argue that attempting to cause shame in others as a tool for self-reformation is likely to misfire in a number of ways.

So far, the moral status of shame has been discussed with regard to its *immorality*. Even if the above defense of shame were on the right track, however, there are those who take shame to be a *non-moral* emotion, as its evaluations fail to conform to fundamental structural constraints of moral discourse (Kekes 1988). In particular, the evaluations involved in shame (i) do occur in connection to things for which the subject is not morally responsible (e.g., shame for one's ugly nose), and (ii) do fail to be autonomous as they may well be triggered by the judgment (or the gaze) of others, even when the subject disagrees with the judgment. These challenges can be met in a variety of ways. One strategy denies (i) and (ii) by making a distinction between rational or "properly focused" shame, on the one hand, and irrational shame, on the other and then claiming that properly focused shame occurs when we hold ourselves responsible for our failures and when the norm to which we respond is a legitimate one, one that the (autonomous) subject should accept. There are, however, those who think that there is nothing irrational or out of focus with episodes of shame that fail to satisfy these constraints. Another strategy denies that (i) and (ii) do (or should) define our moral discourse. Williams (1993), for example, shows that there are other more openly heteronomous moral practices, such as those of the Greeks of the classical period, that involve a different understanding of moral responsibility, and that shame played a fitting and fundamental role in such practices.

More positively, one may argue that shame is a moral emotion along the lines of the third view discussed in the previous section. Shame, that is, would make a constitutive contribution to central elements of morality. Thomason (2015, 21), for one, argues that "[a] liability to shame prevents us from taking the way we see ourselves to be the primary authority in our self-estimation." This specific liability enables us to understand that it is not simply because we think or believe that we are just, that we are in fact just. In order to accept Thomason's argument, however, one should also be prepared to accept the assumptions on which it rests. In particular, one should agree with a radically heteronomous view of shame according to which an individual feels shame when aspects of her identity that are not a part of her self-conception (i.e., the way others see her) are experienced by her as defining her as a whole (2015, 11).

The next important point about the morality of shame was already hinted at in the last paragraph as the idea that emotions such as shame involve the self as a whole. The alleged *globalist* or *totalizing* nature of shame casts a dark shadow on its moral status. The idea is that shame involves a negative evalua-tion of one's self as a whole (Lewis 1971, 30). In other words, unlike emotions such as guilt and resentment, where what is negatively evaluated is a person's action or one of her specific traits, shame evaluates persons as entirely bad because of some trait that they have or of an action that they have under-taken. This point applies even more spectacularly to contempt, the difference being, however, that the global negative evaluation is not that of one's own self, as in shame, but that of another self (Bell 2013, 40).

The globalist nature of contempt is just one of the worries likely to be raised when evaluating its moral status. As a matter of fact, standard characteriza-tions of contempt include a host of features that together seem to exclude the very possibility that it may be considered as a good or moral emotion in any sense. According to Bell (2013, 37–44), for example, beside (i) being globalist, contempt (ii) is a dismissive and insulting attitude that manifests *disregard* for its target, presenting him or her as low in status by some standard of value that the subject cares about; (iii) is comparative or reflexive; "the contemnor makes a comparison between herself and the object of her contempt, and sees the contemned as inferior to her along some axis of comparison" (41); (iv) typically involves action tendencies such as shunning or withdrawing from involvement with the object of contempt (note here the parallel with shame and hiding).

Kant is often mentioned in connection with the idea that contempt should be proscribed as immoral (Hill 2000, 88).[1] That is because holding another in contempt is to deny her all moral worth and thereby the possibility that she can ever be improved, as if she had lost all predisposition to the good. This, according to Kant, is morally objectionable as incompatible with a fundamen-tal duty of respect. To complete this bleak moral picture, note that the globalist and dismissive nature of contempt (features (i) and (ii) above) goes hand in hand with its action tendencies (feature (iv)). By withdrawing in contempt, one is communicating the message that one is "neither interested in what another might say in defense of herself, nor willing to be held accountable for one's own contempt" (Abramson 2010, 195). Contempt seems to express the idea that the contemnor does not hold the contemptible person responsible, and does not hold herself to account with regard to that person. In other words, and going back to Strawson, contempt signals a form of engagement such as we would have with non-persons, i.e., things and "lower" forms of life, and unlike the one we have with other persons. If this is correct, not only is there reason to believe that contempt is morally bad, but also that it is an altogether non-moral emotion perhaps like fear or disgust.

There are nonetheless those who defend the moral status of contempt. For one, it may be argued that contempt does count as an emotion properly belonging to the moral domain. Note how we do not think contempt as fitting towards, say, insects or inanimate things. As de Sousa notes (2016, 15), "contempt is reserved not for 'things' but for people who have allowed themselves to *become* 'mere things'." Contempt, then, signals that we are at some level reacting from within the interpersonal standpoint. What is more, not all contemptuous reactions need to leave no space to mutual accountability and thereby exile the contemptible from the moral community: "even if we literally withdraw from the object of our contempt, there are concomitant ways of indicating that mutual accountability remains in place" (Abramson 2010, 203).

Another line of defense consists in denying that contempt is necessarily global. There is indeed good reason to believe that we sometimes feel contempt for this or that trait of a person without at the same time feeling that she is entirely bad or morally worthless in virtue of that trait, or, in fact, while appreciating her superiority with regard to other traits (Ben-Ze'ev 2000, 309; Abramson 2010, 198–201). If contempt can be local in this way, it makes sense to conceive the withdrawal that goes with it to be similarly limited in scope. Not all instances of contempt deny a person her status as someone fundamentally worthy of dignity or exile her from the moral community. There may indeed be nothing morally objectionable about instances of contempt that are local in their evaluation and their reactions.

There is, finally, at least one author who is prepared to defend the view that contempt can be morally justifiable or virtuous even in its globalist guise. Bell (2013, 137–226) claims that (globalist) contempt is the *best* answer to a category of individuals that are themselves viciously contemptuous, namely, the arrogant, the hypocrite and the racist. These vices have the effect of convincing people of the superiority of those who display them and the inferiority of their victims, or of respectively influencing their perceptions thereof. Thereby, they fundamentally damage our moral relationships and undermine the self-esteem of those who have to endure them. Writing about the case of racism, Bell (2013, 226) argues that when confronted with such a vice, civility may not be the right response, as it condones this abhorrent attitude and puts the self-esteem of the victims in danger. A progressive moral consensus, she claims, can be respectfully brought about through contempt's characteristic disruption. One may have doubts, as Roberts (2016) does, that meeting (globalist) contempt with (globalist) contempt can be the *best* moral response. In the light of Bell's and Abramson's discussions of contempt, however, the idea that there is nothing moral in any sense about it needs to be argued anew.

Note

1. Bell (2013, 171–83), however, shows that Kant was surprisingly sympathetic to contempt.

References

Abramson, Kate. 2010. "A Sentimentalist Defense of Contempt, Shame and Disdain." In *The Oxford Handbook of Philosophy of Emotion*, edited by Peter Goldie, 189–213. Oxford: Clarendon Press.

Bell, Macalester. 2009. "Anger, Virtue, and Oppression." In *Feminist Ethics and Social and Political Philosophy: Theorizing the Non-ideal*, edited by Lisa Tessman, 165–83. Dordrecht and New York: Springer.

Bell, Macalester. 2013. *Hard Feelings: The Moral Psychology of Contempt*. New York: Oxford University Press.

Ben-Ze'ev, Aaron. 2000. *The Subtlety of Emotions*. Cambridge, MA: MIT Press.

Calhoun, Cheshire. 2004. "An Apology for Moral Shame." *The Journal of Political Philosophy* 12: 127–46.

Deonna, Julien, Raffaele Rodogno, and Fabrice Teroni. 2012. *In Defense of Shame: The Faces of an Emotion*. Oxford: Oxford University Press.

de Sousa, Ronald. 2016. "Is Contempt Redeemable?" Accessed December 21, 2016. http://homes.chass.utoronto.ca/%7Esousa/CONTEMPT.pdf

Hill, Thomas E. 2000. "Must Respect Be Earned?" In *Respect, Pluralism, and Justice: Kantian Perspectives*, edited by Thomas Hill, 87–118. New York: Oxford University Press.

Kekes, John. 1988. "Shame and Moral Progress." *Midwest Studies in Philosophy* 13: 282–96.

Lewis, Helen B. 1971. *Shame and Guilt in Neurosis*. New York: International Universities Press.

Luyten, Patrick, Johnny R. J. Fontaine, and Jozef Corveleyn. 2002. "Does the Test of Self-Conscious Affect (TOSCA) Measure Maladaptive Aspects of Guilt and Adaptive Aspects of Shame? An Empirical Investigation." *Personality and Individual Differences* 33: 1373–87..

Nussbaum, Martha. 2004. *Hiding from Humanity: Disgust, Shame and the Law*. Princeton: Princeton University Press.

Rawls, John. 2003. *A Theory of Justice*. Cambridge, MA: Harvard University Press.

Roberts, Robert C. 2016. Review of *Hard Feelings: The Moral Psychology of Contempt*, by Macalester Bell. *Notre Dame Philosophical Reviews*, 2013.09.03. Accessed December 21, 2016. http://ndpr.nd.edu/news/42299-hard-feelings-the-moral-psychology-of-contempt/

Rodogno, Raffaele. 2008. "Shame and Guilt in Restorative Justice." *Psychology, Public Policy, and Law* 14: 142–76.

Strawson, Peter F. 1962. "Freedom and Resentment." *Proceedings of the British Academy* 48: 1–25.

Tangney, June P., and Ronda L. Dearing. 2002. *Shame and Guilt*. New York: The Guilford Press.

Taylor, Gabriele. 1985. *Pride, Shame, and Guilt*. Oxford: Oxford University Press.

Thomason, Krista K. 2015. "Shame, Violence, and Morality." *Philosophy and Phenomenological Research* 91: 1–24.

Velleman, J. David. 2001. "The Genesis of Shame." *Philosophy and Public Affairs* 30: 27–52.

Wallace, R. Jay. 1994. *Responsibility and the Moral Sentiments*. Cambridge, MA: Harvard University Press.

Williams, Bernard. 1993. *Shame and Necessity*. Berkeley, CA: University of California Press.

13 Negative Emotions and Racism

Luc Faucher

On March 17 2017, James Harris Jackson, a white man, climbed in a bus and went to New York City. Once there, he roamed the streets of the city looking for a victim. When he found one, he stabbed to death Timothy Caughman, a 66-year-old African American. Jackson did not know his victim, but by his own admission, he hates African Americans and he wanted to kill one. According to the District Attorney Cy Vence: "James Jackson wanted to kill black men, planned to killed a black man, and then did kill a black man" (Silva 2017). Jackson's crime is one in a long list of a recent hate crimes that involves white men killing or hurting African Americans purposively (a non-exhaustive list includes Dylan Roof, Philip Wade, Darnell Hall, Aaryn Snyder). Though it has proved hard to agree on a definition of racism, no one would dispute that these crimes are an expression of racism. They are motivated by hate towards a racialized group, a kind of hate so intense that it leads someone to kill others only because they belong to that racialized group. Indeed, some philosophers claim that these crimes express the very essence of racism. For instance, Anthony Appiah claims that, at its core, racism is motivated by "hate-filled or contemptuous thoughts and feelings about other races" (2002). Jorge Garcia (1996/2003, 258) proposed a similar account: "[i]n its central and most vicious form, [racism] is a hatred, ill-will, directed against a person or persons on account of their assigned race". If hate and ill-will towards a racial group are at the core of racism, Garcia suggests that other forms of racism consist of a different form of racially-based disregard, based on callous indifference or contempt. In other words, racism is a form of race-based disaffection or lack of regard. The advantage of this way of conceptualizing racism is that it makes obvious what is wrong with racism: at its core, racism is an unjustified, undeserved form of hatred, ill will or contempt. It is a form of disregard for individuals based on an unjustifiable criterion, that is, their assigned race.

Appiah and Garcia's theories propose what could be called a "unified theory of racism". According to such theories, all forms of racism are reducible to one thing: for instance, disregard or disrespect. For some reasons about which I won't elaborate, I am not convinced by the possibility or the interest of unified theories of racism (see Faucher 2017).[1] While I will not pursue this project or discuss it further here, I want to explore one form of racism that bears a family resemblance with the one mentioned above. I call this theory the "emotional theory of racism". I call it an *emotional* theory of racism because it is interested in distinguishing different forms of racism through the kind of emotions that dominate the attitude one has towards individuals or groups based on their assigned race. Basically, the view I want to oppose has it that racism expresses or emanates from one emotion, typically "hate" or one attitude, typically "malevolence" or "disregard". Because they conceptualize racism as flowing from one (sometimes two) emotion or attitude, I will call these theories "monistic". As against this view, I want to suggest that racism results from or involves many different types of emotions and that racism can as a result take many different forms depending on the emotion that dominates one's attitude towards a member of a racialized group (or the racialized group as such). My proposal is therefore "pluralistic" in spirit.

Let me start with a few words about "racism." If we are interested in racism, it is because of its negative effects on individuals and groups. If racism had never led to any actions of which we morally disapprove, if those who are racist had never hurt, maltreated or segregated people or groups on the basis of their assigned race, it is questionable if we would care about it to the same degree. This is not to say that there is a necessary link between racism and actions (i.e., that one could not be racist and not in position to act on the basis of racism), but rather that it is because of its effects that racism is important to track and to understand.

To say that someone or something is racist is to raise a flag or to attract attention to a (or some) kind of moral ill(s) related to race. Claims of racism usually serve to deplore, denounce or condemn. They are also ways to raise consciousness in those in position to do harm about the effects of their practices or behaviors on racialized individuals or on racialized groups. Often, they are a way to request a change (and/or amends or even reparation) from either the person, or in the group, the institution, etc. accused of racism. Racism is therefore not a mere descriptive concept; it is predominantly a normative one. For instance, to say that an idea or a joke is racist is not merely to say that it belongs to a class of ideas or jokes (as one would speak of an existentialist's idea or a philosopher's joke). To say that an idea or a joke is racist transmits or communicates a *negative* evaluation of that idea or that joke. It is not simply saying that you don't like the idea or the joke, but that it displays morally objectionable content, or that it emanates from a morally objectionable intention or desire. With this general conception of racism in mind, let us turn to what I have called the "emotional theory of racism".

In developing the emotional theory of racism, I take my cue from several psychological theories: the duplex theory of hate (Sternberg 2003), the stereotype content theory (Fiske, Cuddy and Glick 2006) and the threat-management approach to prejudices (Neuberg and Schaller 2016). What these theories have in common is that they postulate that (i) the emotions we tend to experience towards out-group members and out-groups are partially determined by the way we conceptualize these very group members and groups;

and (ii) we conceptualize various social groups very differently and experience consequently different emotions towards them. What is of interest for us is that these theories can be used to provide a more nuanced, detailed picture of racism. The emotions and conceptions that are behind what we denounce as racism need not necessarily be the same. Racism takes different forms depending on the context of conceptions and practices; this is what monistic conceptions of racism are missing.

Helm's Theory of Import and Respect

In order to understand the point I want to make, let me borrow from Bennett Helm's way of conceptualizing "import" and "respect" (2011). If something or someone has import for someone else, that person *cares* about it in one way or another. One of the ways one can care about someone is to *respect* him or her as a person. So far so good. But how are we to understand import so that respect can be described (at least on the subjective side) as a kind of import?

We need to introduce two background elements. The first element is that our emotions are responsive to the value things have for us. Take the following illustration: lately someone has been throwing full coffee cups on my porch at night while I was sleeping. This person has become the *target* of my anger. I have this emotion because I consider what she does to be offensive (the action's offensiveness is the *formal object* of my emotion). The reason why I am angry at her is because I value my porch (Helm calls what I value—in that case, my porch—the *focus* of my emotion).

The second background element is the fact that import is constituted by a rational and projectible pattern of emotions. If I value my porch, I will be sad if I accidently scrape the porch with my bicycle; I will be angry at someone who intentionally and without apparent reason, soils it; I will be happy if friends of mine decide to paint it for my birthday, etc. These reactions, which all have the same focus (i.e., my porch), are *rational* given that I care about my porch. In other words, if I value my porch it would be irrational to take pleasure in destroying it with an axe. They are also *projectible*: if you know that I value my porch, you can not only predict that I won't be happy if someone soils it out of pure malice, you can also predict a particular pattern of emotions that I will have given certain counterfactual circumstances. In addition, given the value I ascribe to my porch you can predict a particular pattern of desires, evaluative judgments and actions I might have or take. For instance, you can predict that I will have the desire to keep it clean and in good shape, that I will think of extreme weather as bad, that I will call the carpenter if it breaks, etc. Valuing something is to have a multi-track disposition to undergo various kinds of emotions, desires, evaluative judgments and motivations.

How does this relate to respect? According to Helm, respect is "caring about someone simply as *being* a person, regardless of her identity; it is an evaluative attitude responsive to her dignity" (Helm 2011, 227). If you respect someone *as a person*, you are expected (and here, the expectation is *normative*, it is about something that you *should* do or an attitude you *should* display, something that you could be blamed for not doing or not displaying) to show a rational and projectible pattern of emotions (as well as desires, evaluative judgments and actions) towards that person. You are expected to show a reasonable degree of goodwill or regard to her, regardless of her social identity. You are supposed to display some "affective openness" towards her (Bell 2013, 213), i.e., not to foreclose the possibility that her choices, actions, qualities or character traits shape your attitude towards her by prejudging her based on her assigned race. Moreover, without good reasons to the contrary, you are expected to be kind to her, not to interfere with her autonomy, to be angry if someone is unfair to her, to feel guilty if you harm her, etc.

What Psychology Tells Us About Racism

Let's return to the theories of racism centered around hate or contempt. According to these theories, racism involves withholding from a person "the respect she is owed and the deference and trust that properly express that respect" (Garcia 1996, 10). By manifesting ill will, malevolence or disregard towards some people based on their assigned race, one does not value them as would otherwise be expected for people in general.[2] More precisely, someone who hates another might try to hurt that person (by either inflicting them physical or psychological pain or by ostracism), find pleasure in their pain or bad luck, hope for something bad to happen to them, etc. If I show disregard, I might just not care about them being treated unfairly, not feel guilty if I discover that I have harmed them and not try to remove obstacles that impede their flourishing as persons, etc.

What is wrong with that picture? As I said, I think it does not capture the plurality of forms taken by racism. Let us turn to what psychologists studying hate and prejudice have been telling us, and how this contributes to presenting a more nuanced image of racism that substantiates this pluralism.

Sternberg (2003) is among the rare psychologists who have studied hate. According to his "duplex theory of hate", hate is to be understood on the model of another emotion which Sternberg has studied, i.e., love. According to him, hate has potentially three components that are the mirror image of the components of love. These are: negation of intimacy, (negative) passion[3] and devaluation or diminution of decision/commitment. These components combine differently in different situations, giving rise to different kinds of hate. The first component is negation of intimacy: in hate, someone may try to stay at a distance, to pull away from and to avoid contact with of the target of the emotion. Disgust and repulsion might be experienced. The second component is (negative) passion: hate might be cool and dispassionate, but it can be fuelled by intense anger or fear in response to threat. Anger and fear might lead to different actions: in anger, you might approach the target to punish it; in fear, you might try to protect yourself from the danger it represents. The third component is devaluation or diminution of decision/commitment:

haters may feel contempt towards the target; it is represented as less than human, as not respecting group norms (a cheater, a freeloader or simply a non-human, because he or she fails to comply with norms that are thought of as criterial of humanity) and, therefore, someone unworthy of respect. Because of this, haters might refuse to display the sort of moral concern that is usually due to human beings.

As there are different kinds of love (friendship, infatuation, romantic love, platonic love, companionate love, love of kin, etc.), there are different kinds of hate which result from combining these different components. For instance, you have what Sternberg calls "cool hate", where one feels disgust towards the target, but without anger or the desire to diminish commitment; another form of hate is "cold hate" where one only diminishes commitment towards the target, without disgust or anger; "seething hate" is a mix of anger and devalu-ation/diminution of commitment; and in "burning hate", one feels disgust/revulsion, anger/fear and contempt.

Using Sternberg's framework, it is easy to show how racism against Jews in Nazi Germany, against Afro-Americans in the Jim Crow era or in present-day United States, against Muslims in Europe or against members of the First Nations in Canada exemplifies the various kinds of hate identified above. Since different combinations of emotions motivate different actions (or inactions), they also predict different motivations or actions that people feeling these different kinds of hate will have or take (or not take) towards those different groups.

The other part of Sternberg's theory of hate is the fact that hate emerges from different "stories" that haters (and sometimes, victims as well) tell them-selves. Sternberg proposes a taxonomy of stories capturing the paradigmatic narratives that contribute to the emergence of hate: stories concerning the impurity of the target group, the fact that it is morally bankrupt, barbarian, greedy, animal-like (pest), etc. What Sternberg underlines in this part of his theory is the fact that different kinds of hate respond to the way the hated group is perceived; different conceptions of the groups will result in different forms of hate.

The second theory I wish to turn to is Suzan Fiske and colleagues' "Stereo-type Content Model" (Fiske, Cuddy and Glick 2006). Like Sternberg, these psychologists are sensitive to differences in the way groups are conceptualized and to different types of discrimination that result from these different con-ceptions, and their model gives a prime place to emotions.

The Stereotype Content Model conceives of the social perception of groups as revolving around two dimensions: warmth and competence. As Fiske and her colleagues put it: "the warmth and competence stereotypes respectively stem from appraisals of the (a) potential harm or benefit of the target group's goals and (b) the degree to which the group can effectively enact those goals" (Cuddy, Fiske and Glick 2007, 632). According to these researchers, a group that is conceived of as having the intent to cooperate with the subject's in-group will be thought of as warm; while a group conceived of as trying to take advantage of the in-group will be thought of as lacking warmth. The second dimension evaluates the capacity of the out-group to achieve or enact their goals. For instance, an out-group that is perceived as menacing the in-group can be thought of as competent or incompetent, that is, as able to enact its goals or not. This way of framing out-groups along two dimensions gives rise to four possible categories: warm/competent, warm/incompetent, not warm/competent and not warm/incompetent. For US respondents (which were mostly white Americans), groups like Christians, Irish, black professionals and middle-class Americans, all fall in the first category; the elderly, mentally retarded and disabled, into the second; the rich, whites, the British, Jews and Asians in the third; and poor blacks, welfare recipients, the homeless, Arabs and feminists in the last category.

As stated earlier, different combinations of warmth and competence give rise to different types of discrimination that are mediated by different emotions felt towards the groups. Groups that are conceived of as warm and competent are the object of admiration or pride, emotions that dispose the subject to interact either "actively" with members of that group (e.g., by cooperating) or "passively" with them (e.g., by trusting them). Groups that are conceived of as low in warmth and in competence are objects of disgust and contempt, emotions that motivate harmful interactions, be they active (e.g., by expelling forcefully or obliterating the stimulus) or passive (e.g., by neglecting or distancing oneself from these groups). Groups that are conceived of as of low in warmth and high in competence are the targets of envy or jealousy, emotions that motivate passive facilitation (passive or convenient affiliation, like shopping at a minority group's store), but active harm (for instance, in time of social breakdown, treating the same minorities as exploitative and unleashing anger towards them). Finally, groups that are conceived of as high in warmth and low in competence are subjects of pity, an emotion that is positive in that it motivates helping behavior, but also negative as it implies a superiority, a distance that can have negative effects by motivating patronizing behavior or disregard for autonomy.

In a study, Fiske and her colleagues (Cuddy, Fiske and Glick 2007) suggest that in the case of ambivalent prejudices (those resulting from conceiving of a group as being high in one dimension, low in the other), the reaction to the group might depend on which dimension is made salient. For instance, for a group with warmth but low competence, if warmth is made salient, motivation to help and protect might be activated; while if low competence is made salient, motivation to avoid or to demean might be activated instead.

The third and last body of work I am interested in rests on an evolutionary "socio-functional" theory of emotions. Theories that explain why we are prejudiced against a group are, for the most part, undiscriminating in that their predictions ascribe different valence-based attitudes (negative or positive) to different groups, but without precision concerning the *content* of these attitudes. They usually conceptualize prejudice as an unreasonable negative attitude towards a group (Allport 1954; Fishbein 1996). But "why", Neuberg and Cottrell ask,

> do gay men often evoke [for some of the subjects they tested] disgust and desires to distance one's school-aged children from them, whereas Native Americans often evoke pity and desires to establish community outreach programs for them, and African Americans often evoke fear and desires to learn new self-protection techniques?
>
> (Neuberg and Cottrell 2006, 163)

This failure to account for differences in the forms and content of prejudices has motivated some scholars, inspired by the theory of evolution, to propose a different, more textured conception of prejudice. Such a view is put forward by Cottrell, Neuberg and Schaller in a series of papers which adopt a "threat-based" framework for understanding prejudice (for a summary, see Neuberg and Schaller 2016). This model is based on a "socio-functional" theory of emotions, according to which each emotion (fear, disgust, anger, embarrassment, etc.) is a specific response, or a set of coordinated responses, to a specific problem.

This socio-functional theory is a version of the functional approach. In contrast to other functional approaches, which focus on the problems posed by the physical environment (for example, avoiding toxic food or avoiding predators), it highlights problems related to our social lives. The problems posed by members of other groups to members of our own group are amongst these problems, and according to the social-functional approach, some emotions are adaptive responses to these problems. So, emotions underlying prejudices and evoked by a particular ethnic or racial group should correspond to the problems—more specifically, threats—that this group is perceived as posing. Because perceived threats posed by different groups are themselves different (threat of interpersonal hostility, of contamination, of being cheated out of valuable resources, threat to group shared values, etc.), they elicit different psychological processes that produce different responses. And because different threats demand different responses (contamination demands avoidance, hostility demands either fear or preparation to fight), it is expected that different groups perceived as posing different threats will activate different specialized emotional responses. In a nutshell, different groups are expected to have different "prejudice profiles" (Schaller and Neuberg 2012, 10) and for this reason, "the psychology of prejudice might best be understood as the psychology of prejudices, plural" (Neuberg and Schaller 2016, 2). Also, because a given ethnic or racial group might be seen as posing several problems, it might evoke a combination of emotions. This account even allows for differential responses to sub-groups within these groups, which may be seen as posing different threats and may thus evoke different emotions. Finally, because vulnerability to threat is likely to change over time, the mechanisms that are responsible for processing information about the out-group and producing adaptive responses to the threat should exhibit "functional flexibility" (Schaller and Neuberg 2012, 15).

These predictions are supported by the results of experiments run by Cottrell and Neuberg with white subjects in Vancouver. When white subjects were asked what types of emotion African Americans, Asians and members of First Nations evoked, it was found that African Americans evoked mostly fear (but also disgust and anger), members of the First Nations evoked pity (and some anger) and Asians evoked envy. Notably, each group evoked an equivalent measure of prejudice (that is, whites were equally negatively prejudiced against each group); thus, levels of prejudice that are superficially similar may in fact conceal a striking diversity of emotions. Cottrell and Neuberg also examined how subjects perceived the problems posed by these racial groups. They found that African Americans were seen as posing problems for property, health, reciprocity, social coordination and security. Other groups (such as Asians) were seen as posing problems for the economy and dominant values, but not for social coordination or reciprocity. They also showed that there is a link between perceived threat, emotions and behavioral dispositions (see Cottrell, Richards and Nichols 2010) so that, for instance, "people who are viewed as a threat to physical safety (e.g., African Americans) elicit not only fear but also inclinations to learn new self-defense strategies and to increase police patrols" (Schaller and Neuberg 2012, 11).

Finally, Schaller and Neuberg report the effects of manipulating the feeling of vulnerability in subjects (for instance, by placing them in a darkened room, or making them watch a horror movie). They found that this manipulation increases the activation of specific stereotypes related to danger about a group (like "murderer", "rapist"), but not unrelated negative stereotypes (like "lazy" or "ignorant"). They also found that it had the effect of increasing particular prejudices against specific groups: for instance, manipulating the degree of perceived vulnerability to illness has an impact on xenophobic attitudes towards immigrant groups that the subjects were not familiar with, but not towards groups of immigrants more familiar to them (Faulkner et al. 2004).

Conclusion

What are the lessons about racism one might draw from these various theories? One of them is that it is a mistake to think of racial prejudice as a single, unitary phenomenon, motivated by only one or two kind(s) of emotions. They help us reject what Edouard Machery and myself have elsewhere called a form of "psychological monism" about racial prejudice, whereby "hate" or some other negatively valenced emotion or attitude is central to the explanation of prejudice (Faucher and Machery 2009). To illustrate this, let's return to Helm's account of import and respect.

Psychological monism about racism places hate or contempt at the core of racism.[4] Seen through Helm's theoretical lens, racism should thus be explained by patterns of emotions, motivations, judgments and actions that are characteristic of hate and contempt. As observed earlier, if you hate some-one, it is rational (in the sense that it is understandable) and predictable that you'll rejoice if something bad happens to him or her. It is also rational and predictable that, if given the chance, you'll try to hurt that person, etc. If you feel contempt for that person, you might be indifferent to her miserable conditions of existence, denigrate or do not even recognize her success, etc. However, as we've come to realize, this way of thinking about racism is too simplistic for many reasons.

One reason to oppose psychological monism about racism is that the moral ills caused by racial prejudices are not only caused by hate or contempt, but can also be caused by fear, anger, envy, disgust and different mixes of these emotions. The patterns of emotions, motivations, judgments and actions that follow from these attitudes are expected to be diverse as well. If I fear members of your racialized group, I might keep my distance from you, grab my valuables when in an elevator with you, forbid our children from playing together at your home, etc. You will feel all of this as hurtful and disrespect-ful. But it is different from the patterns of emotions, motivations, judgments and actions that I will show if I am envious of or angry at members your racialized group.

Another reason to oppose the psychological monism is that attitudes towards members of a racialized group are not monolithic. For instance, white Americans have differing attitudes towards young Afro-American men versus young Afro-American women, towards Afro-American professionals versus Afro-American single mothers receiving welfare, etc. These variations in the way members of a particular social group hold differing attitudes will affect members of the Afro-American community in different ways.

A last reason why monism should be rejected is that, as we have seen, social and cultural factors such as the perception of a particular threat posed by an out-group, or feelings of vulnerability, influence both the content of prejudices and their activation. Because of this, attitudes towards racial groups might fluctuate as a function of the social or cultural context. News and pictures showing the ravages of war experienced by Syrian children might spark an attitude of benevolence towards Syrians; yet a terrorist attack and the result-ing fear might activate motivation to close the borders of one's country.

Notes

1. So my proposal has a limited scope in that it does not intend to capture all forms of racism. It is content to capture some "individual", "agent-based" or "psychologi-cal" forms of racism. It leaves open the possibility that some forms of racism do not involve psychological states.
2. Racism can thus be conceptualized as a "negative form" of care based on racial assignation.
3. I put "negative" in parenthesis because Sternberg does not present it this way (he only talks about "passion"), but I think it helps to make salient the mirroring rela-tionships of the components of love and hate.

4. We talked of psychological *monism* not to say that these theories postulate that to be racist is to exhibit only one type of emotions or of mental states, but rather that they construe racism as centrally explained by one or two kinds of emotions rather than many, as my account does.

References

Allport, Gordon W. 1954. *The Nature of Prejudice*. Cambridge, MA: Addison-Wesley.

Appiah, Kwame A. 2002. "Racism: History of Hatred." Review of *Racism: A Short History*, by George Frederickson. *New York Times*, August 4.

Bell, Macalester. 2013. *Hard Feelings: The Moral Psychology of Contempt*. Oxford: Oxford University Press.

Cottrell, Catherine A., David A. R. Richards, and Austin L. Nichols. 2010. "Predicting Policy Attitudes from General Prejudice Versus Specific Intergroup Emotions." *Journal of Experimental Social Psychology* 46: 247–54.

Cuddy, Amy J. C., Susan T. Fiske, and Peter Glick. 2007. "The BIAS Map: Behaviors from Intergroup Affects and Stereotypes." *Journal of Personality and Social Psychology* 92(4): 631–48.

Faucher, Luc. 2017. "Racism." In *The Routledge Companion to Philosophy of Race* edited by Paul C. Taylor, Linda M. Alcoff, and Luvell Anderson. New York: Routledge.

Faucher, Luc, and Edouard Machery. 2009. "Racism: Against Jorge Garcia's Moral and Psychological Monism." *Philosophy of Social Sciences* 39: 41–62.

Faulkner, Jason, Mark Schaller, Justin H. Park and Lesley A. Duncan. 2004. Evolved "Disease-Avoidance Mechanisms and Contemporary Xenophobic Attitudes. " *Group Processes & Intergroup Relations*, vol. 7(4), 333–53.

Fishbein, Harold D. 1996. *Peer Prejudice and Discrimination: Evolutionary, Cultural, and Developmental Dynamics*. Boulder, CO: WestView Co.

Fiske, Susan T., Amy Cuddy, and Peter Glick. 2006. "Universal Dimensions of Social Cognition: Warmth and Competence." *Trends in Cognitive Sciences* 11(2): 77–83.

Garcia, Jorge L. A. 1996/2003. "The Heart of Racism." *Journal of Social Philosophy* 27, no. 1; reprinted in B. Boxil (Ed.), *Race and Racism*, 257–96. Oxford: Oxford University Press.

Helm, Bennett 2011. "Responsibility and Dignity: Strawsonian Themes." In *Morality and the Emotions*, edited by Carla Bagnoli, 217–34. Oxford: Oxford University Press.

Neuberg, Steven L., and Catherine A. Cottrell. 2006. "Evolutionary Bases of Prejudices." In *Evolution and Social Psychology*, edited by Mark Schaller, Jeffry A. Simpson, and Douglas T. Kenrick, 163–87. New York: Psychology Press.

Neuberg, Steven, and Mark Schaller. 2016. "An Evolutionary Threat-Management Approach to Prejudices." *Current Opinion in Psychology* 7: 1–5.

Schaller, Mark, and Steven Neuberg. 2012. "Danger, Disease, and the Nature of Prejudice(s)." *Advances in Experimental Social Psychology* 46: 1–54.

Silva, Daniella. 2017. "White Supremacist James Harris Jackson Charged with Terrorism for Killing Black Man in NYC." *NBC News*, July 18, 2017. www.nbcnews.com/news/us-news/terrorism-charges-white-man-accused-hunting-down-black-men-n739146.

Sternberg, Robert J. 2003. "A Duplex Theory of Hate: Development and Application to Terrorism, Massacres, and Genocide." *Review of General Psychology* 7, no. 3: 299–328.

14 How to Think Yourself Out of Jealousy

Ronald de Sousa

Not long ago, psychologists commonly regarded emotions as disruptions of organized and rational thought and action (Leeper 1948). A functionalist approach, fostered by an adaptationist conception of evolution by natural selection, has in the past few decades led to a very different consensus. Other things being equal, our more enduring capacities must be good for something—though not necessarily for someone: some genes, perhaps, of which organisms are but vehicles (Dawkins 1976); or perhaps for a population or a species as a whole (Gould 2002). That consensus is not, however, committed to the uniformity or universality of our emotional repertoire. The extent to which our emotional potential is malleable remains an open question.

A McDonald Emotion?

The desirability of such emotional malleability is attested by a corollary of the adaptationist approach: namely that we should expect to encounter a number of what we might call McDonald emotions. Our innate taste for fats, sugar, salt and protein doubtless proved essential to our survival during periods of evolutionary adaptation in which these nutrients required some effort to procure. In current advanced societies, these tastes do not encourage healthy diets. Similarly, emotions that were once adaptive may now be worse than useless. As examples, we might cite the emotional and temperamental dispositions, mostly affecting males, that explain the fact that homicide, regardless of its frequency in any given culture, are committed by men around 95% of the time (Daly and Wilson 1988). Whatever adaptive function was served by a disposition to murderous behavior is now more often maladaptive. Such an emotional disposition is particularly undesirable for the individuals involved when it takes the form of road rage or war crimes. Similar considerations apply to many of the other "negative emotions": racism, xenophobia, disgust at unfamiliar sexual practices or gender identities, envy and jealousy.

In this essay, I shall focus narrowly on sexual jealousy. The "green-eyed monster" has undoubtedly been regarded as a "negative" emotion. But what does that mean?

Several philosophers have pointed out that "negative emotions" do not form a clear or coherent category (Kristjánsson 2003; Solomon and Stone 2006). But jealousy seems to be a clear case in that it exhibits three clearly undesirable features. First, it is painful for the subject experiencing it. Second, it is painful and potentially harmful for those whom it targets—both the direct target and the "co-respondent" because of whom it is felt. Third, the actions motivated by jealousy—and to a lesser extent its mere expression and even the suspicious attitudes that unexpressed jealousy may foster, are frequently counterproductive: while jealousy is often said to aim at preserving a loving relationship, it is likely to have the opposite effect.

These features of jealousy should suffice to motivate a desire to eliminate it, or at least to eliminate those negative aspects. In what follows, I will briefly argue, against some recent champions of jealousy, that certain forms of jealousy would be best eliminated. But I will mostly be concerned to explore how such elimination might be possible. More specifically I will argue that jealousy can be stripped of its negative character, by being converted into a kind of mirror image of itself. The resulting positive emotion is defined as applying to precisely those situations that give rise to at least some paradigmatic forms of jealousy, but differs from it in that its valence is positive. The painful emotion associated with witnessing the pleasure that my beloved takes with another, I shall suggest, is sometimes capable of being transformed into *compersion*, which is pleasure taken in precisely the same circumstances.

The Biological Function Defense of Jealousy

Jealousy has provided a juicy opportunity for adaptationist evolutionary psychologists to speculate on the advantages it might have afforded our primitive ancestors. This holds particularly for males. One of the very few incontrovertible differences between males and females is that the former can never be quite certain of their paternal status. From that fact, it takes only a few logical leaps to infer that males must be hard-wired for jealousy. That would naturally result from the successful perpetuation of hypothetical genes for desiring to sequester one's mates, and protecting them from any other males who might want to protect them. It is well known that among some species such as lions, genes fostering an impulse to kill previous offspring of a new mate seem to be well entrenched. In the same vein, David Buss has not only argued that jealousy is an innate emotional disposition, but also claimed to find a gender difference in the character of that emotion. Given the problem of uncertain paternity, he has argued, male jealousy should focus specifically on sexual relations. Females, by contrast, should be expected to feel jealousy in situations that appear to threaten the emotional bond tying a partner to the common venture of raising a child (Buss 1994). While these expectations of a gender asymmetry appear to be confirmed in North America, however, they seem to fade in Northern European countries characterized by lower levels of gender inequality (Hupka and Bank 1996; Harris 2004). That suggests that this particular gender difference, like most of those allegedly discovered by social science is largely driven by ideology. By ideology, I understand a system of normative expectations the justification of which appeals to a conventional—and changeable—conception of "immutable human nature" (Jordan-Young 2010; Fine 2011). I shall argue that it is just such an ideology that accounts for the perceived "naturalness" of jealousy. At the same time, the fact that ideologies are built on mythical rather than real features of human nature, together with the existence of cultural diversity, should encourage some degree of optimism about the possibility of cultivating emotional dispositions more conducive to individual contentment and social harmony.

The Social Constructionist Perspective

In contrast with evolutionary psychologists, many other scholars regard our emotional repertoire as largely determined by social convention (Averill 1985; Mesquita, Bolger and De Leersnyder 2016). An even more radical view is that the social construction of emotions is built on the basis of a very limited range of dispositions to "core affect", the inherent range of which is limited to the dimensions of intensity and valence (Russell 2005; Barrett 2013). I need take no position here on the question of whether there are basic, modular evolved emotions. If there are not, it might seem reasonable to expect that some changes to social arrangements might conceivably lead to psychological adjustments conducive to individual emotional thriving in the world of complex, technologically sophisticated, culturally diverse urban societies. But even if our emotional repertoire is rooted in a small number of relatively autonomous "basic" emotions, we may hope that, just as many of us have developed gastronomical tastes that place McDonald's foods rather low on our scale of preference, we may also develop more sophisticated emotional repertoires. Consider, for example, the emotional configuration characteristic of those cultures that favor "honor killing" of girls who have been raped (Nordland 2014). Even those of us who are concerned to avoid ethnocentric bias would agree that this is one cultural tradition there is sufficient reason to deplore, and which other cultures find it easy to renounce. The same goes for racist or xenophobic hatred. And for jealousy.

What is jealousy? A very general definition is offered by Daniel Farrell, who distinguishes it from envy in that it targets not just one other person but two:

> jealousy is an essentially three-party emotion in which one person—the jealous person—is in some way bothered by the fact that, as he believes, someone else whom he wants to favor him in some way, and who he believes has thus favored him for a time, currently favors (or is likely to begin to favor) someone else in that way instead.
>
> (Farrell 1997, 166)

The Moral Defense: Jealousy as Virtue

As it stands, this definition can apply to a number of circumstances, from professional to sexual. The same is true of some other recent treatments, such as those of Peter Toohey (2014) and Kristján Kristjánsson (2002). I want to narrow down the topic somewhat to the specific case of sexual jealousy. I thus leave aside professional jealousy, as well as the gray area of overlap between jealousy and envy (a two-party emotion). Instead, I shall focus on only those cases that arise in the context of affectionate sexual relationships.

Farrell's definition leaves out an important component of jealousy that is particularly though not exclusively pertinent to the sexual kind. This is the conviction that one not only *wants* a certain sort of favor—namely, in the range of cases I am concerned with, attention and sexual favors—but regards oneself as *entitled* to them.

The addition of a condition of entitlement is actually somewhat paradoxical, since, as Kristján Kristjánsson has pointed out, it involves "the belief that a person has treated you undeservedly through failing to love you romantically as much as another person . . . an apparently unreasonable belief . . . because . . . romantic love has by its very nature nothing to do with deserts" (Kristjánsson 2002, 166). That observation suggests an additional reason for the aversiveness of jealousy: namely that it involves an inherent measure of cognitive dissonance, in so far as it is both a claim to entitlement and an acknowledgement of radical contingency. Unsurprisingly, therefore, jealousy is frequently buttressed in its claim to entitlement by a promise of "fidelity", interpreted as a commitment to sexual exclusivity. In that situation, the granting of "favors" to another can clearly be regarded as breaking that promise. But the offense taken in cases of "sexual infidelity" seems disproportionate to the mere breaking of a promise. Rather than focusing on the hurt attributable to the breaking of the promise, then, we might ask why it should be thought to be a good idea to make such a promise in the first place. For an undertaking of sexual exclusiveness is more frequently grounded in the hope of avoiding jealousy, rather than the other way around.

Most of what follows will concern the *possibility* of reversing the aversive character of jealousy without necessarily modifying its cognitive content, in the sense that it is occasioned by the very situation type that is generally taken both to motivate and to justify a lover's falling into the grip of the green-eyed monster[1]

Both the desirability and the feasibility of overcoming sexual jealousy have been denied. Jerome Neu has claimed that despite the best efforts of the 1960s' experiments in "free love", jealousy remains "ineliminable no matter what the social arrangements" (Neu 2000, 43). And Kristján Kritjánsson (2002) has argued that jealousy, in the right amount, might actually be regarded as an Aristotelian virtue:

> Jealousy qua virtue . . . would then constitute a mean between two vices: too much sensitivity to undeserved treatment which overshadows other

appropriate responses, such as forgivingness, benevolence, etc., and too little sensitivity to such treatment which is the sign of excessive magnanimity toward others or servile sheepishness.

(Kristjánsson 2002, 163)

If we try to apply this formulation to sexual jealousy, it immediately raises the question of what constitutes "undeserved treatment" for which forgiveness might be an option. As we have seen, the feeling of betrayal often identified as jealousy does not always depend on the entitlement warranted by a promise. Kristjánsson claims that this is justified. His reason is that "exclusive affiliation is typically valued from the very start of a loving relationship; and indications of complete indifference in this matter are likely to be considered morally defective". Hence, "those who have high-mindedly overcome the tendency to become jealous", far from being entitled to "moral superiority", are "seriously misguided" (Kristjánsson 2002, 158, 163).

This rather blatantly begs the question of the rationale for promising or for wanting sexual exclusiveness in the first place. The reason for his assertion seems to amount to no more than an appeal to "typical" attitudes. And that is precisely what polyamorist reject (Jenkins 2017).

In modern liberal societies, sexual relations are doubly disconnected from procreation—by the existence of contraception on the one hand, and by the fact that only a tiny proportion of sexual encounters are linked to a wish for procreation on the other. The imperative taken for granted in the evolutionary psychologists' perspective has no correlative in conscious desire. Moreover, the distinction between lust and romantic love is assumed both by the attitude of those who disapprove of lust and by those who regard its exercise as a merely pleasurable diversion. That makes it puzzling that the indulgence of lust outside the bounds of a relationship of romantic love should be regarded as a threat to such relationships. All the more so if one thinks of love as compounded of affection and lust: for neither lust nor affection in themselves make any claim of exclusiveness.

The Polyamorist Alternative

I surmise that the best explanation for the enduring prejudice in favor of sexual exclusiveness lies in its self-confirming character: the ideology of monogamy includes the idea that an intense love connection must be accompanied by exclusive desire and sanctioned by jealousy. That assumption supports the inference from the fact that a lover has experienced sexual pleasure with another to the conclusion that they no longer love their partner.

Several lines of evidence point to the falsehood of that assumption. In fact, spouses often "cheat" precisely in order to safeguard their love relationship rather than give up on it. That fact is at the basis of the success of businesses like Ashley Madison: in "cheating", most spouses have no intention of dissolving their current loving partnership or marriage. The same holds for the practice of "swinging", the somewhat ritualized exchange of sexual partners among married couples. Most explicitly, polyamorists and others in "open" relationships are frequently committed to fidelity to one or more partners without sexual or emotional exclusiveness (Easton and Hardy 2009).

Lovers in such open or polyamorous relationships would find it absurd to claim, with Kristjánsson, that "jealousy is a necessary condition of pridefulness, and hence . . . acts as an important guardian of self-respect" (Kristjánsson, 158). Why should I take pride in forbidding my beloved pleasure unless I am its sole provider? It is a truism that love entails a concern for the beloved: if I love her, I am supposed to make her desires my own. Should I then not rather take pride in feeling vicarious joy in whatever she enjoys? Kristjánsson notes that it is "considered proper" for lovers to make "mutual sacrifices" (Kristjánsson, 163). But why *should* my beloved sacrifice a harmless pleasure? (Answering that her pleasure intrinsically harms me is, of course, just more question begging.) The very fact that it is desired, and must be sacrificed, suggests that I have already lost the single-minded attention to which I thought myself entitled. Any claim on my part to police that single-minded attention is a hubristic attempt to curb the autonomy that lovers should above all prize and respect (Velleman 1999). It is also, in effect, already an admission of defeat. The exercise of such a putative right to limit another's freedom is the very mark of possession. Possession of persons is frowned upon in general; so it is difficult to see why it is so unquestioningly approved of in the context of loving relations.

Anthropological Proofs of Possibility

Let these few remarks suffice to suggest that in at least some cases it may indeed be desirable to do away with sexual jealousy. I now want to make four suggestions intended to counter Jerome Neu's conviction that jealousy is ineliminable. The first simply alludes to counter-examples gleaned from anthropology. The second stresses an analogy with the dual nature of pain, in which a sensory content can be distinguished from its aversive character. The third relates to the demonstrated possibility for a condition of physiological arousal to be construed as radically different emotional states, depending on the framing context. And the fourth exploits certain facts about the multiple conditions that commonly underpin our attribution of emotions both to ourselves and to others. Together, these four sets of considerations will support the conclusion that much of the aversive character of sexual jealousy is due to an ideology of love that remains pervasive in our culture. Recalling that an ideology, in the sense I intend, is a set of beliefs in the desirability of certain attitudes or behaviors that are justified by otherwise groundless myths about "human nature", one might reasonably strive to cultivate alternative attitudes that will allow one to re-gestalt occasions of jealousy as instead worthy of compersion.

Arguments derived from anthropology are liable to be met with skepticism, if only because of the difficulty of securing a reliable translation of the relevant vocabulary. To the very same extent that facts of cultural variation undermine confidence in our interpretations of alien cultures, however, they confirm us in the assumption that people in other cultures experience life in significantly different ways. We do best to concentrate on evidence derived from behavior and the institutions that sustain it, rather than in translated expressions of attitudes and values.

· In that perspective, two notable counter-examples stand out to Neu's assertion of the universality of jealousy. The first is afforded by the practices of the Mosuo, an ethnic group living in the West of China. Mosuo women do not marry; when they have reached sexual maturity, they are free to invite any man to spend the night with them in the bedroom to which they control access. If they have children, these are brought up by their brothers as well as their female relatives. From the biological point of view, it is clear that such a system would greatly lessen the need for males to worry about paternity. Although fathers do still play a significant part in the education of children (Mattison, Scelza and Blumenfield 2014), their genes are reliably transmitted to the next generation through their sisters. As a consequence they do not experience the same pressure to be possessive of their sexual partners, and indeed their language is reported to have no word for jealousy (Blumenfield 2009).

A second example from anthropology is provided by the "parti-paternity" practiced in certain Amazonian tribes. In those tribes a woman will have a number of sexual partners, each of whom is deemed to have contributed his strengths to her offspring, and all of whom share the responsibilities of fatherhood (Beckerman and Valentine 2002). Again, there is in such a system very little motivation for jealousy or even rivalry based on the biological imperative of paternity.

The Analogy of Pain

These reports, and others like them, provide sufficient "proof of possibility" to undermine Neu's assertion about the inevitability of jealousy. They provide no support, however, for the possibility of inverting jealousy's valence. The analogy of pain may begin to provide some such support.

The normal experience of pain is compounded of two separable phenomena: a sensory component that can be described in terms of its characteristic qualia (jabbing? throbbing? where exactly is it felt?) and an aversive affective character, "painfulness", which motivates avoidance behavior. Nikola Grahec has summarized evidence that in certain circumstances, it is possible to experience "pain without painfulness" (Grahec 2007, 61). Patients suffering from "pain asymbolia", in whom the aversive character of pain is absent even though they feel its sensory component, sometimes respond to pain by smiling or laughing:

> the main reason pain asymbolia patients laugh at the pain they feel is that they are not experiencing or perceiving it as . . . horrible, frightening, or

awful. . . . But pinpricks, particularly severe ones, are 'supposed to' evoke strongly aversive or frightening sensations . . . [so they laugh because] the pain that asymbolics feel on such occasions flies in the face of these expectations.

(Grahec 2007, 74)

By analogy, aversive jealousy might also have a cognitive core, analogous though more cognitively complex than the sensory component of pain, to which it might be possible to attach opposite valences. That would explain the many attitudes possible in the face of the type of situation that "normally" induces jealousy. And it might pave the way for a conversion of aversive jealousy into joyful compersion.

There is also a crucial disanalogy between jealousy and pain. When asymbolics miss the role of the pain stimulus as a danger signal, their response fails at the level of pain's biological function. It is the function of pain's aversiveness to trigger an avoidance response. In the case of jealousy, by contrast, there is no good reason to insist that there is, in the same sense, a correct interpretation of the situation and a true sense of the "signal" being conveyed.

In sum, the analogy with pain suggests that conversion of aversive jealousy into joyful compersion might be possible. The disanalogy just noted further implies that this would have no undesirable effects. But by what mechanisms could it be achieved?

The Indeterminacy of Arousal

This question brings me to the third reason to think the aversive character of jealousy can be reversed. A much discussed experiment conducted by Stanley Schachter and Jerome Singer showed that physiological arousal caused by purely chemical means—an injection of epinephrine—could lead a subject to report experiencing a very different subjective emotional state depending on the narrative context in which it was embedded. When a stooge behaved in an annoying way in the presence of the subject, the subject became angry. When a stooge was amusing and entertaining, by contrast, subjects felt happier (Schachter and Singer 1962). While the experiment and its interpretation have been subject to a number of criticisms (Reisenzein 1983), it remains highly suggestive: the story we tell about any situation we find ourselves in can have a determining influence on the emotion we ascribe to ourselves, including its felt valence.

Ascription by Entitlement

I come finally to the fourth cue that could explain the possibility of reversing the negative character of jealousy by showing it to be extraneous to the actual content of its object. This rests on the fact that our normal ascriptions of emotion seem to be guided by three partly independent factors, or "semantic attractors", which can sometimes conflict: (i) a "dictionary definition", which typically refers to a subjective experience (*she feels sad, or scared*) and its characteristic outward expression; (ii) the social norms, or "feeling rules", that regulate both that experience and its expression (*it's understandable she should feel that way in this situation*); and (iii) the way in which feeling rules, display rules and the relevant construal of the situation are all anchored in a standard scenario (*she failed her driving test, so she is expected to feel sad and look sad*). In different circumstances, the weight assigned to each attractor in warranting the ascription of an emotion (whether to oneself or to another) can vary. In particular, the third attractor (iii) is easily overlooked, yet it may in some situations be the only real basis for an ascription. We assume that certain situations are *normally* and *legitimately* met with certain emotional responses. So we infer without direct evidence that a response of type (i) has occurred, on the basis solely of (ii) and (iii).

Recall that in Farrell's definition of jealousy the experience focuses on the frustrated desire to be "favored". This makes sense of its aversive character. That desire is entirely congruent with (ii). For jealousy will be met with social approbation from many people who, like Kristjánsson, would regard its absence as "morally defective". One can, of course, want things that are generally disapproved of. I might want recognition for my ability to ride a unicycle, or move my ears; and I may resent the low status that others accord to my special talents. But I will likely regard myself as *entitled* only when sanctioned by my peers. And the class of those things I am entitled to is identified by the objective facts of the situation, specified in (iii), the third attractor. Anyone who regards a given situation as a normal trigger for an emotion will assume that the subjective experience associated with that emotion "must" ensue. The social conventions that constitute the second attractor (ii) owe their normative power to the assumption that *people will feel what is normal in that sort of situation*, which again is (iii). That assumption needs no evidence about the actual quality of the experience. On the contrary, the ascription of a subjective experience—typically, a painfully aversive jealousy—is inferred from the presumptive fact that the situation warrants it.

In this way, attractor (iii) introduces an element of confabulation into the identification of an emotional response. This is likely to affect not merely an observer, but the subject herself. Confabulation on the basis of what is expected, substituting for what is experienced, is a familiar phenomenon in several domains. In extreme pathological cases, patients will blithely explain their own behavior in terms of completely fictional motives derived from assumptions about what might normally account for behavior of that type (Hirstein 2005). If an emotion is regarded as normal and expected, then it will be ascribed not only to others but even to the subject herself—regardless of what she is actually experiencing.

Conclusion

Insofar as an emotional attitude can be ascribed on the basis of an ideology that defines what is deemed to be both normal and justified, a change in that ideology might result in changing the character of the emotional response. More specifically, I have argued that the *valence* of a response might be reversed without necessarily modifying the *content* of the experience. Facts do not by themselves determine the attitudes we take to them. If one is sufficiently imbued with the desirability of valuing and respecting both the autonomy of one's beloved and their potential for pleasure, the contemplation of the very same content of experience (my lover is happily in the arms of another, and I want to know every detail of her pleasure) may not motivate anguish or a sense of abandonment. Instead, it could give rise to a wholly positive experience of compersion in which I can feel I share in my lover's pleasure rather than being excluded from it.

I conclude that the replacement of a certain form of sexual jealousy by compersion is both desirable and feasible. The literature on polyamory and "open relationships" acknowledges that such an inversion of valence is not always easy to achieve. That literature is full of concrete advice about how best to cultivate desirable alternative attitudes (Easton and Hardy 2009; Deri 2015). I have not attempted to add to this literature of self-improvement. I have only sought to advance some reasons to think that the attempt is both worthwhile and not merely utopian.

Note

1. Note that if, as Farrell's definition implies, aversiveness is part of the *definition* of jealousy, it cannot be the *same* emotion once its valence has been reversed. In so far as its cognitive *content* is the same—the contemplation of an affectionate or sexual relation of one's loved one with others, however, one might regard compersion as the same emotion as jealousy, but with inverted valence. This will not matter for the purposes of my argument here.

References

Averill, James R. 1985. "The Social Construction of Emotion, with Special Reference to Love." In *The Social Construction of the Person*, edited by Kenneth J. Gergen and Keith E. Davis, 89–109. New York: Springer Verlag.

Barrett, Lisa Feldman. 2013. "Psychological Construction: The Darwinian Approach to the Science of Emotion." *Emotion Review* 5, no. 4: 379–89.

Beckerman, Stephen, and Paul Valentine. 2002. *Cultures of Multiple Fathers: The Theory and Practice of Partible Paternity in Lowland South America*. Gainesville: University Press of Florida.

Blumenfield, Tami. 2009. "The Na of Southwest China: Debunking the Myths." https://web.archive.org/web/20110720025007/http://web.pdx.edu/~tblu2/Na/myths.pdf

Buss, David M. 1994. *The Evolution of Desire: Strategies of Human Mating*. New York: BasicBooks.

Daly, Martin, and Margo Wilson. 1988. *Homicide*. New York: A. de Gruyter.

Dawkins, Richard. 1976. *The Selfish Gene*. Oxford: Oxford University Press.

Deri, Jillian. 2015. *Jealousy and Compersion in Queer Women's Polyamorous Relationships*. Toronto: University of Toronto Press.

Easton, Dossie, and Janet W. Hardy. 2009. *The Ethical Slut: A Practical Guide to Polyamory, Open Relationships and Other Adventures* (2nd Ed.). Berkeley: Celestial Arts.

Farrell, Daniel. 1997. "Jealousy and Desire." In *Love Analyzed*, edited by Roger E. Lamb, 165–88. Boulder, CO: Westview Press.

Fine, Cordelia. 2011. *Delusions of Gender: How Our Minds, Society, and Neurosexism Create Difference*. Jossey-Bass Social and Behavioral Science Series. New York: Norton.

Gould, Stephen Jay. 2002. *The Structure of Evolutionary Theory*. Cambridge, MA: Harvard University Press, Belknap.

Grahec, Nikola. 2007. *Feeling Pain and Being in Pain*. Cambridge MA: MIT Press.

Harris, Christine R. 2004. "The Evolution of Jealousy." *American Scientist* 92, no. 1: 62–71.

Hirstein, William. 2005. *Brain Fiction: Self-Deception and the Riddle of Confabulation*. Cambridge, MA: MIT Press.

Hupka, Ralph B., and Adam L. Bank. 1996. "Sex Differences in Jealousy: Evolution or Social Construction?" *Cross-Cultural Research* 30: 24–59.

Jenkins, Caroline Susanne. 2017. *Love: What It Is. And What It Could Be*. New York: Basic Books.

Jordan-Young, Rebecca M. 2010. *Brainstorm: The Flaws in the Science of Sex Differences*. Cambridge, MA: Harvard University Press.

Kristjánsson, Kristján. 2002. *Justifying Emotions: Pride and Jealousy*. London: Routledge.

Kristjánsson, Kristján. 2003. "On the Very Idea of 'negative emotions'." *Journal for the Theory of Social Behaviour* 33, no. 4: 351–64.

Leeper, Robert W. 1948. "A Motivational Theory of Emotion to Replace 'emotion as Disorganized Response." *Psychological Review* 55, no. 1: 5–21.

Mattison, Siobhán M., Brooke Scelza, and Tami Blumenfield. 2014. "Paternal Investment and the Positive Effects of Fathers Among the Matrilineal Mosuo of Southwest China." *American Anthropologist* 116, no. 3: 591–610.

Mesquita, Batja, Michael Bolger, and Jozefien De Leersnyder. 2016. "The Cultural Construction of Emotion." *Current Opinion in Psychology* 8: 31–36.

Neu, Jerrold. 2000. "Jealous Thoughts." In *A Tear Is an Intellectual Thing: The Meanings of Emotion*, 41–67. Oxford and New York: Oxford University Press.

Nordland, Rod. 2014. "Rape Killing Faces Honour Killing." http://hbv-awareness.com/rape-victim-faces-honour-killing/.

Reisenzein, Rainer. 1983. "The Schachter Theory of Emotion: Two Decades Later." *Psychological Bulletin* 94, no. 2: 239–64.

Russell, James A. 2005. "The Circumplex Model of Affect: An Integrative Approach to Affective Neuroscience, Cognitive Development, and Psychopathology." *Development and Psychopathology* 17: 715–34.

Schachter, Stanley, and Jerome E. Singer. 1962. "Cognitive, Social, and Physiological Determinants of Emotional States." *Psychological Review* 69: 379–99.

Solomon, Robert C., and Lori Stone. 2006. "On 'positive' and 'negative' Emotions." *Journal of Theory of Social Behavior* 42: 417–35.

Toohey, Peter. 2014. *Jealousy*. New Haven: Yale University Press.

Velleman, David. 1999. "Love as a Moral Emotion." *Ethics* 109: 338–74.

Index

affects, nasty emotions and 23–5
Allen, Woody 97
Alston, William 72, 73
anger: moral concern and 99–100; as
    negative emotion 96
Anna Karenina (Tolstoy) 36, 37
anxiety 95–103; anger and 99–102;
    cognitive-behavioral therapy and
    102–3; as component of virtuous
    character 99–102; instrumental value
    of 97–9; introduction to 7; overview
    of 95; understanding 96–7
Appiah, Anthony 122
aretaic value 99
arousal, indeterminacy of 139
ascriptions of emotions 139–40
Ashley Madison 136
asymmetry: between factual/evaluative
    contents 30–1; imaginative resistance
    and 31–2

Bain, Alexander 55
being moved, emotion of 60–6;
    appropriate emotional responses and
    62–3; distinctive function/distinctive
    action of 64–5; at experiential apex
    64; introduction to 5; negative cases
    of 65; phenomenology of 63–4;
    semi-negative cases of 65–6;
    triggering conditions of 63
beliefs, conflicts between emotions
    and 39–42
Bell, Macalester 119, 120
Belle du Seigneur (Cohen) 77; disgust
    towards one's beauty in 81–5; love
    in, exploration of 83–5; narcissism in
    81–2; *vanitas* in 82–3

Biran, Adam 89
Bowlby, John 110–11
Broad, C. D. 53–4
Buss, David 133

Capgras delusion 70–1, 73, 74
Carr, David 46, 48
Caughman, Timothy 122
Claparède, Édouard 64
cognitive-behavioral therapy
    (CBT) 102–3
Cohen, Albert 77, 78, 83
coherence, failure of 74
compassion 113
contempt 119–20
contrary emotions 39
Cotard delusion 70
Cottrell, Catherine A. 128–9
Cova, Florian 60
Curtis, Valérie 89

Damasio, Antonio 20
desire representation of valence
    11–12
de Sousa, Ronald 2, 20, 120
disbelieving, being displeased
    and 44–6
disgust 77–85; in *Belle du Seigneur*
    81–5; envy and 80–1; introduction
    to 6; mediated 78–9; moral 78;
    olfactory 189–92; overview of 77–8;
    resentment and 80–1; of satiation
    79–81
doxastic analysis of feelings 71–3;
    defined 72; existential feelings
    and 73
Dreyfus, Hubert 35

emotional rationality 39–48; beliefs and 39–42; conclusive evidence and 42–4; contrary emotions 39; criticizing other accounts of 46–8; disbelieving, being displeased and 44–6; introduction to 4–5

emotional theory of racism 123–4; *see also* racism

emotions: anger as negative 96; ascriptions of 139–40; attitudes towards 1; being moved as 60–6; conflicts between beliefs and 39–42; contrary 39; criteria for 60–1; evaluative aspect of 115; extrinsic faults of 25–6; fear as negative 11, 96; hedonic balance of 113; imaginative resistance and 32–5; immoral/non-moral status of 114–16; intrinsic faults of 23, 24, 26; introduction to 1–9; joy as positive 11, 95–6; negative 10; positive 10; reactive attitudes and 116; sensory perceptions and 25–7; socio-functional theory of 127–9; studies of 1–2; understanding 95–7; valence and 10–18; values and 15–18; *see also* nasty emotions

emotion theory: psychological states and 16–17; representation and 15–16

envy, disgust and 80–1

Epictetus 106

evaluative content 31–2, 37

existential feelings: defined 69; doxastic analysis and 73

extraordinary feelings 70

extrinsic faults 23–4, 25–6

factual content 31–2, 35

familiarity, feeling of 70–1

Farrell, Daniel 134, 140

fear, as negative emotion 11, 96

feelings: doxastic analysis of 71–3; fusions of 55–7; general 53; salient 53; *see also* mixed feelings

feeling theories of emotion 21

Fiske, Suzan 126–7

Fregoli delusion 74–5

Freud, Sigmund 5, 69

Frijda, Nico H. 63

Garcia, Jorge 122

Gervais, Ricky 41, 42, 47

Grahec, Nikola 138–9

Greenspan, Patricia 39, 52

grief 105–11; case against 106–8; complexity of 109–11; as continuation of love 109; introduction to 7; as irrational 106–7; overview of 105–6; as psychological disorder 107–8; as recognition 108–9; stages/phases of 110–11; value of 105

Gustafson, Donald 107, 109, 110

hate: burning 126; cold 126; cool 126; duplex theory of 123, 125; seething 126; types of 126

hedonic balance: described 52; feelings of general condition and 53; mixed feelings and 52–5; moral status of emotions and 113; in one *vs.* several individuals 53–4; salient feelings and 53; smell and 92–3; valence and 12–15

Helm, Bennett 8, 124, 129–30

honor killings 134

Hume, David 3, 30–1, 32

imaginative resistance 30–7; adultery example 35–6; as asymmetry between factual/evaluative contents 31–2; emotions and 32–5; introduction to 3–4; overcoming 35–6; overview of 30–1

intentionality 61

intrinsic faults 23, 24, 26

Jackson, James Harris 122

James, Williams 69–70

jealousy 132–41; anthropological proofs of eliminability of 137–8; arousal and, indeterminacy of 139; biological function defense of 133–4; definition of 134, 140; entitlement and 135, 139–40; features of 133; introduction to 9; McDonald emotions and 132–3; overview of 132; pain and, analogy of 138–9; polyamorous relationships and 136–7; social constructionist perspective of 134; universality of 138; as virtue 135–6

Jollimore, Troy 108–9

joy, as positive emotion 11, 95–6

judgmental theories of emotion 21

Kant, Immanuel 1–2, 95, 103, 119

Kelly, Sean Dorrance 35

Kristjánsson, Kristján 135–6, 137, 140

love, exploration of 83–5

Machery, Edouard 129
Madame Bovary (Flaubert) 36, 37
Mangan, Bruce 72
Marsh, Henry 97–9, 102, 103
McDonald emotions 132–3
mediated disgust 78–9
mixed feelings 50–7; defined 50;
    existence of 50–2; fusions of feelings
    and 55–7; hedonic balance and 52–5;
    introduction to 4; overview of 50
molecules, stench and 88–90
monism about racism 129–30
Montague, Michelle 47–8
moral concern 99–100
moral reasoning 2
moral status: of emotions 113, 114–16;
    of shame and contempt 116–20
Mosuo peoples, paternity and 138
Mulligan, Kevin 31–4
My Age of Anxiety (Stossel) 97

narcissism, in *Belle du Seigneur* 81–2
nasty emotions 20–8; introduction to
    3; and nasty affects 23–5; overview
    of 20–1; perceptual theory and
    21–3; sensory perceptions and
    25–7; solution to 25–7
negative emotions: of racism *see* racism;
    sexual jealousy and 132–3; value of
    see anxiety
negative existential feelings 69–75;
    extraordinary feelings 70; introduction
    to 5–6; sense of reality and 73–5;
    strangeness or non-familiarity, feeling
    of 70–1; uncanniness, feeling of 69–70
Neu, Jerome 135, 137, 138
Neuberg, Steven 128–9
non-familiarity, feeling of 70–1

olfactory experiences *see* stench,
    olfactory disgust and
omnivore's dilemma 89
On Certainty (Wittgenstein) 73
open relationships 137

pain: bodily, varieties of 12–13;
    dissociation cases of 13–14; jealousy
    and 138–9
pain asymbolia 138–9
parti-paternity 138
perception of absence 72–3

perceptual theory of emotions 21–2;
    nasty emotions and 22–3
Plato 13, 106–7, 110
pleasure and displeasure, feelings of
    50–2; *see also* hedonic balance;
    mixed feelings
polarity *see* valence, emotions and
polyamorous relationships, jealousy
    and 136–7
psychological monism about racism
    129–30

quasi-beliefs 33–5

racism 122–30; emotional theory of
    123–4; examples of 122; Helm's theory
    of import and respect 124–5, 129–30;
    introduction to 8; overview of 122–4;
    psychology of 125–9; socio-functional
    theory of 127–9; Stereotype Content
    Model and 126–7; Sternberg studies
    of hate and 125–6; theories of 122–3;
    unified theory of 122
Ratcliffe, Matthew 69, 73–4
Rationality Constraint for Belief 42–4
representation, in emotion theory 15–16
Republic (Plato) 106
resentment, disgust and 80–1
Roberts, Robert C. 120
Rowling, J. K. 33
Rozin, Paul 89
Ryle, Gilbert 53

Sartre, Jean-Paul 72–3
satiation, disgust of 79–81
Schachter, Stanley 139
schadenfreude 113
Schaller, Mark 128–9
Scheler, Max 55, 57
semantic attractors warranting ascription
    of emotion 139–40
Seneca 95, 106–7
sense of reality, negative existential
    feelings and 73–5
sensory perceptions: amorality of 26–7;
    nasty emotions and 25–6
sexual jealousy *see* jealousy
shame and contempt 113–20; immoral/
    non-moral status of emotions and
    114–16; introduction to 7–8; moral
    shadows of 116–20; overview of 113
Sherman, Nancy 102–3
Singer, Jerome 139

smell: as chemical sense 88–9; olfactory disgust and 87–8; pleasant and unpleasant 90–1
social constructionist perspective on jealousy 134
socio-functional theory of emotions 127–9
stench, olfactory disgust and 86–93; chemical molecules and 88–90; hedonic dimensions of 92–3; introduction to 6; Janus-faced nature of 86–7; pleasant/unpleasant character of 90–1; smell and 87–8
Stendhal syndrome 80
Stereotype Content Model 123, 126–7
Sternberg, Robert J. 125–6
Stokes, Dustin 30
Stossel, Scott 97, 98
strangeness, feeling of 70–1
Strawson, Peter 116, 119
swinging married couples 137

Tangney, June 116–18
Tappolet, Christine 47, 48
theory of import and respect 124–5, 129–30
Thomason, Krista K. 118–19

threat-management approach to prejudices 123
Time Machine (Wells) 30
Toohey, Peter 135
Turin, Luca 92–3

uncanniness, feeling of 69–70
Uncanny, The (Freud) 69
universality of jealousy 138

valence, emotions and 10–18; desire-based accounts of 11–12; hedonic states and 12–15; introduction to 2–3; overview of 10–11; reactions to 17–18; values and 15–18
values, emotions and 15–18
vanitas, in *Belle du Seigneur* 82–3
Vence, Cy 122

Walton, Kenneth 30
Wells, H. G. 30
Wilde, Oscar 88
Wilkinson, Stephen 107–8
Williams, Bernard 118
Wittgenstein, Ludwig 73
Wundt, Wilhelm 53